WITHDRAWN
HARVARD LIBRARY
WITHDRAWN

*Kibbutz Judaism*

Norwood Editions, Kibbutz, Cooperative Societies, and Alternative Social Policy Book Series: Volume 7

# Kibbutz Judaism

## A New Tradition in the Making

Shalom Lilker

A Herzl Press Publication
Norwood Editions, Darby, Pennsylvania
New York ● Cornwall Books ● London

© 1982 by Rosemont Publishing and Printing Corporation

Cornwall Books
4 Cornwall Drive
East Brunswick, New Jersey 08816

Cornwall Books
27 Chancery Lane
London WC2A 1NF, England

Cornwall Books
Toronto M5E 1A7, Canada

Herzl Press
515 Park Avenue
New York, New York 10022

**Library of Congress Cataloging in Publication Data**

Lilker, Shalom, 1932–
  Kibbutz Judaism.

  Bibliography: p.
  Includes index.
    1. Judaism—Israel.  2. Kibbutzim—Religion.
I. Title.
BM390.L55        296.8′3        80-70886
ISBN 0-8453-4740-3                  AACR2

*Printed in the United States of America*

*This book is dedicated to my wife, Shoshana,
to our children, Tamar and Ari,
and to the memory of my mother, Esther.*

# Contents

| | |
|---|---|
| Foreword: The Roots and the Tree | 9 |
| Social Invention and Spiritual Search: Introduction by Joseph R. Blasi, Series Editor | 13 |
| Introduction by Shalom Lilker | 23 |
| 1  Historical Gleanings | 31 |
| 2  Ideas on Trial | 43 |
| 3  Hansen's Law in the Kibbutz | 57 |
| 4  The Religious Mentality | 72 |
| 5  Jewish Issues in Kibbutz Society: Past and Present | 87 |
| 6  Equality | 107 |
| 7  Ritual and Culture | 121 |
| 8  Holidays and Rites of Passage | 142 |
| 9  Conclusion | 229 |
| Appendix: The Kibbutz and Martin Buber | 236 |
| Notes | 246 |
| Glossary of Hebrew Terms Used in the Text | 252 |
| Bibliography | 254 |
| Index | 263 |

# Foreword: The Roots and the Tree

In this rapidly changing world one must continually evaluate the events of each passing day. One must view the constantly changing present with the perspective of a historian. One must transcend the given reality, merge diagnostical and normative projectional thought, and prognosticate the ideals of a better world. In our time utopian ideals are not restricted solely to the narrow literary confines of an ahistorical procrustean bed. People do exist who are ready to devote themselves to the task of transforming their ideals for a better world into a society that truly practices them. The Israeli kibbutzim are such utopian societies. These societies demonstrate the possibility of living together in a community as a "we subject" rather than as an egotistical, atomistic aggregate of individuals.

The intricably woven fabric of human existence traditional to Western societies for the last 100 years is currently being pulled apart. Philosophy, sociology, art, and literature reflect modern man's growing insecurity, fear, and alienation. The hedonistic consumer attitude of man dominates more and more realms of his existence. His competitive behavior disrupts the delicate balance that has prevented Western societies from toppling into the dangerous zone of apocalyptic catastrophe. The path indicating the values and ideas inherent in common responsibility and humane living must be found and rebuilt. Numerous movements have been developing that foster "alternative realities." Among the most active of these movements have been the proponents of communal living. A great deal of interest has been developing toward the conceptual framework as well as the achievements of already successful "laboratories" of communal existence. The two main laboratories that have been most successful and should be considered are the religious Christian communities (the Hutterites and the Society of Brothers as well as the once-successful Shakers, Amana, and Ephrata) and the Israeli kibbutzim.

The reasons for the worldwide interest in the kibbutz movement are many. First of all, unlike the Christian religious communities with their specific spiritual demands, the kibbutzim seem to be open and pluralistic. Second, the Israeli kibbutzim are not isolated from the streams of the current technological culture as other communities are, but are utilizing as well as humanizing its features. Hence the reality of the kibbutz intimates that a viable alternative to traditional industrial society is now possible. It behooves those who dream of a better world to inquire and discover the secret behind the success of the Israeli kibbutz.

The question that must be asked is why are the kibbutzim unique to Israel, or, more specifically, why are the kibbutzim an inevitable outgrowth of Jewish culture—its world view, its tradition, and its historical reality? If one accepts the fact that the kibbutz is a distinct outcome of something within Jewish tradition, then the corollary is, what is the precise meaning of Judaism for the kibbutz, or, more importantly, what is the meaning of Judaism as expressed by the kibbutz community?

The book presented here by Shalom Lilker, a trained Reform rabbi, and a long-time member of Kibbutz Kfar Hamaccabi near Haifa, is an important contribution, one that adds a great deal to our understanding of the above questions. The book presents the historical development of the kibbutz from its roots in the Labor Zionist movement right up to the early 1970s. Shalom Lilker's book is not merely a historical narrative or a description. It is a brilliant analysis of the spiritual grounds on which the edifice of the Jewish Rebirth movement was established and realized. The reader of Lilker's work will be well equipped to evaluate the later developments and trends in the kibbutz movement.

The Jewish Rebirth movement was an outgrowth of the European Enlightenment of the nineteenth century. Having anticipated fulfillment of their hopes, the Jews were left disappointed when the developing democracies failed them. Although the physical existence *of* Jews was insured by enlightened rulers, their existence *as* Jews certainly was not. Jews were welcomed only if they could contribute to the well-being of the economy. As a result many Jews either became assimilated into the predominant European culture or emigrated to America. Those Jews who remained steadfast were obliged to conceive of their Jewishness in two ways: 1) in the context of the current Western notion of independent peoplehood (similar to the way in which the Italians, the Germans, the Hungarians, the Poles, and after World War I, the Estonians, Lithuanians, Latvians, and Czechs understood their own national consciousness); 2) in the context of traditional, closed Jewish life—

an existence completely detached from the surrounding cultures. For the majority of the Jewish people this second option seemed unacceptable. The younger generation, educated in the enlightened atmosphere of the time, considered anything connected with their ancient traditions as promoting spiritual and social retardation. They felt that the ancient traditions were responsible for the Jewish economic, social, and spiritual decline. The Jews of the Enlightenment viewed the ancient traditions as primarily concerned with service to God. Judaism as a *total* way of life, pertinent to everyday affairs, had disintegrated. Thus the younger generation, seeking to escape from the narrow social reality of decadence, abandoned the ancient tradition, the religious tradition.

National integrity quickly became a top priority. Two different schools of thought soon developed on how to attain national integrity: 1) continue Jewish life in the Diaspora but establish a nationally oriented consciousness to replace the traditional religious ones; 2) revolt—begin anew in self-ruled institutions and rebuild a healthy society in a independent nation. This independent nation was to be the never-forgotten Jewish homeland—Israel.

The continuity of traditional Jewish life was radically disturbed. Surrogate forms such as folklore, rituals, and existential attitudes soon developed. The Rebirth movement, including the Labor and kibbutz movements, was just as diversified. One common mistake people make is to identify the kibbutz movement solely with Eastern European Jewish history. It is true that Eastern European Jewry had a tremendous impact, but it is well to remember that Jews from Western Europe, Central Europe, North Africa, and Israel (formerly Palestine) also made a contribution based on their own unique spiritual and historical experiences.

In the 1950s and 1960s we learned a surprising lesson: surrogate practices remain surrogate practices. They do not promote creative growth. They can serve a limited task as long as the former, unaltered traditions continue to suckle the newly born practices. The first kibbutz generation, though critical and opposed to traditional Jewish forms, was fundamentally shaped and nourished by them. Ignorant of traditional practices, the second generation relied upon new surrogate forms for its spiritual nourishment. Lilker points out, metaphorically, that these new forms of Jewish ritual do not work: "We intended to grow a high, strong tree of new Jewish life; but it is impossible for a high strong tree to send its roots into a tiny pot." In other words, a sociopolitical revolution may be possible, but a cultural revolution is impossible. Nobody can begin history anew—the human being is a carrier of spiritual continuity. This is manifested in his language, in his way of thinking, and in his demeanor. Human deeds are derived and motivated from this continuity—if it is lacking, the deeds will vanish.

The maturing kibbutz movement apprehended the meanings of these lessons. Dr. Lilker wrote at a turning point in the movement's awareness and reevaluation of its attitude toward its radical beginnings. The last decade has seen the rise of Jewish education at the kibbutz schools. *Shedemot*, the important periodical of the younger generation, which originally grew out of Martin Buber's existentialist interpretation of Judaism, has now turned to more traditional ways of interpreting and learning. More and more, once-rejected rituals and customs are now being accepted and practiced. Some of these rituals, such as the wedding and the funeral, are even being performed in a traditional Jewish way. The high degree of transformation that has recently occurred within the kibbutz movement can be measured by noting the many new synagogues that have been established on the kibbutzim.

The Orthodox establishment has misunderstood this trend in the kibbutz movement. The Orthodox perceive the kibbutz movement as finally accepting the absolute truth of *their* principles and institutions. It seems to me that the contrary is true. The kibbutz has come to recognize specific and authentic Jewish roots in *its own substance*, in its *own* spiritual forms and its own realms of embodiment. The kibbutz movement has also recognized that the continuity expressed in its ideals and its realization of these ideals may be more adequately expressed through the symbolic language of Judaism—rituals, customs, and the means that form a Jewish atmosphere. This process is still very young. Its future character is very difficult to forecast. The symbolic language of yesterday's unacceptable Orthodox forms is now welcomed in the kibbutz movement because it is being reinterpreted.

The involvement of the kibbutz in modern technological culture is a necessary outgrowth of the Jewish world view, its history, and its tradition. This involvement endows the kibbutz idea with important distinction in the search by the Jewish world and other alternative life movements for a better society. The kibbutz's contribution to the spiritual and sociopolitical renaissance of modern Jewish culture is unique—it understands Jewish tradition in its *fullest* sense; a tradition working toward bringing the messianic idea and the idea of the just to this world, through human effort.

Dr. Lilker's study should stimulate interest in this important field.

—Alexander Barzel

# Social Invention and Spiritual Search
# Introduction by Joseph R. Blasi, Series Editor

The Project for Kibbutz Studies at Harvard University's Center for Jewish Studies is pleased to present Volume 7 of the Kibbutz, Cooperative Society, and Alternative Social Policy Book Series. This new edition is a result of a much appreciated collaboration between Cornwall Books, Herzl Press, and Norwood Editions.

## The Kibbutz and Judaism

The relationship between the kibbutz and Judaism has long been an ignored question in Jewish studies and kibbutz research. Shalom Lilker's book suggests one possible explanation of this relationship through an examination that relies mainly on one of the four kibbutz federations, the Ichud HaKvutzot vehaKibbutzim (Union of Kibbutzim), which is today combined with Kibbutz HaMeuchad (The United Kibbutz) into one United Kibbutz Movement. The original Ichud federation has long been recognized by scholars and contemporary observers as very tolerant of individual diversity, kibbutz community autonomy, options in social arrangements, and varied ideological and political approaches among its members. However, it would be a tremendous mistake to explain the historical gleanings and the contemporary developments regarding Judaism in this federation of kibbutz communities by the fact that it has been the most "centrist" of the three secular kibbutz movements. There is a widespread and as yet uncrystalized renaissance of interest in Judaism throughout the so-called "secular" kibbutz communities. A generation of careful social science research has established quite clearly that there are more similarities than differences among these communities as they cope with social, economic, and political change. There is little evidence that their encounter with Judaism—however initial, deep-seated, or established—is an exception. For example, representatives of these federations have been conducting ongoing planning and exploration of common interests for the strengthening of existing communities and the development of new kibbutzim or youth groups with Reform and Conservative congregations in the U.S. Some kibbutz leaders consider this cooperation as central to the future of their movements.

The reader should not mistake the explorations and hypotheses made herein for a finished analysis. These are the first questions, which hopefully will motivate scholars and interested observers to engage in a further process of observation, study, and argument. Today, the major center of practicing Judaism in the kibbutz federations lies in HaKibbutz HaDati (The Religious Kibbutz Federation) where Orthodox Judaism and kibbutz community structure guide the life of about fifteen communities. Major comparative studies of the "religious" and "secular" sectors of the kibbutz movement are simply not available and claim and counterclaim are more readily accessible than scholarship in this area. The Religious Kibbutz Federation has combined social ideas and religious tradition, and within that movement considerable religious thought has developed. Developments in both movements should be studied in parallel.

Important questions for the sociology of religion, the theology of social justice, the future of the kibbutz, and future developments in Judaism come to bear on these observations. What is the relationship between culture and social invention? Is the kibbutz movement increasingly drawn to Judaism by virtue of its clear participation in Jewish and Israeli culture, unlike the well-documented alienation of other utopian experiments from their surrounding society? The problem of the boundary mechanisms between the kibbutz and Israeli society and the mutual relations between the kibbutz as cooperative sector and the State are questions that are increasingly concerning students of the kibbutz. What is the relationship between religion and culture? Can the secular kibbutz movement dabble in the values, the readings, the themes, the occasional rituals, the feelings, and the obligations of Judaism and still experience its essence? In other words, to what extent does religious change in a mainly secular movement constitute mainly a context, an atmosphere, and a concern versus a commitment?

Does the kibbutz require a spiritual grounding to insure its future? Does the increasing fragmentation, urbanization, industrialization, and bureaucratization of contemporary Israeli society threaten religious ideals? Does the kibbutz as an alternative society represent a plausible home for these ideals? How is the important practice of improving the world and reducing hierarchy, stratification, and alienation to find its place in religious life? What specific structural arrangements, social inventions, and resource commitments can organized religious men and women bring to bear on the struggle for democracy, quality, and fellowship?

## *Problems of Methodology*

In a recent issue of *Daedelus* (1982) devoted to religion, scholars raise a number of issues that can justly be applied to the kibbutz. Mary Douglas inquires why scholars did not anticipate the most important of religious developments. She asks whether religion frequently summons up elements of deep cultural bias which make us virtually incapable of objectively treating religion and correctly prophesying its trajectory. Douglas's claims that religious studies have continuously been taken by surprise because of the rigid nature of their assumptions and her ideas for studying the effect of modernization on religious change can serve as a guide for future studies of the kibbutz and Judaism, where religious stirrings were also not predicted. Her proscriptions bear further examination as this research continues.

In the same volume, Louis Dupre, writing about "Spiritual Life in a Secular Age," appropriately sets the tone for the Lilker discussion by summarizing the existing barriers of an a-religious kibbutz tradition:

> In the eighteenth century, the idea of God ceased to be a vital concern for our intellectual culture. Almost without transition, deism merged into a practical atheism. In the nineteenth century, this secularized consciousness, no longer satisfied with a de facto absence of any meaningful transcendence, attempted to convert its attitude into a de jure, justified one. Thus originated the virulent antitheisms of scientific positivism, of sociological structuralism, and of axiological humanism. These antitheist trends have survived into our own day, yet they no longer dominate the religious situation of the present. Today's atheism by and large considers its position sufficiently secure to feel no need for defining itself through a negative relation to faith, nor does it exclude the range of religious experience. Indeed it has ex-

tended its territory to include the significant, yet previously neglected, area of spiritual phenomena. It certainly has abandoned the nineteenth century dream of a purely scientific humanism. As a rule it no longer expects an integral world view from science, and it is even beginning to abandon the previous identification of science with human progress. In short, contemporary humanism is less polemical, more comprehensive, but also more thoroughly immanent than that of the recent past. [P. 21]

Dupre believes that it is impossible to replicate the spiritualism of an earlier age which was grounded in a direct experience of the sacred.

The traditional distinctions between the sacred and the profane—in respect to objects, persons, and events—must seem increasingly foreign. In a secular age, men will tend to take the representational content of their spiritual life straight out of their daily secular experience. This is a new kind of religious engagement, a spirituality that reflects the changed place of religion in our lives. Where ecclesiastical power, discipline, and doctrinal authority have all waned, personal decision takes on a new importance; it alone makes possible the implementation of certain religious ideals. In the end it creates whatever community exists. [P. vi]

It must be questioned however, if this view applies to the kibbutz. For religious studies the kibbutz is quite unique in being a community which is modern, intentional, and growing—not traditional, coincidental, and declining. It is a community which is returning to religion, or at least reexperiencing its religious roots in some very definite ways. As a part of modern society, Dupre might view the increased religious interest within the kibbutz as individual-centered, based on "personal decisions." Yet, both Alexander Barzel and Lilker indicate that there is an increasing institutional commitment to Judaism on the part of the kibbutz federations that parallels the more scattered and growing individual interest. Dupre's model accounts for alienated individuals in a fragmented society who find religion and then join a community to express membership. Lilker's analysis suggests individuals who are already a part of a community whose wholeness in confronting the dignity of the human experience becomes one of many complications in a new religious crisis.

# Introduction by Joseph R. Blasi, Series Editor 17

What then is the effect of the coherence of the kibbutz as a society on expected religious change within it? Peter Berger, in *The Homeless Mind* (1974), analyzes in detail the impossibility of a moral community and ethical wholes because of the dizzying onslaught of modernization. According to Berger, religion becomes implausible. As Douglas notes:

> *The Homeless Mind* is in a direct line of descent from his earlier work. It is a cogent summary of how bureaucracy, work organization, and scientific ways of thought combine to isolate, confuse, and reduce the individual's subjective consciousness. In all his early work, the idea of plausibility structures connects social life intimately with belief and knowledge and thus with culture. My criticism of *The Homeless Mind* is the passive role it gives to the knowing subject. As if in a rabbit warren, the mind runs in one direction, finds it closed off, burrows another way, only to find it closed off too. Loops are cut, exits blocked, there is no space to turn around, all directions are closely regulated. According to Berger, modernization means that the mind cannot return upon itself to reflect or travel far enough to discover its limits, cannot confront others enough to find identity. The book convincingly exposes the insulating and isolating controls on responsibility and consciousness. [P. 17]

In an alternative to modern society where this control is not well-exercised is the soil more fertile for religion? Douglas's criticism of Berger cautions us not to view the absence of religion as a predictable result of social structuring.

## World and Universe

Mainline religious organizations that exist in spite of the destruction of the human community around them are continually criticized to show their just effect on the world by reorganizing it. It is as if the secular world asks what the effect is of this soul-searching and this commitment. The secular kibbutz has gone very far in confronting these tasks of reorganization, but the effects of the social renewal without the soul-searching and the spiritual commitment itself are not enough for the member. The crisis is not one of social reform but of spiritual development.

In illustrating the strains when actual social reconstruction confronts the ground of religious experience the kibbutz exemplifies a critical conflict among the students and the practitioners of religion. Are we concerned about the world or the universe *or* the world and the universe?

The spiritual challenge faced by some kibbutzim creates a further problem: how does one distinguish between popularization and the thing itself? Can a simple worldly concern be passed off as a universal commitment? Hasidism has a place in the early history of the kibbutz movement and it has been an attraction for some kibbutz members. A solid case for its strong effect on the movement has yet to be fully documented and the implications of this attachment for the issue of this book are as yet unclear.

Elkana Margalit, a noted historian of the kibbutz movement, has pointed out that even the most left-wing federation, HaShomair HaTzair, was influenced by Hasidism. Yaacov Chazan, one of the early central leaders of that federation, spoke openly and enthusiastically of this recently when Israeli Radio looked back on the fiftieth anniversary of the kibbutz movement. Margalit points out that this otherwise atheist kibbutz federation published an important book called *The Seven Beggars* by Rabbi Nachman of Bratslav in the formative years of the movement. The book appeared without commentary. Margalit, however, notes that Judaism was a climate in which the kibbutz grew and its influence should not be exaggerated (personal communication, 1982).

The current strains of religious sentiment in the secular kibbutz movement continue to arise without a clear formulation or policy and without a clear goal in mind. The distinction between popularization and the thing itself does not however exhaust the argument, since Lilker also explores a different kind of "strain" between sectors of the kibbutz movement and organized religion. This strain is the political conflict, interest group struggles, and mutual criticism over who represents worldly values and who speaks for universal values. It is the struggle over idealistic turf between the kibbutz movement and the religious establishment in Israel. Lilker alludes repeatedly to this conflict.

### Religion in the Sociology of the Kibbutz

While Lilker's work represents a pioneering study of the subject, religion has received some attention by sociologists who have examined the kibbutz. In the fifties, Melford Spiro (1956, 1958) cited numerous indications of strong antireligious feeling among those he interviewed. He was working in a left-wing kibbutz. Blasi (1978), working in the same federation, suggested that the spiritual tradition of Judaism had direct relevance to the spiritual, social, and cultural conflicts that he found engulfing the modern kibbutz community.

Sociologist Aryeh Fishman has provided a general description of the religious kibbutz in its formative years (1957) and a more detailed sociological analysis (1976). Fishman's recent research uncovers startling differences in the economic performance of religious versus secular kibbutzim—they perform much better and have a much higher rate of saving—which is leading to a better formulation of the mutual influences of religion and social invention (1980). Other publications on the religious kibbutz movement include Bahad (1944), Fuchs (1960), Gabovitch (1956), Miller (1962), and Unna (1971).

In 1968 and 1969 Menachem Rosner and his associates conducted one of the most far-reaching studies of kibbutz members. He analyzed the attachment of kibbutz members to Judaism, Zionism, and the State of Israel, their view of Diaspora Jewry and the dangers faced by Jewish communities around the world, their attitudes toward religion, and their stand on an important religious question in Israel—how one is defined as a Jew (1978, 1981).

Rosner notes:

> The question of whether Jewish national identity is possible in the absence of religious affinity is a fundamental issue which has concerned the Jewish national movement since its very foundation. This question also pertains to the dilemma of Jewish affinity by virtue of common destiny versus that which stems from personal decision and free will. The search for national form and content of a non-religious nature has characterized Zionism from its very outset, particularly among members of the Jewish community in Palestine . . . In light of this approach the aspirations for traditional and even religious Jewish form and content expressed by second generation kibbutz members in the post-1967 war dialogues are rather surprising. As one participant declared: "The question is whether the Jewish People have not been preserved thanks to their faith, thanks to their traditions which they carried on . . . It appears to me that we are overlooking the problem that we are Jews thanks to thousands of generations of grandparents who truly believed in some sort of higher value called God and maintained a framework which is called tradition." [P. 225–26, English edition]

Rosner sought to examine (1) the connection between the role attributed to religion in Jewish history and the function ascribed to it today and (2) whether the trend toward tradition is unique to the second generation or whether it affects the founders as well. In brief he discovered that secular kibbutz members viewed religion as more of a disintegrating and disunifying factor in the present. They were extremely concerned about the relationship between religion and politics in Israel. (For further work on this topic, see Clement, 1971.) They saw religion in Jewish history as functioning more as a unifying source of moral values than in the present situation. No differences were found between the founders and the second generation, while the federations did differ slightly. (The more left-wing the federation the less the contemporary role of religion was emphasized.) Rosner nevertheless comments on indications of a reassessment regarding attitudes toward religion among the left-wing kibbutzim as manifested in the Ein HaShofet Conference on Jewish Affinity held in 1967. He concludes that kibbutz members with generally a more sensitive minority among the second generation clearly desire to attain a closer feeling of Jewish identification but they want it based on conscious choice rather than external compulsion. Mordecai Bar-Lev at Bar-Ilan University's School of Education is now completing a similar study of the second generation of the religious kibbutz movement.

It is perhaps in response to a strongly expressed desire to consciously expand that identification that Judaism has gained a more central place in the School of Education of the secular kibbutz movement at Oranim and in individual kibbutz schools. A recent study by Snarey (1982) allows for some initial sketchy evaluation of the first changes that have taken place. He found that kibbutz youth experienced accelerated moral development and that when Israeli city children were raised in the kibbutz after being rescued in their teens from broken homes and broken lives, they showed startling development in the moral area. The kibbutz adolescents referred to the Bible in justifying their moral claims as much as the urban youngsters. This may be an indication that kibbutzim are providing their children—the third generation—with the opportunities for conscious identification requested by the first and second generations. In relate findings, Snarey discovered that the North American founders of a radical left-wing kibbutz in the late forties were heavily motivated by Jewish ethnicity, Jewish historical continuity, and clear connections they consciously made between their Socialist-Zionism and their religious backgrounds. Finally, kibbutz members themselves have continued to write about the kibbutz and Judaism (see Admanit, 1977; Gelb, 1971; Kerem, 1973; Kerem, Maron, and Tzur, 1978; Langer, 1977, 1978; Maron, 1978; Twersky, 1976; and Yassour, 1977).

Shalom Lilker's exploration opens a door in the field of religious studies and Jewish studies that may have a very wide swing (see Fleik, 1971). It can clarify some basic issues on the relationship between religion and society. While it is a significant contribution, the surface has just been scratched. Parallel textual studies of fiction and poetry by kibbutz members and the exposition of the role and symbolism of the kibbutz itself in decades of Hebrew literature would be important contributions to this task. Such work will continue the promising directions pioneered by the author of this volume. We must recognize however, that there is a parallel renaissance of religious interest and religion throughout the country of Israel (in Haifa and in Tel-Aviv, too—not just in the kibbutzim). The scope and aspects of these developments need to be observed, studied, and compared to developments within the kibbutz before further observations can be made about developments within the kibbutzim. This does not minimize the significance of rustlings inside the kibbutz given its own special structure and its centralized antitheist tradition.

> Joseph R. Blasi, Director
> Project for Kibbutz Studies
> Center for Jewish Studies
> Harvard University

# Introduction by Shalom Liker

Israel's spiritual scene suffers from a penchant for ready labels that its society attaches to various segments of its population. Heading the list are the *Dati'im,* or religious Jews. They include all variants of Orthodox Judaism, from the black-robed inhabitants of Me'ah She'arim in Jerusalem to the casually dressed members of the Orthodox kibbutz movement. The small number of Conservative and Reform Jews in Israel are not included in the category of "religious" Jews, attendance at synagogue notwithstanding. The second category are the *M'sorati'im,* or traditional Jews—a nonorganized body of Jews who observe the customs and practices of Judaism within the limits of their capacity. Some of them are practically Orthodox in behavior, while others select those elements of tradition that have special meaning for them. The third and largest group constitutes the *Hiloni'im,* or secular Jews. Primarily national or ethnic in outlook, their attitudes to the religious heritage fluctuate among passive admiration, indifference, and militant distaste.

Uninformed Diaspora Jews visiting Israel often arrive with the astounding notion that all Israelis should be their religious surrogates. Expecting religiosity, the non-Israeli visitor is taken aback by what he observes. Equating the "spiritual" with organized "religiosity," he concludes that Israel is not religious. This error is only optical, for a spiritual Israel does exist, although not necessarily among those Israelis who make claim to religiosity; it also exists in that part of the population which is stereotyped as secularist. Israeli society does not turn to Orthodox Jewry for illustrations of exemplary spiritual and moral behavior. For this it has another source—the secular Jews.

The present situation in Israel bears some reverse resemblance to the state of affairs described in Will Herberg's classic essay on religious sociology, *Protestant, Catholic, Jew.* When Herberg wrote his book, America was undergoing a religious revival, yet thinking, feeling, and acting secularly. In Israel there are certain elements of the secular community who, despite their protestations to the contrary, think, feel, and act religiously.

A major hazard encountered in an attempt to understand the nature of religion lies in the tendency to simplify reality by classifying and compartmentalizing it. Easily recognizable categories afford a conscious saving in thought and in expenditure of mental energy. To use an academic analogy, religion has become another discipline, along with sociology and psychology, physics and chemistry. But just as these subjects have become increasingly interdisciplinary, utilizing and exploiting the knowledge of related fields, religion, too, has emerged from the narrow confines that were fixed by setting organizational affiliation and attendance at worship services as criteria.

With the broad prospects offered by this study of comparative religion, history, sociology, psychology, philosophy, and anthropology for the expansion of religious perspectives, the claim of most of the traditional religions to absoluteness of belief and customs becomes intolerable.

The infinite variety of religious expression transforms such words as "religious" or "irreligious" into little more than subjective evaluations. To prevent solidification of religion into finely distinct categories, or diffusion into vague sentiment, a definition is required that would set down realistic guidelines based on the best of modern research and on the multiplicity of human religious experience.

Definitions of religion are legion, and little profit can be gained by adding to the overly long list. This study has not led the author to yet another definition of religion, but it has led to discernment of a quality of religion that has materialized in the kibbutz.

The nature of religious faith testifies to the social origins of many of the beliefs of man. Whatever the conception of God or whatever faith a man holds, its applicability to life can only be tested within the borders of his culture. A product of his society, a man's beliefs are restricted by the narrowness of his culture, or extended by its breadth. Nevertheless there occur moments when men break through these confines to something new and unique, while remaining to a certain extent within their former universe. Here the kibbutz enters—a witness to the power of the spirit to move men in ways that are unfamiliar to us.

The kibbutz has succeeded in discovering new frontiers within Judaism through its quest for an authentically human style of life. This search is the cornerstone of its religion. Among the many themes appearing in the history of religious quest, the kibbutz exemplifies the search for unity. This recurrent motif has usually appeared in the history of religion as a metaphysical urge to merge, intellectually or sensually, with encompassing reality, however conceived. This could be accomplished by individuals or small groups. For kibbutz religion, unity has become a social principle. The ideal "one" is society presently divided and fragmented, the achievement of whose organic totality is the aim and purpose of kibbutz "theology." Thus the individual breaks out of his solitude, merging with others to create a society whose social expression is the oneness of human beings.

There is an extensive literature in English on the kibbutz, but even the most cursory examination of this material reveals a curious imbalance.

> While there is a proliferation of writing of a general nature, and a marked interest in problems of family life, education, socialization and mental development of the children, a scarcity of writing on other subjects, such as . . . culture and recreation, is evident. [Erik Cohen, *Bibliography of the Kibbutz* (Givat Haviva, 1964), p. 5]

Indeed, research on kibbutz culture—as Jewish culture—is long overdue. The paucity of material on the subject in English can be attributed to a notion that kibbutz life is irrelevant to the problems of English-speaking Jewry. More puzzling is the indifference shown by Hebrew writers, even within the kibbutz movement itself. For reasons to be discussed later this unique society, the most original creation of the Jewish people returned to their land has never been considered especially Jewish in quality, tone, or style. The kibbutz movement itself has paradoxically fostered this attitude. Denial of identity as Jewish is encouraged by the atmosphere prevalent in the State of Israel, where all things "Jewish" must be organizationally recognizable and "historically legitimate." Under such conditions the nonappearance of works on the subject of Judaism and kibbutz should evoke no surprise.

I have limited my research primarily to one kibbutz movement—Ihud-hakevutzot Ve-ha-kibbutzim (hereafter called "Ihud"). This is not intended to deny the significance of the other two movements—Ha-Kibbutz ha-Me'uhad and Ha-Kibbutz ha-Artzi ha-Shomer ha-Tzair—which merit special study. Relevant articles written by members of those movements have been included, and some of their key figures were interviewed. I hope that the picture presented here is not a monchrome but a colorful blend of the variety of views present in the kibbutz movement. Trends and currents within the Ihud do remain, however, the basic source, if only because problems pertaining to Judaism appear more often in their literature. The following Ihud publications were the most frequently consulted: *Niv ha-Kevutzah,* a quarterly journal; *Iggeret,* a weekly newsletter; and the quarterly *Shedemot,* first published in 1960 by the youth division of the Ihud. The period covered by most of the written literature is from 1952 to 1970. Material pertaining to holiday customs and observances is published by a joint committee of three federations, with provision for expression of dissenting views.

Despite cooperation in certain spheres, the three major divisions of the kibbutz movement remain distinct and retain distinguishable differences in tone, mood, and style. In addition to the reading, thirty-five tape-recorded interviews were conducted with kibbutz personalities whose reputation linked them to the subject of this study. Admittedly, subjective choice determined what material was to be considered related and which people were worth interviewing. This choice was dictated by the author's understanding of the breadth and scope of Judaism.

Few books written about a living society, particularly one as self-conscious as the kibbutz, can escape error or bias. Any errors of fact or interpretation that exist in this work are the author's alone. If such mistakes have appeared it is despite the generous advice and devoted assistance of Dr. Jack J. Cohen of the B'nai B'rith Hillel Foundation at the Hebrew University and of Dr. Ezra Spicehandler of the Hebrew Union College in Jerusalem. They both served as advisers for this work in its initial form as a dissertation for the Doctor of Hebrew Letters degree granted by HUC in New York.

Dr. Zvi Kurzweil, chairman of the Department of General Studies at the Technion–Israel Institute of Technology, graciously reduced the number of the author's teaching hours at the Technion to make more time available for research. Conversations with Dr. Zvi Sobel of the Haifa University contributed immeasurably to the fulfillment of the prime function of any writer: asking the right questions.

Kibbutz Ramat Yohanan kindly permitted the author to live and work there with his family during a sabbatical year from the Technion, for the counterweight of kibbutz experience was necessary to balance theoretical knowledge. Without the support of Haim Hadomi, then general secretary of Ramat Yohanan, this could not have been accomplished.

Dr. Geoffrey Wigoder, of the Oral History Division of the Institute of Contemporary Jewry of the Hebrew University, offered the services of his staff for transcription of the interviews. The vital first draft was typed by Tova Shimron, of the Technion. But my greatest gratitude is to my wife, Shoshana, whose patience and understanding smoothed over the many rough spots encountered during the course of the work.

*Kibbutz Judaism*

# 1
# *Historical Gleanings*

> So little do those who shoot the arrows of the spirit know where they will light.
> —R. H. Tawney, *Religion and the Rise of Capitalism*

## *The Rejection of Eastern European Jewish Life*

The highly regarded founders of the kibbutz movement, the *Vatikim*—veterans—have always been controversial individuals. They comprised the small core who built up the kibbutz from its small beginning at Degania to its present status of 90,000 people and 224 kibbutzim (as of 1970).

The character of their creation is the subject of this work, and it is therefore appropriate, before entering into the contemporary world of the *Vatikim*, also to enter into their past. A history of the kibbutz movement has yet to be written. Nor is there adequate material on its European background. The unique creation of a minute segment of the Jewish community in Israel, the kibbutz is inconceivable without its European origins. "European" as used here is a reference to Eastern European life, both Jewish and non-Jewish. Although various waves of immigration came to the kibbutz from Central and Western Europe, and both North and South America, the tone of kibbutz life was generally set by the Eastern European settlers.

The destruction of Eastern European Jewish life resulted in a tendency to idealize that community, especially since the *Vatikim* are in a sense its survivors. Because the world from which they originated no longer exists, its very martyrdom has tempered their former harsh criticism of it. Nevertheless, it was rebellion against that world that provided a good part of the impetus to abandon

Europe and immigrate to Palestine. Sorrow and mourning for the lost society of Eastern European Jewry need not blind us to the fact that one of the most creative movements in modern Jewish life arose as a reaction to a mode and style of life then prevalent among traditional Jewry in Poland and Russia. The distaste of the *Vatikim* for Orthodox Jewry may be muted today, but there is no doubt about their earlier youthful antagonisms. The hostility was mutual, for prior to World War II, when thousands of Jews asked their Hasidic leaders if they should settle in Palestine, the usual answer was no. The heretical views and outrageously nonobservant behavior of the young *Vatikim* were enough to dissuade Hasidic Jews from fulfilling one of the major commandments of the Torah— settlement in the Holy Land. The demographic consequences of this answer for the State of Israel are felt to this day.

## *The Alliance of Religion and Wealth*

The books available in English on Eastern European Jewry compose in a sense a literature of eulogy. The reader of *Life Is with People* or *The Earth Is the Lord's* and the stories of Shalom Aleichem would have difficulty grasping the hostility toward traditional Jewish life that existed among Eastern European Jews only a few generations ago. It is not from the apologetic defenders or blind detractors of Eastern European Jewry that an image of its world in the late nineteenth and early twentieth centuries can take shape, but through the writings of the late S. Y. Agnon, an Orthodox Jew in practice, but no apologist for his coreligionists in Orthodoxy. In his novelette *Two Wise Men in Our City* Agnon writes regretfully that "three or four generations ago, when the Torah was beloved by Israel and every man's glory was in the Torah, our city was privileged to be counted among those known because of the disciples of the wise who lived there." What accounted for the decline of the Torah? Agnon does not engage in analysis, but he does indicate a few aspects of the spiritual breakdown within traditional Eastern European Jewry.

> Why has the glory of the Torah declined? Because the Rabbis marry their sons to the daughters of the rich. The sons-in-law depend on the money of their fathers-in-law, which buys them

the Rabbinate. Once in the Rabbinate they must satisfy the material appetites of their wives, who are unused to austerity. As a result, they become servile flatterers.[1]

Agnon fixes the blame for the Torah's decline not on unbelievers but on its supporters.

As will be seen later, Agnon's description of the unfortunate alliance between the rabbinate and the rich points to one of the basic factors in the abandonment of traditional Jewry by many of its sons. In place of tradition they adopted a socialist teaching that aimed at eliminating circumstances that might result in the corruption of the spiritual leadership of the Jewish people. Even Abraham Joshua Heschel, whose *The Earth Is the Lord's* is a Kaddish for Eastern European Jewry, admits that "there was not only light but also shadow" in that world.[2] Heschel, however, suggests that the shadows were almost entirely a result of the frightful conditions—economic, political, and social—under which Jewry lived. This view was accepted by those Orthodox Jews who adopted Zionism. They agreed with the Zionist thesis that the degrading conditions of life in the Diaspora twisted and warped Jewish life. Only as free men in their own land could Jews restore Judaism to some measure of its inherent but hidden splendor. What form would be taken by a Judaism released from the shackles of the Diaspora still remains a subject for debate. In essence, the rebellion against Eastern European Jewish life was directed against a particular style of life and not against Judaism as a historical tradition. If, indeed, that tradition and people have been distorted by the Diaspora, then it was in effect only a sick tradition that was being rejected. The "rebellion against Judaism," therefore, applied only to Judaism under certain historical circumstances. *Vatikim* universalized from their particular experience—a common enough error—and convinced themselves that they had rejected Judaism.

Their bitter rejection, however, could not conceal the effect of Eastern European Jewish life on the building of their new society, for while the kibbutz is unique and different, it nevertheless retains features that are part of its Diaspora heritage. Despite its use of the language of revolution, the kibbutz exemplifies features of the patterns of social solidarity and mutual self-help that existed there. "The community, a whole made up of many closely welded parts, is felt as an extension of the family."[3] Similar phrases appear in kibbutz literature to this day. There are some observers who go so far as to claim that the successes of the kibbutz are comprehensible only in light of the Eastern European origin of many of its founders, who brought with them the best of that world, despite their apparent repudiation of it. What are these commendable qualities? In *Life Is with People*, it is claimed that despite poverty and suffering there hovered above the communities a Jewish soul characterized by love, respect for others, a striving for justice, study, and messianic vision.

It is doubtful whether Jewish urban socialists from the West could have created kibbutzim. The Eastern European had some model to follow, although its very core—the religious culture of Eastern European Jewry, was found wanting. At first sight the religious world would seem inextricably tied to those very qualities enumerated as existing in the Jewish soul—but by the end of the nineteenth century and the beginning of the twentieth, the Jewish socialists had already separated social justice from its religious origins.

The Jewish working class of Eastern Europe was among the most antireligious groups on the Continent, and the tradition they created retains some of its antireligious force in present-day Israel. This antireligiosity was closer to an anticlericalism, for its major target was the rabbinate and the control it wielded over the people, together with its allies among the wealthy. This does not mean that there were no poor rabbis or that they did not sympathize with and assist the Jewish working class. But the fact remains that the prestigious rabbis, the men in positions of communal leadership, stood in opposition to Jewish workers' movements. From the moment it arose, socialism, like Zionism, was opposed by the rabbinate. The czarist government, at the turn of the century, pressed the rabbinate to issue warnings alerting the Jewish community to the dangers it faced through the establishment of revolutionary groups. This may well have been a factor that set the rabbinate in opposition to the workers; the rabbis might have been more sympathetic had they been left alone. There were indeed some who helped form workers' groups, but it was already too late, for the saying "A rabbi honors the rich" had become dogma in workers' circles.

Rejection of Jewish tradition was relatively easy for Eastern European Jews, since Orthodox Jewry had been unable to discover a means of relating itself to the intellectual and social problems of society. It was a simple matter to describe traditional Judaism not only as reactionary, but also as irrelevant.

To this very day many *Vatikim* in the kibbutz prefer to view Judaism only in terms of its past. The reason is not dificult to see. This model of Judaism presents no challenge to them and can be easily shunted aside. But their aggressive rejection of Jewish tradition inevitably arouses suspicion. Gordon Allport, in his writings on the phychology of religion, remarks that a militant atheism betrays a deep interest in the religious mode of life. The kibbutz would seem to offer a justification of this statement, with the addition that it did more than betray a deep interest—it actually built a religious mode of life.

## *Early Halutz Types*

The intellectually exhilarating atmosphere within Eastern European Jewry attracted swarms of youth to the different movements springing up in that Jewish world. Of the small number who eventually came to Palestine, only a minute percentage went to kibbutzim, and of that percentage most left, to settle in cities or in other types of rural settlement, or to return to Europe. *Vatikim* who were interviewed warned against attempts to romanticize the early period of kibbutz settlement. At all times, from its earliest moments until this very day, the kibbutz has remained the creation of and for a minority group within Israeli society. Certainly in the years before children were born there, the kibbutz could be considered a very selective group. The *Vatikim* comprised an elite among the Jewish people. The attributes of this elite have been described by many writers, among them Martin Buber, who was a close friend of the kibbutz movement and a firm supporter of many of its goals. Buber's friendship was not uncritical, especially in his later years.

During the middle and late 1930s Buber spoke and wrote about the *halutz*, enumerating the characteristics that made this new type an elite. His remarks, perhaps somewhat naive, are of interest as we trace the development of the "new type of man" emerging out of the Israeli experience. The new man, says Buber, is prerequisite to the success of a national movement. Zionism could never have succeeded without an avant-garde able and willing to perform the tasks imposed upon it by Jewish history. Buber saw the duty of the *halutz* not only in the realm of physical development of the land, but also in the creation of a new life, a new type of society. He calls the *halutz* the "regenerative type within the Jewish people," who ties his own personal good to the general good of the people, and whose self-realization is dependent upon the achievement of that immemorial goal of the Jew—an authentic association of human beings. Buber uses the term "halutzic elite" in describing this avant-garde, claiming that the proper place and the proper way of life for this elite is in the communal village. The kibbutz way of life is possible for an elite only, and it serves the function of preserving and renewing the characteristics essential for the leadership class of the Jewish people.

Today a visitor to an established kibbutz can see three and even four generations living together, and he may forget that the *Vatikim* had to create not only a new society but also a new family. Contrary to the usual pattern of Jewish migration, the *Vatikim* arrived without family groups, as young unmarried people who had left their parents behind. Without denying the human tragedy involved, especially for closely knit Jewish families, it was their departure from the physical confines of the adult world that allowed them the freedom to build a new society. Once youthful rebels, they became older. This often nullifies the rebellion of many revolutionaries, but the *Vatikim*, through their migration, "could detach themselves from the existing territorial and institutional structure and realize their rebellion by creating an entirely new society."[4] The very youth of the founding generation affected the structure and appearance of the kibbutz, giving it the character of a youth camp.

Today they realize that a permanent form of settlement can no longer retain the features of youth villages. Most of the youth who entered the kibbutz did not remain, and those who did have more staying power were not supermen, despite Buber's elitism. One of the founders of Degania, Joseph Baratz, describes the loneliness of the early settlers. Life was not a continuous revolutionary "happening." He tells of his longing for parents and family, and of many nights when he would weep with despair. This loneliness, and not only ideology, was a factor in the foundation of a communal form of life, especially for sons and daughters of the shtetl. The dreams and visions of a new society prevalent at that time provided intellectual motivation, but the sense of isolation felt by the *Vatikim* deepened the psychological need fulfilled by a communal settlement. No matter what their reasons for settlement in the kibbutz, most of the young people failed to survive its rigors or to contend with its demands. The *Vatikim* who remain today constitute a minority of the numerous types who, exalted by their social visions and dreams, had passed through the kibbutz over the years.

> A kvutza is not an organization, not a party grouping. It is a life lived together. It is not just a question of agreeing about principles, but of give and take, of understanding, of putting aside selfishness; we learned that it was not easy, and that it did not suit everyone.[5]

What Baratz suggests is that few individuals could pass the test of character required for kibbutz life. Further confirmation is afforded in the diaries kept by early settlers, who often ask the question, Will people learn to live with one another? A picture of some of the people who passed through the kibbutz explains the frequent appearance of that question in settlers' diaries.

> Only those groups with a nucleus of strong and sober minded leaders could make the grade, for they alone knew how to direct emotional upsurge into channels of daily work. The others, after abandoning themselves to ecstasies, were exhausted, and could not cope with the exacting routine of cooperative farm life. Some of the extremists among them grew beards, because it was unnatural to shave; they declared war on European bourgeois dress, and donning sacks, with a hole for the head and two for the arms, were celebrated as the "Kvutza of sacks."[6]

Such eccentrics were eventually weeded out, leaving only a small minority with the stamina to undertake the tasks they imposed upon themselves. This small group, until recently a main focus of Israeli identity, were fond of using revolutionary terminology, thereby accentuating the break with the past. The life they chose undoubtedly did require a "leap of faith," if only because their path was so different from that of previous generations. The question of continuity was of no concern to the *Vatikim* in their youth, when they were so deeply involved in the physical rehabilitation of the land. Of late, however, when there is somewhat more time to be reflective, articles have appeared that emphasize the ease of transition from the "tents of the Lord" to the tents of *halutzim* in the Jezreel Valley. For some the move from the *yeshivah* or *heder* to the *halutz* movement seemed not only natural, but to be taken for granted.

## *Kehiliyateynu: A Nontheistic Mystic Brotherhood*

The document entitled *Kehiliyateynu* (Our Community) was printed in 1922 and contains letters, notations, and confessions of twenty-seven of the one hundred members of Kibbutz Alef, the first kibbutz of what was later to become Ha-Kibbutz ha-Artzi ha-Shomer ha-Tzair. This group, which had worked previously in road gangs in the Galilee area, later became the nucleus of Bet Alfa. Whoever reads *Kehiliyateynu* has the impression that he has stumbled across a variation of William James's *Varieties of Religious Experience*. The entire book evokes the setting for a mystical religious sect and is charged with religious feeling and symbolism. God as the partner of mystic union, or the object of mystic devotions, does not appear. For *Kehiliyateynu* is a form of what Erich Fromm calls nontheistic mysticism. Anyone familiar with the rationalism of contemporary kibbutz life would be amazed by the revelations appearing in the pages of *Kehiliyateynu* that reveal that the beginnings of the kibbutz movement were infused with a mystical spirit.

A selection of short readings from the book will illustrate its tone.

> Then came the moment when the love of each for his friend created wonder: souls were revealed in their true light and joined. . . . On the altar of common creativity a group soul was formed. . . . Arms were joined and wild song burst forth. The next day all were loyal brothers, who looked at each other with love and affection. That night the Kvutza was formed. [P. 24]

> We called that night Yom Kippur night, when we sat until morning and confessed to each other. It was as pure prayer, overflowing from heart to heart. [P. 23]

> A miracle! As I reached the peak of the hill I felt as if a holy "Shechina" enveloped me and conquered my heart, pushing away all the black clouds that hovered over me for the longest time. I rested on the peak of the hill. . . . My heart full and overflowing with reverence, awe and joy, a joy I had never known before. I felt as though I would hear the voice of an angel of God, decreeing and commanding, "Take off your shoes for you are walking on holy soil." [P. 96]

> We believe that our extreme love for the idea of the new

society is our greatest strength, our most Jewish strength. [P. 116]

The family meal—the secret from which grows the mystery of every religion, every messianic and hasidic movement, every community and commune: the altar table. Without the altar table there is no commune. [P. 129]

You have sought an eternal Sabbath and failed to understand that it is the week that creates the Sabbath. [P. 177]

It appears that the Kibbutz ha-Artzi was not overly eager to publish *Kehiliyateynu*. For a movement that took pride in "scientific socialism," the document seemed inappropriate. One respondent, an intellectual of Kibbutz ha-Artzi, claimed that the best source for an understanding of the spirit of the kibbutz is in *Kehiliyateynu*. Whatever the disagreements about this book, it remains a prime source for understanding the spiritual odyssey of the kibbutz.

Almost all the *halutzim* appearing in *Kehiliyateynu* came from one area of East Europe—the province of Galicia of the pre–World War I Austro-Hungarian Empire. Once having left Europe, these young people did not immediately join or form kibbutzim, but worked in road gangs under severe conditions. These youths, in their late teens or early twenties, came from middle-class homes. They were delicate and somewhat spoiled. Driven by grandiose ideas about the nobility of proletarian life and culture, they were bitterly disappointed by their contact with fellow workers on the road gangs. Despite their appreciation of the positive qualities of the workers—in particular their willingness to assist each other—they were disillusioned by the narrow reach of proletarian cultural life. Sensitive youths who had been accustomed to some quiet and solitude at home were unable to stand the mass conditions of living in the road gangs. In short, they refused to adjust to the way of life they found, and instead sought a means of implementing an idea they had brought with them—the idea of brotherhood. Now they were able to form a communal brotherhood because the setting was just right—they were without family, estranged from their new environment, and suffering from physical conditions of life for which they were unprepared.

The establishment of Kibbutz Alef, while they were still working on the roads, seemed a genuine catharisis for many of its members. Contemporary descriptions of that period reveal a depressing scene. The heat, the severe physical effort, fatigue, poor diet, and disease resulted in nervous breakdowns. At night weeping could be heard from the tents and suicide was not unknown. Under such circumstances, the founding of Kibbutz Alef as a communal brotherhood provided relief from the severe tensions experienced daily. A release was also afforded by group confessionals, which became a tradition in Kibbutz Alef and remained a practice in the earlier years of Bet Alfa.

While immediate circumstances undoubtedly were a factor in the creation of Kibbutz Alef, it would be oversimplification to claim that loneliness alone was behind the will to build a communal brotherhood. The founders' departure from Europe was partially motivated by a rejection of the European society they knew, which they saw as hypocritical and philistine. In reaction, they sought to build a brotherhood whose dominating features would be solidarity, mutuality, and a sense of communal oneness.

The success of such an ambitious venture depended upon having a mixed group of members. Although mostly from the same youth movement and the same region of Europe, they were not of one cultural stamp. Some were from assimiliated Polish-Jewish families, far from Judaism or Zionism, others from a Hasidic background. Followers of Buber shared a tent with anarchists and a few who were disposed to Jesus. It is no wonder that outward religious behavior appeared in the life of Kibbutz Alef. The members would frequently burst into Hasidic song and in the evenings go as a group into the surrounding hills, searching for unity with the natural world. It is hardly surprising that their neighbors looked upon Kibbutz Alef with some skepticism. A variety of interpretations were current, because of the air of mystery surrounding the group. Some thought they were a free-love society, and probably all considered them strange visionaries. There is, of course, some justification for the common opinion that Kibbutz Alef was composed of unusual people undergoing a deep psychological crisis. The introspective tone of *Kehiliyateynu* reflects this crisis and the longing of many of its contributors for psychological balance. Throughout its pages there appear phrases that give evidence of fear, despair, uncertainty. The goal sought, to use the Hasidic phrase appearing in *Kehiliyateynu* was a "straightening of the tortuousness of the heart." The hope was constantly expressed for the creation of a new life through brotherhood through the formation of a "spiritual family." The never-ending emphasis on individual renewal—through the group—inevitably brought in its wake a reaction, both within Kibbutz Alef and from its friends. Within *Kehiliyateynu* itself the accusation appeared that the members of Kibbutz Alef were too intensely interested in themselves and in their own subjective problems.

The most damaging criticism of the atmosphere that prevailed in Kibbutz Alef came from Meir Ya'ari of Merhavia, longtime head of Mapam. Ya'ari attacks the ceaseless search after Olympian experiences and the unwillingness of many members to reach their vision by way of the routine and dull path of daily life. He blames the youth movements in Europe, which preach "youth culture," the cult of youth, the "eternity of youth," and a mélange of contradictory notions culled from conflicting sources such as Buber, Nietzsche, Freud, and Landauer. The result is the "spiritual egocentrism" of *Kehiliyateynu*, which he sees as the "swan song of exaggerated religiosity."

In the reality of the early 1920s, the poorly digested ideas brought from the European youth movements had no chance of survival. Ya'ari was proved correct by the many who abandoned Kibbutz Alef when it settled on the land to become Bet Alfa. Their reason was simple: that ultimate brotherhood they had sought did not exist. Those grand dreams of a new type of social relations shattered on the "prosaic rock of daily work." The free life on the roads, the stimulation of imagination that existed in Kibbutz Alef had to give way before the rational tasks of building a settlement with its demands for discipline, constancy, sobriety, and complete concentration on the problems of the settlement. There is no need to conclude, however, that Bet Alfa became so grimly efficient that it was emotionally poverty-stricken. It still retained many of the customs of Kibbutz Alef—the communal confession, Hasidic enthusiasm in song and custom, and a generally emotional and "religious" atmosphere. Everything was still wrapped in mystery and saturated with questioning—and there were no answers. The society and surroundings outside seemed too simple, secular, and even cynical.

The need to restore a balance among those young people desperately seeking their individual salvation did not lead Ya'ari to cold pragmatism or to rejection of the search for self-renewal. He contended that, without a world view, the newly emerging communes would have little future or meaning. This emerges from a statement in his article "Unattached Symbols," in 1923:

> An entire people cannot ensure its existence and continuity for any length of time without a metaphysical principle and a religious symbol. Without it, it will cease. Here no economic or social concept will suffice. It is also clear to me that a religious symbol which can serve as the heritage of all the community can be born only among us, the mass of toilers, who are disgusted by luxury and willingly accept. . . . a material asceticism. We do not have the religious symbol today—and since it is not here—no amulets, whisperings or momentary excitement will help. In our path, the path of labor, we shall continue without it. We are obligated to start from the beginning and have to search without false images. Perhaps, as we search, we shall find a source of living water under the gloom of grey reality. The work is not ours to finish. Generations come and go, groping in the mist, until the redeeming symbol will again be discovered. But this is not intended to encourage those who wait in the corridor out of boredom, and then try to break into the parlor.[7]

This passage is quoted at length to forestall any conclusions that *Kehiliyateyna* was little more than an episode best forgotten. Its spirit, despite the bizarre expression it found, still remains beneath the surface of the kibbutz, and is a prime source of the social creativity necessary for kibbutz living.

# 2
# *Ideas on Trial*

> Issues which were thought to have been buried by the discretion of centuries have shown in our day that they were not dead, but sleeping.
> —R. H. Tawney, *Religion and the Rise of Capitalism*

## The Kibbutz as a Believing Community

Today the kibbutz movement has become, in large part, a stable society composed of a number of generations. In a few cases even great-grandchildren have appeared on the scene. The growth and development of the kibbutz in its early years was dependent on an influx of committed youth from the various branches and divisions of the Zionist movements—in other words, through converts who abandoned their former way of life and attempted to live the kibbutz way. Population increase, therefore, was dependent almost entirely on external sources. The so-called internal immigration—children born in the kibbutz—was quite negligible. Since World War II and the establishment of the State of Israel, the external sources have not renewed themselves, and the kibbutz movement has been forced to base its forecasts for growth upon internal renewal. This does not mean, however, that all endeavours to attract outsiders have ceased, or that the kibbutz has despaired of attracting urban elements from Israel and the Diaspora. Efforts to this end are still made today, although it is too early to determine what measure of success has been achieved.

In its edition of April 2, 1971, the newspaper Ha-Aretz, one of the few in Israel not officially affiliated with a political party, ran an advertisement headed "The kibbutz wants to be your home." The notice sought to outline those advantages of kibbutz life which might reasonably convince a reader that the kibbutz is a good place to live in.

The advertisement, published jointly by all the kibbutz movements, emphasized the opportunities available to potential members in a wide variety of occupations, the excellent educational system, decent standards of living, and the respect of the kibbutz for a person's individuality. There was no immediate reaction to this advertisement, but a promotional pamphlet published during the period of economic recession in Israel prior to the Six-Day War, and written in a similar spirit, aroused the anger of some *Vatikim* who saw in it another indication of ideological decline. They felt that the kibbutz was being presented as a society whose material and social advantages rival and surpass the city—and not as a society where values play a key role. At no point has the kibbutz been against material comfort, though some tension does exist between the materially good life and an ascetic tinge in kibbutz life. In the 1970s the appeal to potential members is: "Live in the kibbutz and see if you like it"—certainly a realistic and reasonable approach in a pragmatic society.

The question raised by the advertisement in *Ha-Aretz* is: Can a pragmatist or realist live in a kibbutz? While the kibbutz is certainly a rationalistic society in the choice of means, it nevertheless remains a believing society in its choice of ends. Is the practice of kibbutz life possible without some prior commitment to its cardinal tenets? Perhaps the kibbutz is returning to an old and tested approach found in Jewish tradition—that practice of the commandments without proper intention is preferable to nonpractice. The assumption is that automatic, even unthinking observance will eventually result in emergence of the appropriate intention. Life in the kibbutz, and its values and commitments will become self-evident and will perhaps be absorbed.

One possible reason for the absence of a kibbutz "Torah" or teaching in its promotional literature is that a clearly formulated "Torah" does not exist. All the movements have platforms, and articulate individuals have written stirring expositions of kibbutz belief, yet in oral interviews respondents resisted its formulation. This may indicate either uncertainty, an unwillingness to be doctrinaire and rigid, or the realization that the kibbutz is engaged in a reevaluation of its primary values. Be it as it may, all respondents agreed that their society is a believing one.

Many Israelis are unimpressed by formulations of kibbutz belief and see in the kibbutz only a refuge from the struggles of living, a shelter for the unambitious and the fearful. One needs a heavy dose of prejudice against the kibbutz to accept such a narrow view.

People who view life almost entirely in material terms, or according to current standards of achievement and status, see in the kibbutz only failure and retreat. An approach to the kibbutz from a spiritual viewpoint will result in a different conclusion. The material body of the kibbutz is more than just a sprawling collection of buildings, homes, and fields. Similar structural groupings can be found elsewhere. Where the kibbutz transcends its material limitations is in the realm of the spirit, for it has become, with all the attendant problems of implementation, a living embodiment of a set of values and principles. It transcends itself. What these values are determines the nature and direction of that transcendence, whether for good or for evil.

Value tied to reality is a significant kibbutz contribution, for even the most noble and aristocratic values have little use other than for intellectual sport if they remain unrooted in actuality. Life in a kibbutz where it must be lived as a constant example, primarily for the children, has the qualities of a pedagogical exercise.

> Everything you say is worthless unless we leave the classroom and see such examples in life.

This remark—directed at a kibbutz teacher by his pupil—indicates the difficulty of building a society on principles. Like the works of creation, it must be renewed every day.

Anyone who has spent time in a kibbutz will recall the inability of the people there, particularly the youth, to express their inner beliefs. Yet without a spiritual world is it possible to remain in a kibbutz? Unfortunately, this inner world remains locked and barred; few seem to know how to open it or where the key is to be found. A spiritual movement need not necessarily be metaphysical or cosmological. It may leave untouched the big questions of human purpose and of man's relationship to the universe in favor of the more prosaic problems of everyday existence. The kibbutz at this stage is unwilling or unprepared to grapple with a cosmology. This does not mean that it loses its right to be considered as a spiritual movement. Flight beyond the confines of actuality remains an option for the kibbutzniks who are willing to encounter the dangers entailed—as long as they fulfill their responsibilities to their "earthly" society. Unless this demand be met, and a man has his feet planted on the ground while his head reaches to the heavens, ideas and spirit lose their ultimate value as guides to life.

## *Rationalistic Faith*

In discussions of a society built upon faith there is a tendency to evaluate that quality in irrational terms, as opposed to reason or common sense. This is especially so with supernatural religions, which the metaphysical dimension places beyond the boundaries of the natural world and of verifiable evidence. The faith of the kibbutz is not a supernatural one, though it may very well be metaphysical—for it certainly is not verifiable in the commonly accepted sense. Because it neither engages in cosmological speculation nor seeks a revelation, does the kibbutz thereby lose its right to be considered a community of faith? It might well be claimed that any community of faith lacking revelational overtones can never fully achieve the potentialities of the faith dimension, and must remain a pseudo-faith. The kibbutz could retort that its faith is the more genuine because it is rational and based upon "one's own experience, in the confidence of one's power of thought, observation and judgment."[8] This type of faith, called "rational faith" by Erich Fromm, is called "secular humanistic faith" by Ze'ev Gazit of Kibbutz Ein Dor (Ha-Kibbutz ha-Artzi). In his important article "Secular Faith," he outlines those characteristics which lift the kibbutz above existing reality, yet allow it to remain rooted in that reality. In other words, kibbutz faith as he understands it is realistic, going beyond the present toward a yet unrealized future—but this future, the object of the faith, remains at all times natural, not supernatural. Gazit admits that religious movements gave birth to secular faith, but that secular faith picks up and develops the realistic trends within supernatural religion. He believes that man is not just a rational creature, but possesses the quality of faith as an inherent trait. Without this characteristic he would be unable to summon the zealousness sometimes necessary for the bold steps his beliefs dictate. However, these steps always lead toward the possible, for if the object of faith remains beyond human achievement, few will make the attempt. Zionism and the Second and Third Aliyah all demanded the belief that their goals were attainable. Were this not so, no one would have come to Palestine and attempted to build a different society.

According to Gazit, the source of a visionary faith planted in realism can be found in the gaps between the ability to act and the ability to understand. Only when this gap is spanned—by faith—can man act and operate. Belief, then, is activistic and perhaps even situational, arising in response to challenge, when faith in the value of an ultimate aim can provide the strength and impetus for its successful achievement. This can be illustrated through the example of messianism, a belief that seemed unrealistic, unrealizable, and perhaps even dangerous until Jewish nationalism arose and messianism appeared achievable as Zionism.

Like all analysts of the nature and goals of faith, Gazit asks how to prevent it from being petrified and dogmatic. He answers by demanding an open faith, free from conservatism, infantilism, emotionalism, and dogma (dependence on the written word, which turns all those who disagree into heretics). The open faith does not tie itself to sacred principles, and is willing to doubt anything. Gazit does not deny the risks of that faith. It is a faith without assurance. It rewards, yet offers no certainties.

A view of faith similar to Gazit's is found in Gordon Allport's *The Individual and His Religion*, in which faith is defined as "man's belief in the validity and attainability of some good (value). The goal is set by desires. They include such complex, future-oriented states as changing for a better world, for one's own perfection, for a completely satisfying relation to the universe. . . . Some sort of idea of the end is always bound into the act itself. It is this inseparability of the idea of the end from the course of the striving that we call faith."[9]

Because the kibbutz feels under no obligation to take its faith beyond the natural world into a theological realm, the question arises of the permanence of its faith structure. Without their having a base in the universe or a guarantor in God, what future is there for the values professed by the kibbutz? Can its members faithfully fulfill the demands of their society if these demands lack the stamp of eternity? The kibbutz movement realizes that it bears certain absolute values, such as equality, for example, but it is reluctant to speculate upon them abstractly.

The debate between sociologists and theologians on the religiosity of different patterns of faith is relevant in any discussion of the kibbutz. Except in the Orthodox kibbutz, the kibbutzniks are not consciously religious in the traditional sense. The kibbutz has been called a religion without revelation, or a humanistic religion, or a substitute religion. These terms all point toward religious overtones in the kibbutz and a different understanding of what the objects of faith should ideally be. If the term "religion" can be used as descriptive of the kibbutz, it is because kibbutz society takes hold of the second pole of all theology—man—which has been underplayed in most traditional religions. Perhaps here the kibbutz is acting as a precursor of future trends in religion. The answer to this question will become clearer at the conclusion of this work.

In a world where faith is not considered a progressive characteristic, the kibbutz must engage in constant struggle. The nonbelievers ridicule all believers, of whatever kind. The religious believers ridicule the "neoreligiosity" of a nontheological faith. Within the kibbutz itself a small minority of young people are asking whether they can do without God.

Above all, the kibbutz is a society created for the good of the members. As a voluntary society the kibbutz would never be able to impose courses of action that its members could not accept. The traditional Jewish saying—that the Sabbath was created for man and not man for the Sabbath—applies to kibbutz life. The forms and patterns of Kibbutz life derive their validity from their success in shaping a more satisfying sort of life for those who live by them. "And you shall live by them"—this biblical precept revealing the aim of the Bible's laws and codes certainly applies to the kibbutz way of life. What occurs when a conflict arises between principle and the demands of human nature, whether in traditional Judaism or in the kibbutz, would be a good indicator of how spirit and letter find a delicate balance.

## Trust in Man

Berl Katznelson, the "Rav" of many *Vatikim*, stated unequivocally that the kibbutz, despite its broadly national and social aims, seeks basically to create a human society worthy of man. Katznelson was very much the activist, constantly involved in the institutions of the Jewish community's political life and in the Histadrut, but his major concern always remained the soul of the *haver*.

This concern for the soul of each member is more than altruism. Unless the kibbutz is worthy of man and is built for man, its future holds little promise. To make man the center of society is actually a kibbutz imperative. Placing man in the center does not, however, mean constant satisfaction of his wants or the fulfillment of all his needs. While the centrality of man does include provision for a higher standard of living, its major aim is improvement of human behavior and the realization of man's humanity. These goals cannot be achieved without struggle. As a result, the kibbutz, contrary to a commonly held view, becomes a difficult rather than an easy way of life. It takes on the character of a moral movement. The measure of success is not pertinent here. Of moment is that the kibbutz sees itself as a contributing agent to the development of human character. Today there is little of the naiveté of the early years when *Vatikim* believed that finer people and better human relations would result from a society that is liberated from individual competition and freed from the competitive struggle for existence. Today the kibbutz realizes that people are too complex to be remolded merely by changing the conditions of life. This does not mean, however, that the goal has vanished. It remains, and more sophisticated means are now being sought for its achievement.

Not all kibbutzniks agree that the kibbutz should be made responsible for the needs of the individual. The view that the general good has preference over the individual good now has few supporters. The reason is not difficult to see. Thousands of people left the kibbutz not because of grand ideological issues but because it was unable to respond to individual wants. Once the kibbutzniks grasped this fact, the proper balance between individual and general will was sought—and is still being sought today.

What theory of human nature guides the kibbutz in its daily relations? Though it is quite possible to claim that "human nature" is not a separate entity, being just the sum of a person's social relations, the kibbutz does operate on certain assumptions about human beings. It believes that man is basically good. This seemingly naive premise has practical consequences, for without it there would be no kibbutz. Complete trust prevails in daily life—no foreman checks one's work.

The results of this trust are difficult to gauge. Sometimes its consequences go beyond the confines of the kibbutz. Young men and women from broken homes or backgrounds conducive to delinquency often return to their homes better people, less given to the suspicion and hostility so common to the average urban society, after having lived in the kibbutz. During their stay in the kibbutz they have gained a heightened respect for humanity that serves them well in adult life. In this respect the kibbutz has functioned as a clinic, helping to heal the psychic wounds suffered by many youthful unfortunates, who live for the first time in a society that believes in its members. This is its strength and its weakness. If someone says he doesn't feel well and can't work, he is believed. Whatever one has done is the best one can do. On the outside this is considered a naive attitude toward people, and obviously it can encourage what the kibbutz calls "parasitism." But it remains the greatness of the kibbutz. A Jewish proverb says, "Honor him, yet suspect him." But the kibbutz cannot live by this standard, for without trust it would degenerate into suspicion, hostility, and finally self-destruction. The kibbutz has become a testimony to the possibilities of the human spirit—attempting to overcome pettiness, meanness, and jealousy. I say "attempt" because fulfillment of the ideal remains remote, and perhaps the kibbutz is doomed to eventual failure in its search for an ever-increasing human perfection.

## *The Future of Humanism*

During the interviews with kibbutz members none was willing to say in so many words that his humanism was religious in origin. Most kibbutzniks would consider themselves "secular humanists" or "socialist humanists." For the few who do consider themselves religious humanists, there is no God-figure as traditionally understood. "God is in his place,"[10] not because of a belief in His existence, but because it can be felt that God exists in the particular way of life found in the kibbutz—a way of life aimed at lifting the individual beyond his material concerns into the realm of values.

Not everyone will accept this concept of godliness, but its recognition is significant for the "theological" future of the kibbutz. In effect, loyalty to the social values of the kibbutz becomes synonymous, if not with God, then with godliness. This philosophy also opens doors for that sense of holiness whose want is so deeply felt in the kibbutz. The respondent who expressed this view belongs to Kibbutz Hatzerim, where traditional services have been instituted for the High Holidays—an indication of the beginning of a search for suitable instruments by means of which to evoke the holiness implicit in the kibbutz way.

On the assumption that the kibbutz is a uniquely Jewish creation (a view accepted by the kibbutz today), its humanism is a Jewish humanism that draws from the sources of Jewish life and literature—a process going on today with greater intensity. The humanism of the kibbutz, whether it is secular, socialist, or religious, is a realization of values basic to Judaism, in whatever guise they appear.

Religious humanism, of whatever kind, remains the position of a minority among kibbutz thinkers. This is understandable in the light of their unawareness of modern religious thought and of their automatic identification of religion with a behavioristic Orthodoxy. Martin Buber, himself a religious humanist, had some minor influence. The kibbutz with a special tie to Buber—Ha-Zorea—drifted away from Buber's religious thinking, yet considered itself loyal to his humanistic teachings. A member of Ha-Zorea claims that Buber himself understood that in these days man must turn to man, because God is difficult for moderns to accept. Turning to man was not to be conceived as a denial of God, but a demand of the hour during this age of God's eclipse.

The kibbutz humanist who denies that a belief in God is a necessity for an ethical person has some powerful arguments on his side. These arguments are based on a comparison between a society without a consciously theistic humanism (kibbutz) and a consciously theistic society (Orthodox Judaism in Israel). In a debate appearing in the journal *Shedemot* on the attitude of Judaism to the non-Jew, a member of Ha-Kibbutz ha-Artzi, while admitting occasional remarks favorable to non-Jews, declared that the dominant tone of Jewish tradition is negative. The conclusion of this debate was that nontheistic humanism is ethically superior to traditional Judaism in all that pertains to the non-Jew, i.e., the human being as human and not as Jew alone. While this is an oversimplification of a complex issue, the truth nevertheless remains that the kibbutz believes it has a moral stature and power sorely lacking within religious Jewry. Nontheistic humanism was considered a satisfactory source for the values of life by many of my respondents, though some admitted that means are lacking for turning the values and faith of nontheistic humanism into a Torah, a lifeteaching.

On the issue of educating for humanism, David Maletz of Ein Harod is the most serious thinker. For many years he served as a teacher of Hebrew literature at the local high school, and is a writer of essays and novels on kibbutz life.

Maletz, as a teacher of the humanities, poses some difficult questions for himself. He cannot teach the value of truth, of justice, other than as nontheistic, but he admits his fear that without the backing of a religious tradition these values will be unable to withstand the pressures of what he terms a nihilistic world. He rejects Dostoevski's view that without God everything is permitted, yet admits that humanism in Europe is bankrupt. This does not necessarily thrust him into the arms of religion as a consequence. We must do the best with what we have, says Maletz, and the best is humanism. Humanism is not easier to accept than religion, for both teach life values that conflict with the *Weltanschauung* of maximum comfort and personal pleasure that Maletz observes in the youth he taught.

The aim of the kibbutz and of its educators—a fully human being—is doomed to failure if humanism has no foundation functionally similar to Providence in religion. Maletz means that in religious thought God sees everything and man is responsible to Him. Humanism can have a foundation if a man believes that he is responsible to somebody or something. He arrives at this conclusion through his belief that no society, however moral it may be in relations between its members, can exist forever on ethical values alone. In Jewish tradition the ethical commandments between man and his neighbor had their counterpart in commandments between God and man. Maletz realizes that kibbutz society lacks this second category of commandments and cannot artificially accept them, and therefore suggests an interpretation of his own—commandments between man and his place in the world. This entails a deepening of the relationship between man and the universe. Again, this in itself is not sufficient. He further suggests that appropriate ceremonial forms be found for expressing this relationship. As far as is known, nothing has been produced in line with this suggested proposal, which is an admission that what Maletz terms the "eternal human values"[11] are in danger in the kibbutz unless efforts are made to provide them with a secure base.

Another motive underlying Maletz's search for a sturdy humanism is the disappointment of the early settlers in the belief that the disappearance of private property and the establishment of forms of life based on equality and cooperation would improve the quality of human relations. This article of faith was shattered on the rock of human nature, which proved more complex and complicated than they had foreseen. The ideal of better human relations still remains the vision—but simple trust in redemption through changes in the forms of society has given place to a more sober assessment of human character. Both Buber and A. D. Gordon opposed the simplistic faith that societal forms are able to shape human behavior. Buber wrote, "The body cannot be healed without healing the soul"[12] and Gordon stated that humans determine more than forms. The brief experience of the kibbutz reveals that neither shifts in societal forms nor a reliance on the individual has proved salutary.

## Asceticism as a Moral Principle

Another factor in the formation of the character of the kibbutz is its ascetic tinge—an odd and unexpected characteristic in a non-religious movement. The willingness to forego material pleasure and advantage has generally been associated with religious sects or movements whose readiness to relinquish material goods was in expectation of greater riches in another realm. The next world and its rewards, fuller and more sublime than this existence, were to be achieved with greater certainty through self-renunciation. For the believer there was really no sacrifice entailed, because the joys of future life would outweigh whatever deprivations were suffered in this existence. But for a this-worldly movement asceticism brings no rewards, neither in this world nor the next. The simple question arises: What possible function can even the mildest asceticism perform in the kibbutz? Socialism is not an ascetic doctrine. Nor is the dominant tone of Jewish tradition especially ascetic. Yet a certain asceticism remains a basic value in kibbutz life, not as physical flagellation or withdrawal from surrounding society, but as simplicity in life-style and a distaste for the externals that often erroneously determine an individual's status and prestige. Even when a member of a kibbutz goes to live outside Israel for a short period, he is expected to continue to live in a modest manner, refraining from show or behavior unbecoming a kibbutz member. Failure to live simply implies a surrender to the surroundings and their standards—which often judge a man by what he has rather than what he is.

Asceticism for the kibbutz, therefore, becomes a means of judging a member's loyalty to the kibbutz belief in man. Once an individual is judged by his material possessions, there remains little possibility of discovering him as a man, for such externals cloak his real personality. By the renunciation of some material goods a man reveals his inner strength, his commitment to self-discipline. Asceticism thereby ceases to be a negative, masochistic denial and instead serves as evidence of a search for content in life. The kibbutz has found that material goods deflect a man from the essential to the secondary, from the permanent toward the temporary. Therefore a simple life-style assists it in the quest for the development of a spiritual outlook on the world. Naturally, this still remains an unrealized ideal. Many people in the kibbutz remain untouched by it.

The religious kibbutzim have discussed the place of material austerity in their movement and concluded that, even though this value has no halakhic foundation in Jewish tradition, they will continue to advocate it, because kibbutz society would crumble were material achievement to become primary. A comfortable life is not negated when it serves the purpose of promoting a higher spiritual and ethical level. The sought-for balance remains extremely delicate and a tipping of the scales toward materialism would be highly dangerous for the kibbutz; a retreat from implementation of its social goals. It would lose the moral stature bestowed upon it by a measure of voluntary austerity.

It was in the first years of settlement that asceticism took root in the kibbutz. The poverty of that period made it not only a virtue but a necessity. Nevertheless, even as physical conditions improved, asceticism remained a constituent value, primarily for the sense of inner power that it conferred upon its practitioners. In addition, revolt against their middle class background made ascetic ideas appealing to many *Vatikim* who sought a simpler way of life as a means of creating a workers' culture, and as a symbol of their distaste for middle-class culture. But whatever the causes, the outcome was a tempered relationship to the material world that stood the kibbutz in good stead over the years and helped supply its spiritual energy. Once the kibbutz had learned moderation and restraint, it moved ahead in its task of constructing the new and different society it sought. If a high standard of living were its central aim, the kibbutz would cease to be a society built upon an ideal and become an unsatisfactory imitation of surrounding society.

## *The Work Ethic*

Acceptance of a standard of living less comfortable than the urban has not resulted in a weakening of the will to work. Even without directly measurable material rewards for work accomplished, the work ethic retains an honored place in the hierarchy of kibbutz values. Spiro's *The Kibbutz* has an excellent description of this society's work ethic. He makes a point, confirmed by personal experience, that one would feel guilty should he be unwilling or unable to do manual work. Not to perform any physical labor at all—even the least demanding—would reveal a reluctance to share in the work that is necessary for the operation of the kibbutz.

By its almost unqualifiedly affirmative evaluation of manual labor, the kibbutz was apparently overreacting to the depreciation of this value in the shtetl. Intellectual prowess was demeaned—perhaps as a defense. Yet within this stream of anti-intellectual emotion a few voices spoke out in favor of a felicitous combination of the physical and intellectual for the kibbutz man of the future, an emulation of the ancient sages whose aim had been to find a combination of worker and intellectual who both labored and studied Torah. This was undoubtedly an exceptional phenomenon in its day, for physical labor was relegated to the slave in ancient Greece and Rome. There is a saying in Jewish tradition that "any teaching that is not accompanied by labor is destined to be nullified and to bring sin in its wake."

But this saying exerted little influence, for in the course of their history Jews moved heavily into professions which demanded minimal physical labor. The balance of the Second Temple period tipped under the weight of a heady intellectualism, and economic conditions during subsequent centuries led Jews away from physical work. The kibbutz, until recently at least, had some success in restoring to manual labor its ancient prestige. Today physical work remains a basic tenet of the kibbutz, but with it there is a growing understanding of the need for study in the complex world of the 1970s. Now that work and study are more evenly balanced, historical perspective allows a calmer evaluation of the significance of labor. The kibbutz was instrumental in eradicating from some elements of the Jewish people what Lewis Mumford calls "the shame of labor, that previous heritage of servile culture."[13] Kibbutz members working outside of their kibbutz, or former members employed by Israeli firms, have excellent reputations as reliable workers. (A quip has it that in addition to the usual credentials such as B.A. or B.S. there is B.K., or Bachelor of Kibbutz—an unofficial degree, the best evidence that such a man is a hard worker.) In kibbutz high schools youngsters must devote part of their school time to special work projects and are expected to engage in some productive kibbutz activity parallel to their studies.

The kibbutz has made a significant contribution to society by raising work to the level of a social value, and divorcing it from direct connection to the profit motive. Society is no longer conceived of as an appendage or handmaiden to an efficient economy. Two realms previously distinct are now united, the societal and the economic, with society's goals having ultimate preference over economic aims. This was accomplished not only without loss of a work ethic (the usual result of a lack of economic motivation), but with the elevation of work to the level of a creative principle.

The social creativity of the kibbutz has drawn upon rich sources in the Jewish and non-Jewish world for the formulation and fulfillment of its values. None of the values mentioned in this chapter are new, nor does the kibbutz claim to be an originator of values. Like Shakespeare, who borrowed his plots from others, yet produced original plays, the kibbutz has disclosed a creativity by the new social variations it has composed upon traditional themes.

# 3
# *Hansen's Law in the Kibbutz*

"What the son wishes to forget, the grandson wishes to remember."

The Kibbutz will provide the motive for greater belief. For in the Kibbutz movement there is idealism, searching, self-accounting, and a striving for truth. You do not find there comfort for its own sake, pleasure-seeking and careerism as in the city. All this can serve as a background for a new awakening in the direction of adopting the eternal values of Judaism. Sometimes I feel that redemption will come, oddly enough, from the kibbutzim of Mapam because of their seriousness. . . .

There is no way of knowing what form this Judaism will take which may grow from the ranks of working Israel . . . for in Judaism there is not one form alone.
—Simha Bunam Urbach, late Professor of Jewish Philosophy, Bar Ilan University

## *The Religion of Pioneering*

The Israeli-born kibbutznik cannot know that his parents, like many Jews in the Diaspora, were ambivalent toward their Jewish heritage and that with the rise of the Zionist movement an avenue was opened for the relief of some of the antagonism between them and their Judaism. One reason for the supposed separation between the kibbutz and the Jewish past derives from its declared intention to create a "new" culture. "New" implies rejection of the old and break with continuity. Especially astonishing in the creation of this image is its extraordinary success, for it contradicts simple historical facts. When the *Vatikim* came to Palestine, they played a central role in reviving the Hebrew language. At all times they considered themselves decent and loyal members of the Jewish people. The "antithesis" to Judaism remained within the borders of Jewish life, not outside of it. Questions of Jewish fate and future were always central to kibbutz thought, even among the most internationalist of socialists. Herzl saw in Zionism a return to Judaism, a correct valuation for Central and Western European Jews who were searching for a means of resisting assimilation without synagogue affiliation. Zionism filled a vacuum in their Jewish life, but for Eastern European Jews it played another role.

> Students of the traditional Bet Ha-Midrash, or those who grew up in homes where Jewish faith and tradition still remained, sought in Zionism a release from the pain of separation from the spiritual world in which they were educated. The demands for personal "realization" were not only the results of the sharper sense of distress experienced by Eastern as against Western European Jews, but were the product of a more rooted Judaism for whom Zionism was a substitute belief and a substitute way of life.[14]

Though Zionism was a substitute religion, it remained within Jewish life, not outside of it. This is its distinction from other substitute religions that have attracted to their ranks many Jews in search of a faith. Critical as Zionists were of tradition, there was no hatred behind their scornful attacks, but more of a feeling of flawed and disappointed love.

Zionism's effectiveness as a substitute for traditional religion was testified to by the zealousness of its Eastern European following, whose willingness to devote their persons and lives to the movement was a proof of its spiritual dynamism. The religious tone of the Zionist movement had an articulate spokesman in A. D. Gordon, a loved and revered figure within the small kibbutz world of the Second Aliyah. Gordon was raised in a traditional home and during his adult life in Europe observed the customs and practices of traditional Judaism. Upon his arrival in Palestine, he continued his observant way of life, but in the course of time dropped the pattern of traditional behavior. In a recent study of A. D. Gordon by Dr. Eliezer Schweid of the Hebrew University, Schweid compares the relationships of Gordon and Rav Kook to the Zionist movement. Both of them (and Buber as well) perceived in Zionism a religious, redemptive movement that sought the spiritual regeneration of the Jewish people. In it Gordon discerned more than an instrument for the physical settlement of the Jews on their own land. To him it was also a means toward religious awakening.

Clearly, the character of this awakening would bear little resemblance to Rav Kook's expectations. Gordon's Zionism was a means for the renewal of religious consciousness, an impetus for a religious renaissance. Gordon even dared to hope that Zionism's success in generating such a renaissance might lead to the renewal of prophecy.

Such visionary hopes lacked the clarity of Rav Kook, to whom "return to religion" meant Orthodoxy, albeit a rejuvenated Orthodoxy. Gordon was not hostile to traditional Judaism, but he did regret what he considered the inhibiting influence of Jewish custom and ceremony upon the spontaneity of a genuine religious experience. What Gordon meant or understood by religion is not set out in clearly stipulated ceremony, practice, or doctrine. He preached a free and spontaneous religiosity that resists definition. This type of religiosity was not Gordon's alone. Though he wrote about it, others living in kibbutzim experienced something akin to it. The free and spontaneous religiosity which existed in the early years of the kibbutz movement took the form of a radical devotion to work. Gordon never used the phrase "religion of labor," which is mistakenly attributed to him. His shift from traditional to "free" religion is closely tied to the process of "Keebush Atzmee" or self-conquest, at the time when he began working in the fields. His morning prayers were replaced by physical labor. Work was not a curse to the early pioneers, but was accepted and experienced with a sense of exaltation. A special and unique relationship to work was a necessity for the *Vatikim* to enable them to overcome the grim reality of Palestine before and after World War I. The religious fervor the early settlers had absorbed at home was transferred to labor, but unless labor was given an exalted meaning, a redemptive value, they would have been unable to withstand its rigors. Work had to become an independent, almost holy value. This is what indeed occurred. "To labor is to pray," Lewis Mumford said in writing about the beginnings of the Benedictine order, and this applies equally to the kibbutz *Vatikim* who transformed physical labor from a shame to an honor.

The effect of work upon their spiritual world appears in a telling remark of a *Vatik*. In the Diaspora, he said, there was a clearly marked separation between the holy and the secular, between daily life and holiday observance. But in those early years of settlement "the whole year was like one holiday,"[15] so brimming with a sense of purpose and dedication that no holidays were needed, no special days had to be set aside for collective remembrance of group goals. There were no holiday observances at all in the early years of Kibbutz Ramat Yohanan. Work and pioneering provided the necessary spiritual content for those difficult years. But the exhilaration of the early years of kibbutz settlement inevitably wore off. Once this occurred, work could no longer perform its former role, though it remains a central value in the kibbutz. Pioneering and work as religious substitutes began to fade, and the holidays left behind in Europe slowly began to resurface, though in new and different forms. Their reappearance was also inevitable, because a movement whose origins are spiritual cannot permit the existence of a vacuum. Once the promethean joy of creation declined something had to replace it. Fortunately, the Jewish past provided the revolutionaries with a hold upon the present when the new culture thay had hoped for failed to emerge. The religion of pioneering ran out of steam but the holidays were there to assure continuity with the Jewish past. As put by a founder of Kibbutz Yif at: "The holidays saved us, and not we the holidays."

## *The Decline of Revolutionary Fervor*

Today in Israel the working class constitutes one of the most conservative groups in the country. The loss of revolutionary fervor was already becoming apparent during the years prior to the establishment of the state. One of the founders of Kibbutz Bet ha-Shittah issued an unusual warning about the dangers facing the Jewish proletariat. He observed a decline in the ardor and zeal of the working class and the onset of fatigue and passivity. This loss of momentum was signified by a gradual turn toward old and established customs unbefitting a revolutionary movement. If a worker's movement seeks to remain revolutionary, it must remain distant from religious tradition, but workers' movements unfortunately tend to become traditional, which results in diminishing their identity as a proletariat.

> Only as they despair of the struggles of humanity do they begin to search for God. The community of workers in Eretz Israel must be immune to religion.[16]

At a Hebrew University symposium arranged by Martin Buber in 1945 on the cooperative village in Israel similar opinions were voiced. Not that the kibbutz was searching for God. It had discovered, instead, that the rejection of God brings in its wake new and unresolved problems. The spokesman for this view, David Maletz of Ein Harod, expressed his misgivings in language accurately forecasting the vacillating spiritual state within the kibbutz today as it confronts Jewish tradition. Maletz praised those members of the founding generation whose *apikorsut* (heresy) developed out of a deep inner struggle, rather than out of indifferent or callous rejection. This type of *apikorsut*, though seemingly destructive, was nevertheless distinguished by what Maletz called its life power. Because some of the *Vatikim* had undergone great psychic strain before they adopted their "heretical" positions, the choice they made became a value. Consequently, they concluded that *apikorsut* was more than just a negation and was worthy of being transmitted to their sons. But, said Maletz, when *apikorsut* is handed down as an inheritance, without choice, it results in superficiality.

> I realize that society cannot remain sturdy for long within the barren wastes of *apikorsut,* but I do not know how to consciously make the leap out of that *apikorsut*.[17]

Maletz saw the start of the search for liberation from the spiritual wasteland of negation, but he realized that these beginnings were not yet serious. Maletz is not pleased with the "neoreligious" direction of the retreat from *apikorsut*, but can only offer as an alternative the humanism he had long before projected. For some youth this humanism remains unsatisfactory and in their rejection of negation they have begun to indicate an interest in what their fathers rejected.

The personal testimonies of a number of young people bear out Maletz's statements. In their reflections upon their education, particularly its relationship to Jewish tradition, they conclude that their education was one-sided and biased. Whether they are justified or not is today the subject of self-searching among kibbutz educators. A conference of educators from Kibbutz ha-Artzi movement met in 1965 to discuss the question of "education for strengthening the connection with the Jewish people." In evaulating past performance a number of educators confessed that "if you want to become an *apikorus,* you have to study first"; or, "we must teach youngsters to hate the Diaspora but love the Jews living in the Diaspora." With characteristic frankness and willingness to face their problems honestly, Ha-Kibbutz ha-Artzi educators admitted their past errors. By overemphasizing the present, their ties to the past had been overlooked. And when the Jewish past was taught, the method was dry, factual, with the stress on information and knowledge. What was missing was the creation of an emotional relationship to the Jewish past, a bond of feeling and not only of mind.

The willingness to admit error does not guarantee its correction. A pessimistic tone prevailed at the conclusion of the conference. The participants realized that kibbutz teachers were products of the rebellion against Orthodoxy, and even with the best of good will they could not significantly modify their relationship to Jewish tradition, or revise their teaching methods.

Because Melford Spiro's book *Children of the Kibbutz* was written after staying with a Kibbutz ha-Artzi community, his statements about the "anti-Semitism" of Israeli-born kibbutz youth should not be surprising. Today that section of Spiro's book is considered out of date by the Jewish Agency officials who compile recommended reading lists on the kibbutz. They were ashamed to admit the truth of Spiro's allegations that some kibbutz youth were taught to despise Diaspora Jews. The issue is complicated by the untold sacrifices made for Israel by this "anti-Semitic" kibbutz youth—thereby strengthening the Jewish people throughout the world. Today the question that preoccupies the concerned youth of the kibbutz, of all streams, is whether living in Israel and being loyal to Israel are enough. The simplistic negations of an earlier period are over.

The question is especially poignant because the leaders of the kibbutz had intended that it should never again be asked. They believed that living in a Jewish state would provide a natural connection to Judaism. But Jewish fate seeks out the Jewish people no matter where they settle, and despite attempts to build a secular Jewish world, the religious tradition remains a challenge that even the most confirmed secularist must take into account. A recognition of the hold that religious tradition still maintains appeared within Ha-Kibbutz ha-Artzi. One of their writers has admitted that the price paid by the kibbutzim for their revolt against the Jewish tradition was very great. But despite their regret at having broken off contact with tradition, they reached the conclusion that the break with Judaism was a historical necessity, justified by circumstances and essential for the future well-being of the Jewish people. But now that the need to rebel no longer exists, could tradition become a "fountain of living waters," a resource for spiritual values? The value of holiness is accepted as a deep human need that even the most revolutionary movement cannot do without. Holiness "elevates and sensitizes man and life, which is also the aim of socialism in its most noble sense."[18] Because socialism lacks the instruments for encouraging a sense of holiness, the Jewish tradition might be drawn upon, to enrich the socialist way of life in the kibbutz.

The search for holiness is only in its beginning and will undoubtedly continue for generations. One reason for the long and tortuous road the seekers of holiness will have to follow lies in the quality of Jewish education in the kibbutz. Ignorance of tradition blocks satisfaction of spiritual wants. In his environment, the kibbutz child has few opportunities to come into contact with different religious communities. He can never see a synagogue unless taken there by his teachers. Synagogues in kibbutzim are peopled by *Vatikim* whose youthful Jewish education gave them the knowledge and experience necessary only for leading in prayer. Services are strictly Orthodox and are characterized by rapidity of prayer and an unwillingness to accept any revisions of form that might make them more palatable to the native-born generation. Kibbutz youth react with a mildly contemptuous smile when a kibbutz synagogue is mentioned.

On the other hand, the kibbutz child knows that the festivals of the Jewish New Year will be celebrated, in the kibbutz fashion, which provides him with more Jewish experience than most urban children have. On balance, therefore, a kibbutz youngster has some feeling for holiday practice, but his knowledge of Judaism is very superficial and distorted. For some young people a crisis occurs when they become aware of their ignorance of Jewish tradition. A few overreact and blame their elders for having cheated them. They do not realize that their fathers were incapable of transmitting the Jewish tradition to them. Had they undergone the same exposure to Jewish tradition as their elders, their reaction might indeed have been similar.

## Hansen's Law

The call for closer ties to the Jewish tradition among the kibbutz generation in the twenty-to-forty age bracket takes a variety of forms. These appeals are mostly vague and misty—a faithful reflection of the confusion prevailing among that group. Specific proposals other than the requirement of study are not forthcoming. Once this requirement is fulfilled, a few of that generation may be equipped to perform what they consider their ultimate objective.

> The contribution of the *Vatikim* was, first of all, to enter into history and politics. Our mission is a new one—to create a Jewish way of life which bears political responsibilities and realizes the values of man.[19]

In addition to yearnings for a way of life with identifiable Jewish characteristics, there are demands for fulfilling the needs of the *nefesh* (soul, or spirit). If secular humanism cannot achieve an inner unity with the world, can Judaism do so? But since a return to Jewish religion is out of the question, what remains? Having arrived at the crossroads, what choice is there? Despite this apparently spiritual dead end, "we are commanded to search for paths to belief, ways of fulfilling the soul." The youthful author of these lines realizes that without "sparks of holiness" slim hope exists for the achievement of his goals, for the elevation of his spirit. Perhaps the elders of the kibbutz experienced a different kind of holiness, one to which this generation is not accustomed. Theirs may have been the holiness of creativity and originality. They did not need to ask the question posed by some of their sons: Is there any meaning or purpose in life? Their life has a clearly defined object of "ultimate concern"—the building of the kibbutz. How shocked they must be to read articles written by some of their own youth that claim that within Israel itself, the Jewish state, one can live in spiritual exile.

The deep-seated alienation from society characteristic of some of today's Western youth has few equivalents among young kibbutz intellectuals. Yet a young man living in a kibbutz in Israel wrote the following lines:

> The exile of the Israel Jew is a spiritual exile. He is a foreigner in the land of his fathers. . . . This position is more than tragic, it is ridiculous and absurd. . . . Actually it is difficult to call this exile. It becomes exile only to the degree that one of us feels a deep sense of belonging to that spiritual world of his father and seeks to link himself with it.[20]

There would be little reason to hold such a forceful position were kibbutz life in its present form able to provide an alternative to a yearning for the Jewish past. It may be reasonably argued that the craving for Jewishness might ultimately result in a degree of alienation from kibbutz life and principles, or even in abandonment of the kibbutz by some. For some youth the kibbutz appears to have lost its major role as provider of spiritual values. Jewish tradition is beginning, for some, to fill that gap. The outcome need not be flight from the kibbutz, for were kibbutz life to integrate with Jewish tradition and to be interpreted as some special form of Judaism, the problems of the kibbutz would become the problems of Judaism, and not just the perplexities of a peripheral group. At this point we note a drive toward renewing contact with Jewish tradition. The reasons given vary, often depending upon the particular kibbutz movement.

Members of Ha-Kibbutz ha-Artzi, whose belief in the ultimate triumph of the socialist world had persisted, have experienced the failure of their gods, and after the disintegration of that belief the young men discovered that they could not exist without some object of faith and commitment. Faith, they learned, was a spiritual need of all men. If a faith proves false, something must replace it. Because the only other major value-centered world in Israel is the world of Jewish tradition, a move in its direction was to be expected. One who is rooted in Ha-Kibbutz ha-Artzi, while his hands are reaching toward the previously forbidden fruit of Jewish tradition, is bound to feel a faint tinge of guilt. Another element of the malaise is that daily life, the holidays, the entire pattern of kibbutz living have lost a spiritual dimension for some. If this is what some of the young people feel, the situation must be grave indeed.

## *The Nature of the "Return"*

As this quest for Jewish content begins, it quickly loses some initial momentum through the caution evinced by a generation that had suffered because of its too eager willingness to believe. The result is spiritual inhibition, which, together with the deficiencies of kibbutz education in Jewishness, prevent the seeker from coming too close to the object of his pursuit or from identifying with it completely. What exists therefore is a desire and a will to believe, tempered by caution learned from previous disillusionment. This wariness exhibits a realistic fear of the possible outcome of religious faith, whether arrived at intellectually or emotionally. A kibbutznik knows from his experience that there is no faith without works.

Were he to accept a religious faith he would be obligated to practice some form of observance. His present groping is therefore hedged with suspicion, anxiety, and fear.

In the literature of the "return," which has been prolific since the Six-Day War, the question mark appears with unusual frequency alongside the usual punctuation marks. For this generation the central problems are in its relationship to Jewish history, the Jewish people, Jewish literature, Jewish identity, Jewish fate. The God dimension is absent from their religious quest. Their interest in ritual is negligible. The absence of theological questions results from a lack of knowledge of religious and philosophical thought of the West. Conceiving of God as a supernatural being, kibbutz intellectuals are unaware of the theological possibilities open to them as naturalists. Were this cognitive obstacle surmounted, the idea of God might add an entirely new dimension to their quests.

Religious symbols have become a major means of expressing the emergence of a greater sense of social-national belonging. This is illustrated by the use of God's name in the poetry written by young kibbutz poets. When one of them was asked why the term "God" appears in his poetry, he replied that by "God" he means "all the good, the exalted, the noble and the beautiful that I am unable to represent." For some of these young writers God serves as an undefined symbol of the exalted, the secret and the unknown.

The kibbutz is not the only group within Israeli society in which young people have been asking questions about their Jewishness. Some urban youth are as deeply engaged as kibbutz youth, but it is the quest within kibbutz society that has attracted the most attention. Because it has at its disposal well-organized and well-financed organs of literary expression, the kibbutz exposes its inner deliberations to the public eye. There is a quality in this society itself that prompts and encourages the type of questioning current today. Interest in Judaism in the kibbutz stems not just from the magnetism of Judaism, but from the inevitable disappointments that kibbutz life generates. This discontent may not be as sharply focused in Israel's urban life because city dwellers expect little from the form of life they lead, but the contrary applies to the kibbutz, whose claims to a more human form of life arouse correspondingly higher expectations among its supporters. A member of a kibbutz anticipates a great deal and therefore his vulnerability is much greater. The kibbutz undertakes to provide both for the material needs of its members and for their spiritual wants. In case of failure a feeling of spiritual vacuum becomes especially acute because the kibbutz, as a movement that demands certain limitations and restrictions on personal freedom, must compensate within the spiritual and cultural realm. When this compensation is not forthcoming or proves to be illusory, the discontent and frustration can be overwhelming. The advantage of the kibbutznik over a comparable urban dweller lies in his liberation from economic struggle, which provides him more time to seek for content in his spiritual life. While liberation from the struggles of material existence does not guarantee solutions for spiritual problems, there is a consciousness within kibbutz society that the kibbutz is collectively responsible for aiding in the solution of such problems. Because spiritual emptiness is a danger to kibbutz life, the collective must accept responsibility for the individual's spiritual needs. In order to maintain the strength of its collective life, the kibbutz searches for forms of living and for traditions that will give its members cultural and spiritual content.

Some young men and women are given time off from their work to devote themselves to the study of Judaism. Organized study circles on Jewish subjects and conferences for Jewish study have existed within the kibbutz movement since the reawakening of interest. Oranim, a kibbutz teachers' seminary near Haifa, has successfully instituted an intensive year's course in Jewish sources. In providing these cultural and spiritual opportunities, the kibbutz is providing necessities, not luxuries.

Behind the emergence of these study groups is an awareness of a pervading ignorance of Judaism, and a desire to discover why the *Vatikim* rejected it. One can also discern a tendency to challenge the idea that a "scientific view of life would make religion untenable." To the surpise and shock of kibbutz educators who sincerely believed that science would be the antidote to religion, it has indirectly served to arouse interest in religion.

> Science seems progressive when one emerges from a religious background. Today, young people learn science first and then ask if it is adequate. What of values, idealism, purpose? This favors religion as a new insight.[21]

Reactions from kibbutz educators to the religious quest have varied from the extremes of contempt for this new phenomenon to virtually uncritical praise of it. The evaluations have also been at odds. Some believed a genuine religious awakening was occurring while others have paid it little heed, expecting time and age to take their toll of what they considered a temporary and superficial phenomenon. The prime target of the critics is the journal *Shedemot*, whose contents might easily lead the reader to unfounded conclusions. The pages of *Shedemot* often contain expressions of a yearning for God, leading readers to conclude that the turn toward Judaism was essentially mystic and contemplative. Were this true, one could expect opposition to such a trend within the kibbutz movement.

Though a mystic approach to religion may result in increased activity among men and within society, the usual outcome is a turning inward, a search for union with a reality outside of society. The danger of passivity, therefore, has alerted some kibbutz thinkers. In a movement as activist as the kibbutz any interest in mysticism holds apparent dangers of retreat from involvement into passivity. In the light of this fear, accusations of pseudo-religiosity have been hurled against the "return." This pseudo-religiosity is viewed as "a vote of no confidence" in the ability of the kibbutz movement to grapple with Jewish tradition and to generate its own living forms of cultural expression.

The term "pseudo-religion" is commonly used by those with Eastern European backgrounds. The kibbitz movement, however, has a number of leaders and thinkers with Central and Western European backgrounds in addition to a few Americans. Their criticism of the move toward Jewish sources tends to be more balanced. One of the severest critics of *Shedemot* said that he understood them, for he had used similar language for the very same reason—he had lived in a "value vacuum." Expressions such as "I hope to reach full belief" or "I don't yet believe" indicate an inner emptiness that will fill eventually—but not with religious belief. Critics argued that maturity would eventually lead today's religiously inclined youth to a more realistic grasp of life's actualities and to the inevitable conclusion that religion is not the answer to the problems of modern man. However painful the disappointment with liberalism, socialism, humanism, or Marxism, these secular teachings were honest attempts to face the problems of society. But a return to religion would be reactionary.

The kibbutz thinker David Maletz is also a partner to the skeptical attitude toward those who "seek paths to the values of religion." Though Maletz admitted in conversation that a belief in God that need not result in the performance of commandments is possible, he failed to see the significance or value of such a belief. The origin of religions, he claimed, is in emotion, but this is not sufficient. The next and basic step must be the transformation of that feeling into a "commanding power," a sense of obligation toward the performance of those commandments which spring out of faith. The strength of a religion lies in its power to convert its believers from passive acceptance to active performance, and to discipline its followers to practice its commandments.

This description of religion hardly applies to the seekers within the kibbutz. They are transforming their own private experience into an object of devotion, because their commitment to religion has not resulted in the one major consequence that could make it meaningful—there has been no change in their way of life. Only when this begins to occur can the new phenomenon be taken seriously. Until that point is reached, however, those who "seek paths toward the values of religion" will remain enclosed in their own subjective little world and have no real effect on the way of life of the kibbutz.

A confirmation of this position was arrived at by a man from an entirely different background, who has engaged David Maletz in a debate on the subject of the kibbutz as a link in the continuity of the Jewish tradition. Moshe Kerem (formerly Murray Weingarten) wrote one of the first English accounts of kibbutz life. Like Maletz, Kerem observes no external change resulting from increased exposure to Jewish sources. The change is internal—in attitude and relationship. Courses in Jewish subjects are much more popular than ever before among the students he observes at the kibbutz teachers' seminary where he teaches. But this has not resulted in any religious ritualism. Kerem would agree with Maletz that "commandment" is absent, as is evident in the fact that no change in life has occurred. But the aim of the seekers is not to seek religious experience and thereby separate themselves from the community, but rather to search within Judaism for a religious base for their way of life. Instead of secular humanistic socialism, they are groping for a Jewish religious socialism. Kerem would deny that the "mysticism" of this group is narrowly egocentric. Its aim is to impart a tone and quality to the kibbutz world that could prepare it to play a role in Jewish society. What is occurring is not a flight from the kibbutz to Judaism, but a reinterpretation of the kibbutz along more recognizable Jewish lines.

The kibbutzim that do practice religious ritual—the Orthodox kibbutz movement—have always tried to bring their kibbutz colleagues closer to Jewish tradition. Among the large concentration of Orthodox kibbutzim in the Beth Shean Valley, an extra evening has been added to the celebration of Simhat Torah for non-

Orthodox kibbutzniks who want to sing and dance with Torah scrolls. They also host kibbutz youth and adults on the Sabbath. The Orthodox kibbutz has held seminars on the question of how to bring Jews closer to tradition. What is their reaction to the "return" within the kibbutz movement?

Though mutual respect exists between the two branches of the kibbutz movement, the Orthodox kibbutz is not content with the level of Jewish knowledge or the degree of Jewish attachment within the general kibbutz. Because of their high regard for the general kibbutz, the Orthodox kibbutzim are disappointed at the minimal role traditional Judaism has played in its life. They believe that the kibbutz will be unable to play any significant role in the future formation of Jewish life in Israel unless it comes to terms with its Jewish heritage. It would be tragic if a spiritual movement such as the kibbutz remained consciously divorced from the major spiritual heritage of the Jewish people. If the kibbutz wants to merge more fully into Jewish life, it must seek to liberate itself from the vestiges of its past revolt—a difficult task, because it must overcome a negative heritage of at least two generations.

Eliezer Goldman, one of the most articulate spokesmen of the Orthodox kibbutz movement, has stated that the non-Orthodox kibbutz must sooner or later come to grips with its Jewishness as the revolt against tradition and religious communal discipline wears off. Now that the traditional Jewish society is no longer a majority, the revolt lacks a target. New questions have to be asked—for example, "Where are our roots?" In Israel, revolt is anachronistic because Orthodoxy is a peripheral element and few people suffer directly from its injunctions.

Among youth of Ha-Kibbutz ha-Artzi the return is an admission that the ideology that justified their settlement on the land is now questionable. They now see that they are not the vanguard of revolution whose task is to unite the laboring classes in the Arab states with their Jewish counterparts in a common effort against class oppression—whether Jewish or Arab. Their socialist and universalist appeals evoked no reaction among the Arab laboring class, who preferred the oppression of their fellow Arabs to Jewish egalitarianism. Arab nationalism rejected the romantic notions of Ha-Kibbutz ha-Artzi, which put a young kibbutznik serving in the Israel army in the ideologically untenable position of having to shoot down his supposedly real ally—the Arab working man. The latter made no fine distinction between socialist and capitalist Israelis.

This is a very grave matter from some of the young people of Ha-Kibbutz ha-Artzi. They are, after all, very serious people, unwilling to live without some *Weltanschauung*. Where they stand today, within the State of Israel, is a vital question to them. Their "Jewish identity" has thus become a major problem. Viewed in its proper perspective, what is occurring in the kibbutz reflects the general problem faced by Jewish society in Israel.

Not all Israelis, of course, are engaging in an identity search. A goodly number are scarcely perturbed and consider themselves Israelis, above all. The question put by Ernst Simon of the Hebrew University—"Are we Israelis still Jews?"—is equally an overstatement. The question should be rephrased to ask, "How are we Israelis Jews?" To the average Orthodox Israeli Jew this question is senseless. The non-Orthodox, however, whose attachment to Judaism is national and cultural, may ask himself if his ties to the country and the land are enough to live by.

Here is the quandary of the Israeli non-Orthodox Jew who rejects the simplicities of Orthodoxy and of Jewish nationalism. The Orthodox definition of Judaism results in sectarianism. Whoever is outside it becomes an antagonist. The national definition has similar results, since belongingness to a national body alone transforms outsiders into strangers, with whom one has nothing in common. This is "the Sabra anti-Semitism" observed by Melford Spiro.

A delicate balance between nationalism and universalism—a recurrent Jewish problem—can be achieved when the Jew is living in two domains—the universalistic Diaspora and the nationalistic Israel. One group needs the other lest they become estranged. Where does the kibbutz fit in? It combines the nationalistic school of Jewish life with a humanistic universalism. Can it succeed in uniting them into a Jewish humanism that is tied to its national heritage, but is also open to the spiritual experience of all men?

# 4
# *The Religious Mentality*

> Religion is not primarily an activity of intellectuals. . . .
> The fundamental religious impulse is not to theorize
> about transcendence but to worship it. . . . The theological enterprise . . . even if it employs the most complex
> tools of the intellectual's trade, will always push towards
> expression in living communities of men other than intellectuals.
> —Peter Berger, *A Rumor of Angels, Modern Society
> and the Rediscovery of the Supernatural*

## *The Kibbutz as a Metaphysical Entity*

The plethora of definitions for the term "religion" can lead a reader to despair. Whether the arguments center around Western as against Eastern religions, or metaphysical belief as against humanistic belief, the basic problem remains the question of a supernatural or cosmic object of worship as opposed to a natural, nonmetaphysical object of ultimate concern. Though the kibbutz can have no objection to its individual members holding metaphysical beliefs, they receive no official approval from the kibbutz itself. Support is granted to anyone who wishes to observe traditional customs and practices—usually through the provision of a synagogue, special kitchen accommodations for kosher food, or a release from tasks on the Sabbath. If there are enough participants, teachers are brought to the kibbutz to conduct study circles in Jewish religious literature. All this is made available to its members by a nonreligious movement, not only because the kibbutz is obliged to fulfill the cultural and spiritual needs of its members, or because "things Jewish" have a new and higher status in Israeli society, but because the kibbutz retains an unconscious identification with religion, and even with the supernatural type.

This identification is no accident. It accurately reflects

similarities in tone and style between the kibbutz and traditional Judaism. That relationship is difficult to trace, due to the radical differences apparent between them. To use the image suggested by a *Vatik*, Judaism in the kibbutz is like a chemical element that loses its physically identifiable characteristics when in solution, but is till actively present. Kibbutz thinkers have not devoted much thought to categorizing their society as a form of humanistic or naturalistic religion. Such questions appeared remote to them during the active period of their growth and consolidation. Nevertheless, even in those years an occasional article would appear in their literature, admitting certain lines of similarity between a religious and a kibbutz experience. In an article written in 1962, Ephraim Reisner of Ramat Yohanan takes note of the desire to return to Judaism. He observed in this interest more than intellectual curiosity—perhaps even an emotional urge to seek an absolute. Reisner suggests that the kibbutz should offer a different kind of transcendentalism in response to this new direction among some sections of kibbutz and Israeli society. He could not be expected to legitimize the supernaturalism of traditional Judaism, because his generation *(Vatikim)* remains steadfastly rationalistic. What the kibbutz should provide is a transcendentalism that would allow its foundations to remain "rationalistic" and yet satisfy the impulse for a metaphysical belief. Reisner finds religion in

> our absolute attachment to the kibbutz as a way towards the regeneration of human relations, to this body which goes beyond the borders of our individual existence and ties us to eternity.[22]

This form of transcendentalism has a place for God but can manage without Him if necessary, because the object of ultimate concern is the kibbutz.

It is difficult to detect the extent of religious consciousness in the kibbutz because of the absence of any organizational mode for its expression. The kibbutz, therefore, cannot be compared with organized religions. Were that the only model for determining religiosity, the kibbutz would fail to meet that criterion, but if religion is something other than its organizational contexts, the kibbutz may well be considered a religious body without the organizational trappings common to religious groups.

In the predominantly Jewish society in Israel the kibbutz was not conscious of questions of Jewish identity until just recently when discussion on "Who is a Jew?" began. It was not their own individual identity as Jews that was the problem, but rather the "Jewish identity" of the society they had created. The question is not superfluous, even though Israel could be defined as Jewish by virtue of its existence as a Jewish state, using the Hebrew language as its official tongue, and teaching Jewish culture and literature in its schools. Yet dissatisfaction has been voiced of late about the Jewish quality of Israeli life, particularly in the urban centers, where its style and pace have begun to approach American patterns. This, in a sense, is an oversimplification, for it would be hasty to underestimate the psychological effect of living within a society with a Jewish majority. However, this does not affect the ever-growing feeling among observers within Israel's society that there is really no significant difference between the way of life of Jews living in Chicago and a Jew living in Tel Aviv. If this evaluation is correct, then the question might well be asked whether the Jewish state has been a cultural failure. This question originates mainly from circles that see Israel not only as a refuge from persecution or as an opportunity to reinstate Jewish sovereignty after a lapse of centuries, but as a cultural and spiritual center for the Jewish people thoughout the world. If this center, instead of actively influencing the Diaspora, becomes a passive recipient of Disapora values, the significance of all the labor invested in the creation of a Jewish state becomes questionable. Interchange between Israel and the Diaspora was anticipated. Israel was not expected to dictate the Jewish culture of the Diaspora, but there had been a hope that Israeli society would provide a variable cultural alternative to Orthodoxy. This hope has not materialized. Israeli cities, even Jerusalem to some extent, have assumed the features of urban centers of the Western world. The large cities of Israel lack a Jewish style of life (except among the Orthodox). An Israeli Sabbath style has evolved; a day devoted to trips, visits to friends and family, and physical rest. Little attention is paid to matters of the spirit.

In the light of this background, the Jewish quality of the kibbutz becomes an authentic question. The non-Orthodox Jew, observing the nonproductive character of Israeli urban society in the sphere of Jewishness, and the increasing influence of America through the communications media, may ask whether any community exists in Israel that is striving to create a Jewish life-style that is not Orthodox. The kibbutz immediately emerges as a candidate to exemplify such a community, if only because it has an overwhelming advantage over urban Jewry—possession of greater freedom and flexibility to decide how it may live. If, therefore, the kibbutz is convinced that it has an obligation to the Jewish people and to itself, to move in the direction of cultural creativity, it can help fill the gap in the spiritual life of non-Orthodox Israel. But does the kibbutz believe that it has such a mission—that it should be a "pioneer of Judaism"[23] now that it has successfully accomplished other pioneering tasks?

Whether it will assume such a function depends upon its Jewish image and those characteristics of its life-style that indicate a sense of continuity with Jewish tradition. The kibbutz has always assumed it should be a avant-garde, leading the Jewish people and serving as an example of sacrifice and dedication. But until recently its pioneering tasks did not demand the type of creativity necessary for it to be a "pioneer of Judaism." Now that the Israeli government has taken over many of the tasks formerly performed by the kibbutz, where can its pioneering drives find a new outlet?

It is generally agreed that the kibbutz is responsible for the formaton of its own cultural patterns. Otherwise, there would be a mindless imitation of city life and consequent loss of creative powers. Within the kibbutz there are various schools of thought on this issue, all at odds with each other about the legitimacy of the kibbutz as an interpreter of Jewish tradition.

## *The Continuity of Judaism*

The opinions and views that follow are those of individuals and should not be considered as reflecting a general surge of interest in these questions within the kibbutz movements. They should be seen as only beginnings among isolated individuals and small groups that are not necessarily representative of the movements. A growing awareness of the kibbutz as an interpreter of Jewish tradition is beginning to spread. A number of respondents repeatedly stressed that the kibbutz was not to be seen as a revolutionary movement sweeping aside traditional values and practices, but as a group dedicated to the preservation and maximal fulfillment of old and accepted values. According to this principle the kibbutz has instituted a conservative revolution, a maintenance of old values within a new mold—a reformation of sorts. The following personal testimony illustrates this line of thought. One *Vatik* remarked that, for him, his entrance into the kibbutz movement did not entail a break with his father, a pious Jewish merchant in Eastern Europe.

To him the basic aim of the kibbutz is parallel to the aim of the commandments—to perfect human beings (*l'tzarayf et habreeyot*). The only real conflict with his father arose over his leaving home to live in Israel. Other than that, they followed similar paths, for even when he became a Marxist, it involved no real change in his God. As his father did, he sought a better world, but while his father's way was by studying the Talmud and observing the commandments, his was by studying Marx and living in a kibbutz. He does not feel that they were radically different, because even though his father addressed God, while he did not, their basic approach to life was similar. They both knew what was meant by the good life, by a good man. His father believed that a good man is one who does not deceive others, studies, fulfills the commandments, believes. His son, living in a kibbutz, has the same conception of the good man.

> In the sense that the kibbutz was an attempt to give a decisive status to the value of the elevation of man and the improvement of his qualities—without entering into the question of the success or failure of the kibbutz—the aim is absolutely Jewish. What is the aim of Judaism? To live in God's image. Orthodox Judaism will say this is possible only through a life of commandments. Only they can lead to the elevation of man. If we ignore the theological side—of obligation to God—then the ambition to create a life and a society which is serious, honorable and responsible (as the Jew says, not to engage in vain matters)—in this sense the kibbutz manifests the best of Jewish thought and will.[24]

For this *Vatik* the kibbutz is very Jewish, because it manifests a life of purpose and content. Similar reasoning was followed by a younger man, a native-born kibbutznik, who also adhered to the "conservative revolution" approach. He understands as eminently Jewish the content of kibbutz life, the values it seeks to achieve, though as in the previous instance, there is no religious expression of a belief in God. The particular values he mentions—respect for man, the right of man to life, aid to the weak, equality among people, justice, striving for perfection of man and the world—are values that neither the Jews nor the kibbutz monopolize. The kibbutz revolution lies in its willingness to take these old and accepted values seriously, beyond lip service.

Few kibbutzniks concerned with these questions would take exception to the views expressed above, but only a small minority would boldly claim that the kibbutz is not only Jewish, but is a legitimate interpreter of Jewish tradition. The State of Israel is Jewish, but is Israel a legitimate interpreter of Judaism? That the kibbutz has a connection to traditional Judaism is a reasonable statement, but can it be established as a rival, together with Conservative and Reform Judaism, to the "supremacy" of Orthodoxy? There are a few personalities within the kibbutz who believe that it has as much right to challenge Orthodoxy as do other movements.

> The kibbutz is more religious than Reform Judaism. If we put aside the question of God for a moment and see Jewish religion as a relationship to Jewish values, ethical values, Jewish history, Jewish festivals and customs, then the average kibbutz is more religious than the average Reform congregation. . . . there are many people in the kibbutz who would believe in a naturalistic God, or that there is something wondrous about Jewish history. . . . What is being discussed? What should be the ethical values on which society should be based? It becomes a theological discussion but people are afraid of being tagged.[25]

Were a naturalistic theology accepted within the kibbutz, it would negate the commonplace of Israeli life that only Orthodoxy deserves to be termed "religious." Liberated from labels, discussion of religion would be emancipated from the secular-versus-religious dichotomy, and would center on another distinction that divides society today—between those who have faith and those who do not. By this standard the kibbutz would pass the test of a faith-centered and religious society. But, granted that the kibbutz possesses a religious bent, should it be permitted to don the mantle of interpreter of religion and of Jewish tradition? With the acceptance of the present-day Jewish world as pluralistic, the kibbutz may claim that it represents a particular interpretation of Judaism with unique patterns of life not found in other spheres of modern Judaism.

According to this interpretation, the kibbutz has succeeded in achieving one of Judaism's prime values—maximum mutuality. Because the kibbutz was established to cultivate brotherly relations and could not survive if they deteriorated, the creation of community feeling is more than just an observance of a prime Jewish value. It is a matter of life and death. Its purpose and character dictate the deep feeling of responsibility among and toward its members that Judaism has so steadfastly urged upon all Jews. The kibbutz has developed certain trends in Judaism to a degree beyond the capabilities of other Jewish social or religious movements. In a Jewish world where the ritualism of Orthodoxy has disengaged it from social questions, the kibbutz emerges as a "religion" dominated by social ethics. This explains the statement of a thinker of Ha-Kibbutz ha-Artzi that there is nothing more Jewish in Israel today than the kibbutz, a remark one may attribute to the centrality of social ethics in his vision of Judaism.

Respondents with a background in traditional Judaism were somewhat more modest in their evaluation. A number of respondents with reputations in the Ihud as "professional Jews" deny that the kibbutz is a legitimate interpreter of Jewish tradition and believe it has no right to make such assertions. Unlike the religious movements of the Diaspora, the kibbutz has no intention of reinterpreting Judaism or "making it more modern." It only wants to fulfill and realize, in its way, those Jewish values it considers socially and ethically significant. It has little interest in confronting abstract questions as, for example, its relationship to Jewish life within the modern world. Only through interviews did views emerge on the kibbutz as the legitimate interpreter of Judaism. There are practically no written materials on this subject. As a practical movement, the kibbutz did not philosophize—it performed. Philosophical conclusions could be drawn afterward.

Western Jews in the kibbutz, who had rarely experienced traditional Judaism in its Eastern European form or undergone the experience of revolt, were more prone to regard the kibbutz as a legitimate inheritor of Jewish tradition. Some Eastern European *Vatikim* stated that they did not reject Judaism because they at one time rose up against it. They observe in kibbutz life and institutions a unique revelation of the Jewish spirit, and would therefore accept the kibbutz as a legitimate interpreter of the Jewish tradition if the word "tradition" were replaced by "spirit."

> The kibbutz is not a Jewish variation of socialistic thinking, but rather a typically Jewish attempt to translate socialism into a way of life.... The kibbutz is the one secular social movement that requires its members to live socialistically.... The idea of socialism as a way of life placing obligations on the individual—that is the reflection of Judaism.[26]

The preoccupation of a small group of kibbutz thinkers with the question of their place as individuals, and as members of the kibbutz movement, within the world of Jewish values and culture, is a hopeful omen of the power of Jewish tradition to attract men who grapple with problems of man and the world. For individuals or movements deeply involved in the struggle of contemporary society, Judaism appeared to have little appeal. The kibbutz world, the world of tomorrow, had to be free of every trace of that past. The present renewal of interest in Jewish heritage therefore raises questions. Is this renewed interest due to disappointment with past idols, or is it an enrichment of the spirit growing out of renewed contact with Jewish tradition? The kibbutz, as a spiritual movement, would not search for replenishment of its own spiritual resources from a dry source. Jewish tradition must pass a severe test. Can it respond adequately to men who seek its wisdom? A community such as the kibbutz, with its "religious mentality," may predispose some of its people to an interest in formally religious groups because they sense certain affinities. Adherents of contrary views often respect each other. If the kibbutz and Jewish tradition could become allies, this union could furnish an additional and modern outlet for a surge of the Jewish spirit into the world. By a return to Jewish sources the kibbutz could become a major instrument in competing with the rival philosophies that draw so many young Jews away from their people.

Notwithstanding the dissimilarities between kibbutz society and traditional Judaism, enough remains in common to explain the tacit respect between them. It is a curious fact that Reform rabbis who visit a kibbutz to speak are often criticized more vehemently than Orthodox rabbis. Instead of considering the Reform rabbi a potential ally against the imposition of Orthodoxy upon Israeli society, liberal Judaism is found at fault. The main reason for its reservations appears to be that substantively the kibbutz stands closer to Orthodoxy than to Reform. "The kibbutz is halakhah without belief while Reform Judaism is belief without halakhah," remarked a *Vatik* who graduated from the Breuer Yeshivah in Frankfurt.

## Halakhah and Aggadah

In the past, connection with socialistic ideals was stronger, and their phraseology expressed kibbutz ambition and thought. With the fading of that tradition suggestions have been made that Jewish thought and terminology direct kibbutz dynamics. Nathan Rotenstreich, professor of philosophy at the Hebrew University, lecturing to a conference of kibbutz educators, perceived the problem of

Israeli culture not as a renewal of prophecy, but of *halakhah*. This opinion in contrary to the usual pronouncements about Israel as the land of the prophets. For Dr. Rotenstreich, prophecy always remains visionary, with no means of action. These are available in the *halakhah*, which he describes as "an active and directive formation of daily reality."[27] The following comment by a veteran founder of a kibbutz is illustrative:

> The workers' movement in Israel, which showed indifference to religion, never tried to release itself from the yoke of commandments because it was convenient to do so. On the contrary, it continually loaded upon itself positive and negative commandments, and in this sense was a continuity of Jewish tradition. I have brought as proof the wide use of the term "acceptance of the yoke" within the workers' movement. Thus it was in the workers' movement in general and even more so in the kibbutz, a form of life which is one complete web of commandments and prohibitions that encompasses an individual's entire life. . . . Is not this way of life the Torah heritage of halakhic Judaism which did not accept Torah without observance of commandments? . . .
>
> It is a great virtue of the kibbutz that its members observe their commandments publicly and not in isolation, out of a sense of unlimited mutual responsibility. Their life is the finest commentary on "all Jews are responsible for one another," always, as a law of life, and not just during moments of danger. The kibbutz cannot exist without love of fellow Jews and without the commandment, "You shall love your neighbor as yourself." . . . I spent the best years of my youth in the Yeshiva. Going from there straight to the Hehalutz movement was natural and to be taken for granted. The tent I dwelt in during my youthful years in the Jezreel Valley . . . was a continuation of the tents of the Lord I dwelt in for a number of years.[28]

This quotation is unique in its tone, for few writers seem willing to transfer the terminology of Judaism to the kibbutz as a descriptive tool for analysis of its life.

The Jewish socialist who arrived in Eretz Israel was dissatisfied with the more abstract type of socialism then prevalent, and the experience of their Jewish past, imbued with Halakhic values, was behind their acceptance of the kibbutz yoke of commandments. Jewish literature is replete with statements about the greater value of action over study and of *halakhah* over *aggadah*. The poetry and faith of the *aggadah* could not survive without the *halakah* to give it flesh. This halakhic conditioning prepared the *halutzim* for the famous appeal of the Hebrew poet Haim Nahman Bialik for a new *halakah*, and it is agreed that Bailik's essay *Halakhah and Aggadah* had a profound influence upon the *Vatikim:*

> All *aggadah* is like iron that has been heated but not cooled. Aspiration, goodwill, spiritual elation, heartfelt love—all these are excellent and valuable when they lead to action, to action which is hard as iron and obeys the stern behest of duty. What we need is to have duties imposed on us.[29]

*Halakhah* is so much an integral part of Jewish living that even a revolt against religion cannot eradicate it. On the contrary, the rebellion against religion led the *halutzim* to look for a new secular Shulhan Arukh. The *halutzim* were not the only people who threw religion overboard. They were in company with millions who found in nationalism and socialism new nonreligious values to give meaning to their lives. But the *halutzim* wanted much more. After having thrown off the religious "yoke of heaven," they voluntarily tied themselves to the secular yoke of the *mitzvot* of the kibbutz.

The close tie between the Orthodox and the kibbutz approach is evidenced by the similar manner of explaining and justifying the limitations on freedom that both must accept. In a famous *aggadah* the rabbis play on words based upon the Hebrew for "engraved" and "freedom." The Ten Commandments were engraved on stone and their acceptance meant acceptance of the "yoke of heaven." But this was not to be considered an unbearable burden, for the word "engraved" *(harut)* should be read "freedom" *(hayrut)*. Thus, a Jew gains his truest and fullest freedom by accepting the discipline of Torah, and under its tutelage becomes a spiritually free man. Limitations imposed upon the individual in the kibbutz are also explained not as a burdensome, mechanical, and oppressive discipline, but as a discipline necessary for the existence of the kibbutz and the protection of the rights of other persons in that society. By accepting self-discipline and the sovereignty of the group a man becomes truly free. When these fences break down, freedom is lost.

The *halakhah* of the kibbutz lacks the authority of a special leadership (such as the rabbinate) that would be devoted to its preservation and development. It is an extension of communal consciousness and a reflection of its consensus. Its obligatory power therefore depends upon the social commitment of the community to its particular way of life. As every society, the kibbutz must transmit its heritage to the coming generations, but in this it faces very special difficulties. The fences of Orthodoxy, however burdensome, can be interpreted as the will of God. In the kibbutz the acceptance of self-discipline must emanate from another source. For the founders it was a quasi-religious commitment to the kibbutz as the reflection of their spirit. But for the coming generations, having an established society, the acceptance of the yoke is a problem of serious proportions. Some believe the kibbutz can assure the continuity of its values and way of life by providing a high standard of living to its members, thereby compensating them for self-imposed restrictions. Although a comfortable life is not incompatible with kibbutz principles, comfort, as a value, will have difficulty competing with the higher standard of urban living in Israel. Ultimately, the justification for the kibbutz way of life derives from a conviction that this form is superior to the patterns of life on the outside. Such a conviction must grow out of community experience and comparison with competitive forms of living.

A lone voice within the general kibbutz movement, Yehoshua Manoah of Degania Alef, has written extensively of the urgent need for the compilation of a kibbutz *halakhah*. He claimed that the teaching of the kibbutz cannot be allowed to remain abstract, but must be a living Torah—which demands a *halakhah*.

> *Halakhot* of work and deed, eating and drinking, protection and concern for the public realm and public property. Kibbutz politeness, courtesy and good manners.[30]

Manoah wants the kibbutz to advance beyond its present oral law to a written law. He disagrees with the assertion that the kibbutz has succeeded in turning *aggadah* into *halakhah*, but believes that it yet remains within the realm of *aggadah* and has yet to pass beyond. He quotes Bialik's essay to show that the kibbutz is still very far from having attained *halakhah*. Since Manoah wrote on this subject in the early 1960s, a *takkanon*, or set of regulations, has been drafted by the Union of Kibbutz Federations to define its goals, its authority, and the privileges and obligations of members. The *takkanon* is in the process of adoption by the kibbutz federations, but it bears little resemblance to the type of *halakhah* suggested by Manoah. He proposed a kibbutz Shulhan Arukh, controlling both the public and private realm of its life. Although Bialik also used traditional terms, he did not arouse a fear of a kibbutz Shulhan Arukh mentality that Manoah's ideas provoked in some. This misgiving derives from the danger posed by a written law—the conservative tendency to sanctify a written document. An oral, unwritten law would be more fluid, more responsive to the changing needs of the kibbutz. But as the kibbutz becomes a more heterogeneous society, the consensus of former years no longer guarantees the effectiveness of the prior oral accords. Some kibbutzim have begun to compile a collection of the rules and decisions adopted over the years. The future will determine the degree of authority these documents will attain over their compilers.

## *The Burden of Commandments:* Mitzva *in the Kibbutz*

The word "commandment," *mitzvah,* appears frequently in kibbutz literature. Has it been transformed into a more neutral secular term, or does it express a quality of traditional Judaism that, like *halakhah,* is operative within the kibbutz? Max Kadushin notes in his work *Worship and Ethics* that *mitzvot* is a conceptual term that is found in the Bible, but once more it is a term whose rabbinical connotations differ from the biblical. In the Bible, while the word often refers to commandments of God, it also refers to the commandments or admonitions of a king, parent, or teacher, or those of any other superior. In rabbinical literature, the tendency is to limit the term to *mitzvot* of God. Kibbutz practice is a return to the biblical usage of including *mitzvah* within the realm of commandments whose origin is not necessarily in divine fiat. Though the term has taken on a different connotation in Yiddish, referring to the performance of good deeds, it still retains in its purer form an association with divine law, whether in the ritual or the ethical sphere. The usage of the term—the burden of kibbutz *mitzvot*—indicates a belief in the practice of kibbutz values as more than a duty but as a commandment, whose origins lie deep within the consciousness of the community. A *mitzvah* is a moral obligation without legal force. But is it pretentious to use the term *mitzvah* for the obligations of kibbutz life? For Orthodox Jews the halakhic tradition is a serious matter, because its obligations are deemed to be of divine origin. For them the *halakhah* and *mitzvot* of the kibbutz would be classified as *minhag,* or custom. Nevertheless, halakhic legitimacy has been granted to customs deriving from popular practice and not rabbinical determination.

The kibbutz is a Jewish culture with a distinct value system in contrast to urban life in Israel. As a society cognizant of its basic principles, the consensus of the community is a real and living option because it grows out of a life lived for more than personal self-interest. Its practices are the outcome of a society with a communal consciousness. Whether their *minhag* can ever achieve the status of *halakhah* and *mitzvah* as understood by religious Jewry is a question for the future to decide. Can the kibbutz develop the tools for achieving this aim? An Orthodox kibbutznik once stated that unless the kibbutz way of life takes on halakhic force it will not be transmissible to coming generations. On the other hand, *halakhah* symbolized petrification to many thinking people within the general kibbutz, though a parallel fear exists that submission to rapid change would endanger the character of the kibbutz and lead to is eventual extinction. Reliance upon communal *minhag* will remain the foundation of kibbutz life, but it will demand a high degree of sensibility on the part of the whole community.

Within the kibbutzim the position of the *mitzvah* has engaged few thinkers, and even among those few there is little agreement. Though present trends would tend to validate those who are pessimistic, it would be premature to consign to the dust the strong sense of *mitzvah* that motivated the *Vatikim* simply because the second generation appears to be living without an awareness of the concept. Despite the indifference of the native-born, the structure of the kibbutz can assure a life ordered through *mitzvot*. An indirect affirmation of this point of view comes from a young Orthodox rabbi of Jerusalem, Adin Steinsaltz. He has often addressed kibbutz audiences and maintains close ties with the intellectuals of the movement. He is one of the few Orthodox Jews who can communicate with a kibbutz audience—including young people—and also respect their views. Rabbi Steinsaltz accepts the premise that the kibbutz is constructed on the lines of *mitzvot*, constituting a "creation within the religious sphere" with a theology of its own. This theology was socialist, but following upon the socialist crisis of faith, it faded, with a consequent decline in the imperatives of kibbutz *mitzvot*.

Steinsaltz does not believe the kibbutz can be indifferent to religion, because it belongs to a believing tradition and the resulting emptiness would strike deeply at its foundations. The kibbutz must therefore fill that void. His analysis is confirmed by different sources, all in agreement that as the kibbutz spiritual world becomes slack and shallow, *mitzvot* turn into *hovot* (obligations) among both the younger generation and the *Vatikim*. The appearnnace of written rules and regulations in interpreted by some as proof of the decline of faith. They believe that faith and *mitzvot* are yielding to legal obligation. Should the kibbutz relinquish its power of creating the inner imperative of *mitzvot*, then it becomes a place in which to live, not a spiritual community. Symptoms of the decline are a diminishing interest in holiday observance and a slow deterioration of that basic principle of the kibbutz, the work ethic. In the past, members felt charged to fulfill tasks. This feeling, too, has deteriorated. Despite the gloomy forecase, *mitzvah* remains a constituent of the kibbutz.

The kibbutz established broad and encompassing social *mitzvot*. In the realm of *mitzvot* that have often preoccupied traditional religion—the purification of one's private character—the kibbutz is reticent. As long as a member fulfills his societal obligations and does no harm to others, his inner purity is of no interest to the kibbutz, except as it affects his ability to perform the tasks required of him. This indifference to the inner man leaves a gap in kibbutz life. For some, societal *mitzvot* are not enough.

What are the basic *mitzvot* of the kibbutz? Although there have been many versions presented, the opinions of David Maletz and Yitzhak Maor are particularly relevant because of the close intellectual and emotional ties they retain with the twin worlds of traditional Judaism and of the kibbutz. Maletz's proposal is:

To live by one's work, not to exploit society, to accept upon oneself societal obligations.[31]

Maor is more specific, suggesting that communal patterns of life constitute the basic *mitzvot*:

Communal life, mutual aid, communal property, communal production and consumption.[32]

Maor believes that the *Vatikim* inadvertently sinned against their sons in the same way that their fathers sinned against them, in assuming that observance of *mitzvot* would lead easily and naturally to the concepts underlying them. This approach was effective when an entire society lived by those *mitzvot*. In today's fragmented world the competition of rival philosophies requires acceptance of the discipline of *mitzvot* with a measure of commitment. The alternative—which is what Maor fears—is the routinization of kibbutz *mitzvot*. His anxiety may be justified. Always known as "doers," the kibbutzniks emphasize action. The fact that these doers brought with them from Europe a strong ideological commitment was overlooked. In the past kibbutzim have split and members came to blows over ideas. With the intellectual foundering of their ideology the *Vatikim* hoped that in living the kibbutz *mitzvot* even without prior commitment, the inherent ideas would be absorbed. This was not borne out by experience.

An example of the type of *mitzvah* essential to kibbutz society is the rotating service required outside of work hours, such as working in the dining room or serving as night watchman for the children's houses. In what sense are they *mitzvot?* They do not fit the definition of a *mitzvah* as " the commands or admonition of a king, parent, or teacher, or those of any other superior." The *mitzvah* of the kibbutz is a command of equals and its performance carries no reward other than the gratitude of the community and the satisfaction of serving others. Although the remuneration for the observance of *mitzvot* in traditional Judaism is ideally contained within the performance of the *mitzvah* itself, material and spiritual rewards are promised—including those of the next world. The kibbutz is unable to offer the material motives that some people require for fulfillment of societal obligations. Consequently the practice of kibbutz *mitzvot* demands a high degree of commitment. An unsophisticated person finds life in a kibbutz difficult, because he is unable to apprehend the demands made upon him. It was not just a coincidence that many of the *Vatikim* were intellectual people, for only an understanding of kibbutz *mitzvot* and their performance with *kavanah* (intention) makes them palatable.

# 5
# *Jewish Issues in Kibbutz Society: Past and Present*

> They are concertedly and in all their pursuits to practice truth, humility, righteousness justice, charity and decency, with no one walking in the stubborness of his own heart or going astray after his own heart or his eyes or his fallible human mind. . . . They are to establish in Israel a solid basis of truth. They are to unite in a bond indissoluble for ever.
> —Theodore H. Gaster, "Of Social Relations" (V, 1–7), *The Dead Sea Scriptures* (English translation)

## Social Ethics

In his work on Jewish ethics, *The Vision and the Way*, Jacob B. Agus argues that the dominating motif of Jewish social ethics is melioristic and not messianic—that is, we are admonished to improve our society, not to impose a perfect plan upon it. Nor are we permitted to force the coming of the Messiah, but only to hasten his arrival by deeds of charity and repentance. Jews are therefore enjoined to be active builders of the Kingdom of God, but also to know that their efforts cannot but be fragmentary, and very often contradictory. The views of Agus can also apply to personal ethics. Although human beings are encouraged to seek the general welfare, the rabbis realized that they should at the same time look after their individual good. Of course, they cautioned against overdoing self-concern. Though human purpose and actions must invariably be just, they should nevertheless be attended by personal advantage. Morals, therefore, become a form of discipline by which a person learns to accept the conditions of life, while bending them as much as possible in his own favor. This attitude is best summed up in the expression "The Torah was not intended for angels."[33]

This approach to Jewish tradition does not expect man to be utterly selfless, steadfastly living a life of service to his fellowman. It does not apply to the prevailing and dominant mode of kibbutz thought and tradition, which takes on a maximalist and totalistic approach. Indeed, foreign visitors sometimes leave the kibbutz convinced that it is a community of saints. The kibbutz comes close to the description of Jewish ethics that appears in Morris Lazarus's classic work *The Ethics of Judaism:*

> Within the Jewish domain ethics are social ethics, in service and for the purposes of human society.[34]

Or, as he states further:

> The aim of morality is the sanctification of life, in other words, the perfect moralization of human society. Not the individual can be holy, but only the community. God is the only single being that is holy.[35]

His insistence on the primacy of social ethics within Judaism leads to the conclusion that the task of ethics should not be individual perfectibility, but a watch on the "stirring of the public consciousness," because the source of moral authority remains the ethical conscience of the people. Lazarus, in referring to the conscience of the Jewish people at large, posits an entity whose existence is beyond any real substantiation, and depends upon a mystique no less irrational than the doctrine of chosenness in traditional Judaism. Regarding kibbutz society, it is possible to accept the existence of a kibbutz conscience that is not fashioned by an organization, but is self-imposed, growing out of a constant collective watchfulness of morality. In kibbutz parlance it is known as public opinion, and it is that area of community life where morality is created and finds its realization. The spiritual energy of a kibbutz is dependent upon the strength and vigor of this collective conscience. The defects of individuals may be overlooked, but the community must pass muster.

Does the kibbutz fit the criteria for social ethics proposed by Lazarus? Some kibbutz intellectuals believe theirs is the first Jewish community in history to manifest authentically the social ethics of the Jewish tradition. Neither the prophets, the Pharisees, the

Essenes, nor the Hasidim succeeded in building a model communal life, an example of Jews living together according to the social principles of Jewish tradition. The Essenes may have come closest, but their error was to renounce Jewish society at large. (It was no coincidence that when the Dead Sea Scrolls were discovered some members of the kibbutz movement were inspired to write poetry about the Essenes.)

Here the kibbutz appears as the bearer of ancient values never consistently put into practice. Solutions to problems rarely tackled in any human society have evolved and in the process, new and different questions arose that are unique to the kibbutz form of life. Whatever success the kibbutz achieved can be attributed to its transcendence of the realistic approach to morality. Instead of a minimal morality securing moderation, order, and peace, it has sought to "produce new desires, higher and nobler than original impulses . . . a spiritual and ideal structure—a moral world."[36]

For the late kibbutz thinker Kadish Luz, justice and love go hand in hand. Unless a society can ensure firm justice it cannot expect improved moral relations between the members of its society. Luz claims that love can never reign among human beings when society is founded upon the right of man to private property. Historical evidence from the Jewish past would seem to confirm this view.

> The Rabbis, discussing the moral attainments and shortcomings of the Jews living during the Second Commonwealth, noted that Jews then studied the Torah, observed the commandments, paid the tithes punctiliously and carried themselves in the grand manner, but they loved money and loathed one another without rhyme or reason.[37]

How did the kibbutz liberate itself from the shackles of monetary competition? This was possible because it dared to attempt what Jewish tradition has always discouraged—"forcing the end." For the kibbutz this entailed becoming a redemptive movement unwilling to live within a faulty and imperfect society that contradicts the content of that redemption. The fulfillment of Jewish social ethics therefore demanded activism. Once the claims of justice had been gratified to a degree that would have been impossible in ordinary society, the kibbutz was at liberty to explore the possibility of building its society on the precept of "love thy neighbor as thyself." This was the redemptive situation that their social ideals produced—a society capable of examining whether it is possible, once freed from the obstacles of competitive life, to live according to the essence of the Torah. The hope has always existed that some day men would live together amicably without the restraints of law or the controls of force. This prospect was left to a messianic age because it seemed hopelessly impractical and unattainable under the prevailing conditions of human society. But because the kibbutz arose at a period in history when "revolution" was in the air and men believed in their ability to shape a new world, its founders could defy the past and its chain of messianic failures. By example this movement would show its people what a messianic society could attain. Though there are many variations of messianic expectation, from the fantastic to the rational, the "end of days" as envisioned for the kibbutz meant harmonious and loving human relations realized through a society that was liberated from the unavoidable resentments and hate of the normal world. Though originating from religious tradition, the messianism of Kadish Luz had united with socialism. This was possible because socialist messianism was not radically different from religious messianism that dreamed of a Kingdom of Heaven on earth. It was blended with longings for a fuller life and creation of a new man and a new society based on justice, love, and peace.

> The workers movement of Eretz Israel is a messianic movement—it forces the end. It sees Zionism as part of human redemption to the Jewish people. . . . There are many clever people who lack the belief that man can be perfected, who suppose that original sin still hangs over us. It is no wonder that a movement which yearns for messianism, to whom it is revealed that the Messiah is approaching, seeks vision.[38]

Today the type of phraseology used by the *Vatikim,* by a Kadish Luz or a Berl Katznelson, is no longer heard. Nowadays human perfection is a function of human-relations workshops. The decline of the messianic urge in the second and third generations can be traced to the failure of the *Vatikim* to educate their sons in the religious tradition that nurtured their messianism. A faith such as theirs, which embodies religious ideals, can have no continuity if the coming generations grow up illiterate. The rich associations that the *Vatikim* brought with them—which gave their life a certain dimension of holiness—are empty of content for the present generation.

## Kibbutz and Hasidism

In the earlier days of the kibbutz a living tie existed between the *Vatikim* and the mass mystic movement of Hasidism from which some of them originated. Remainders of this emotional connection appear in kibbutz ceremonies or parties, at which a Hasidic dance (the dancers with false earlocks) often appears in the program. Scholarly research on the influence of Hasidism on the kibbutz is still wanting. However there is a weighty body of opinion in the kibbutz that believes Hasidism has left its traces. Only certain components of Hasidism made their way into the kibbutz. As is to be expected, the directly religious element was deleted, leaving the folkloristic, emotional, and artistic bond that also appears in general Israel society. The Hasidic Song Festival, for instance, is held under nonreligious auspices. In a kibbutz with members of Hasidic origin, their Yiddish songs, translated into Hebrew in the early years, constituted a considerable part of the hours of singing in the evenings. Today, some kibbutzim still maintain this tradition. Following the conclusion of a holiday ceremony, the singing can go on for hours. Anyone who has participated in community singing in a kibbutz remembers those moments which were reminiscent of the spirit of song among the Hasidim. Despite the obvious differences between them, both the kibbutz and Hasidic movement sought through song to unite their communities in bonds of brotherhood forged through rejoicing and joy. When everyone sings, even those who have no voice dare to join in. But whereas in the Hasidic community the brothers were equal in the sight of God and of the rebbe, they remained unequal in their relations with each other. With Hasidism, differences in status, social position, and class were maintained. The rebbe was the nucleus of the brotherhood; relations between the members of Hasidic society centered around him. His presence was an assurance of the cooperation and solidarity of the brotherhood. The kibbutz has produced some charismatic figures in its history, but none could ever assume the role of rebbe, for he would lack a following that was prepared to accept his dictates.

Despite these differences the kibbutz felt emotional ties to Hasidism because of the common effort to initiate a brotherhood. Also, identification with Hasidism granted the kibbutz an indirect form of Jewish identity. Through identification with the Hasidic movement the *Vatikim* could substitute for their lack of formal religious observance. In addition, there was a similar background of revolt against the alliance of wealth and learning that dominated the Jewish masses of Eastern Europe. Hasidism gained its following primarily from the lower classes of Jewish communities who were engaged in the simple, manual occupations scorned by the upper classes. By their appeal to the working classes Hasidic leaders furnished their followers with a sense of worth that the unlettered Jew had never experienced. Even the most menial occupations were viewed as bearing sparks of divinity. Physical labor was no longer derided and even the most degrading task was accepted as holy, if performed with the proper intention—dedication and consecration to God. For the kibbutz, where physical labor had become a key value, this element of Hasidism served a very valuable purpose, for it attributed significance to the type of menial task most Jews were taught to despise. "It is not true that manure has no divine spark,"[39] said one respondent. The Hasid was raising the divine sparks and striving to reunite them with their ultimate source, while the kibbutznik who performed the *schwarze arbeit* ("black labor") despised by Jews, did so for the Jewish people and for his kibbutz—for the Jewish people so that they would learn to engage in productive labor and not be dependent upon others for menial tasks, and for the kibbutz because his community was built upon mutual support and obligation. The Hasid who labored in faith was aiding God, while the kibbutznik was aiding his community, performing his work faithfully in the knowledge that to clean latrines or wash floors was his contribution.

This transformation of Hasidic mystic intention into a mystique of physical labor succeeded with the generation of *Vatikim* who were unused to physical work and educated in the old values of disdain for it. Today's kibbutz-born generation, trained to work, has a more matter-of-fact, empirical attitude to labor, and appears capable of performing any kind of physical work without having to engage in meditative exercises. *Aggadah* has been transformed into *halakhah*.

Martin Buber has suggested that the degree of Hasidic influence on the kibbutz is beyond our comprehension for the present but will reveal itself at some future period. In his writings he claims that "Hasidism was the last intensive effort in modern history to rejuvenate a religion: yet it seems to have been a failure. But it has produced an abundance of spendid religious life such as the world has very seldom seen and has scattered seed in other spheres, some of which has already come up and the rest of which will probably develop later on. Some day it will be impossible to see and understand the best of what has arisen and is arising now in the way of a new human life in the Jewish settlements of Palestine without connecting it with Hasidism."[40]

## Kibbutz and Socialism

Within the kibbutz movement different interpretations of socialism exist. Ha-Kibbutz ha-Artzi considers itself consciously Marxist, while the Ihud can reasonably claim that there is no tie between the kibbutz and Marx's interpretation of socialism. Kibbutz socialism would have been branded by Marx as "utopian socialism," a pejorative phrase in the Marxist lexicon. Instead of engaging in political revolution and joining with other socialists to overthrow reactionary regimes, utopians retreat from the struggle by building small exemplary socialist communities. The nonidentification of the kibbutz with Marx cannot negate its indebtedness to him. One of his statements, "From each according to his abilities to each according to his needs," serves as a guiding principle in kibbutz society. Acceptance of this principle does not mean that the kibbutz is Marxist, for the kibbutz brand of socialism is closer to what Martin Buber calls "voluntaristic socialism," a socialism that appeals to reason, to justice, to the will of man to remedy the maladjustments of society, instead of his merely acquiring an active awareness of what is "dialectically brewing in the womb of industrialism."[41]

The teaching of socialism as a form of humanism must come as a surprise to those who view socialism as an economic doctrine (and an inefficient one at that) that poses serious dangers to democratic society and its way of life. This is an understandable result of identifying socialism with totalitarian regimes that speak in the name of this doctrine.

An excellent summary of the socialist outlook on life is in R. H. Tawney's *Religion and the Rise of Capitalism*. Though the following quotation refers specifically to medieval thought, it can be extended to socialism.

> Society is a spiritual organism, not an economic machine, and that economic activity, which is one subordinate element within a vast and complex unity, requires to be controlled and repressed by reference to the moral end for which it supplies the

material means. So merciless is the tyranny of economic appetites, so prone to self-aggrandizement the empire of economic interest, that a doctrine which confines them to their proper sphere, as the servant, not the master, of civilization, may reasonably be regarded as among the pregnant truisms which are a permanent element in any sane philosophy.[42]

By turning socialism into a way of life, the kibbutz succeeded in putting equality to the test of experience. Whether its socialism has Jewish significance is a question of moment for some kibbutz intellectuals who have Judaized the socialist idea. In general, Judaism does not insist on one or another economic system, but it asserts the inadequacy of all systems. In a society where free enterprise is the rule, Judaism asserts the constant need to combat poverty and to safeguard the freedom and dignity of the individual. In a socialist society, it would stress the sanctity of the human person and the inviolability of his basic rights.[43]

This independent posture assumed by Judaism releases Jews from the burden of having to justify (unless the system is tyrannical) the social, economic, and political system under which they live through discovery of its affinities to Judaism. Western Jewry, since the Emancipation, has sought the favor of their host countries by assuring them that Jewish values are in close, if not perfect agreement with local national values. This approach is open to many obvious dangers, and yet can be enriching when practiced cautiously. The Jewish heritage has both benefited and suffered from the values and beliefs absorbed over the centuries. By living in the more tolerant, open and democractic society of the United States, the Jews of America, including the Orthodox, are more temperate than their counterparts in Israel.

Something within American society was absorbed by the Jews. Are the principles of American democracy and Judaism in accord, or is it the better part of wisdom to withhold judgment on the compatibility of Judaism and democracy and take a neutral, nonjudgmental view, refusing commitment to any system? This hesitancy overlooks the splendid opportunities for enlargement of the Jewish heritage offered by its contact with other cultures and systems. Reasonably the Jewish heritage should be disengaged from political and social struggles that identify Judaism with any one position. This would preclude overdependence. Despite this reservation, dominate themes in Jewish thought appear closer to certain social and economic systems than to others. Were this not the case, Judaism would be a colorless and irrelevant teaching that abandons the tumultuous world for the security of noncommitment.

Just as it is possible to claim that some cultures are superior to others in their life-sustaining, harmonious power, so certain economic systems may potentially, if not actually, fit the ethical spirit of Judaism. It has been claimed that Judaism can accommodate itself to any system. Within the Jewish heritage capitalism has coexisted with socialism, freedom with slavery, monogamy with polygamy. Yet a rough consensus on essentials remains. The attraction of Jews to left-wing socialist causes, whatever its sociological origins, cannot be dismissed as the quirk of an odd minority group.

Within the Jewish heritage there are only the faintest glimmerings of modern socialism. This is true, says Yitzhak Maor of Ashdod Yaacov [Ihud], but the vision of socialism is not the invention of the nineteenth century; it has deep roots in man's strivings for justice on earth. Socialism and the prophets share common social goals, although the prophets aimed at improving their society from within and not at changing its entire structure. The kibbutz is consciously socialistic, but it is unknowingly prophetic. By Judaizing socialism a thinker such as Yitzhak Maor adds to the stock of ideas and beliefs of Jewish tradition, thereby broadening its base for active confrontations with modern society. Socialism can be an effective modern transplant to Judaism if its teachings are in accord with the spirit of Jewish social ethics. Can the same be said for capitalism, a system through which Jews have benefited materially from Western societies?

> All the social commandments in the Law of Moses have their roots in a world outlook which denies a man absolute ownership of his property. "For the land is Mine, but you are strangers and residents with Me." Man is a passing guest in the world of the Holy One, blessed be He. Property is given to him only as a pledge.[44]

This authority for a kibbutz socialist sermon is biblical and not modern. It does not instantly provide a Jewish origin for socialism, but it does assist the Jew, as socialist, to live his socialism not as a foreign graft, but as an intrinsic, though understated, element in his Jewish past. Few settlers came to the kibbutz because they believed socialism to be a part of their Jewish background, for although considered a solution to the problems of the Jewish people, socialism was rarely connected with the Jewish heritage. To espouse it was another indication of liberation from the burdensome Jewish past. Such was the situation in the early years of kibbutz settlement. But as the attraction of socialism declined, later waves of settlers, particularly from Western countries, envisaged the kibbutz as the peak of Jewish rather than socialist renewal.

## *The Cosmological Dimension*

Living in a moral society can become routine and meaningless unless appropriate ceremony allows one to partake emotionally of that society's meaning—for itself, for the Jewish world, and for humanity. This question leads to the problem of Jewish ritual and ceremonial forms in the kibbutz. If we accept the assumption that pervades this work, i.e., that the kibbutz has the expectations and mentality of a religious society, then its lack of tools for signifying its fundamental temper and mood can turn into a chronic defect. No society in all of Israel can be said to be in greater need of ritual than the kibbutz. An example is in the dining room, whose communal meals symbolize the idea of brotherhood. Today the meal rarely succeeds in representing this concept. Although tentative moves have been made to introduce a brief ceremony prior to the Friday-night meal, meals in the dining room usually have no ceremonial accompaniment. During work days meals are eaten hastily and in shifts. Only when the kibbutz dines together, as on holidays, weddings, or other special events, does the meal include more than food. Most members feel that the kibbutz, as a value-conscious society, cannot exist without appropriate ceremonies to dramatize those values. The question is, What types of ceremony are appropriate for a kibbutz setting?

Israel Bitman, of Yifat, is one of the few individuals who has recognized the need for a renewal of Jewish ritual forms within the kibbutz. Such ritual does not entail a return to traditional structures, but should arise out of the way of life of the kibbutz itself. Until now the kibbutz was almost completely involved in national, political, and social issues. This "religion of pioneering" was sufficient in the early years of settlement, but with the attainment of permanence, man's soul demands answers to questions beyond the social sphere. Bitman thinks that a vacuum still exists in the spiritual life of the kibbutz that social ethics cannot fill, because man has a will to "stride in secret paths." He believes that this will to extend ourselves beyond immediate reality obtains even when our universe is balanced and harmonious.

At one time the kibbutz had hoped that its totalistic approach would fulfill all the social, cultural, and economic requirements of its members. But this proved to be an oversimplification of human complexity. The kibbutz discovered itself unable to span every area of human activity. The totalism of kibbutz life even had the unanticipated effect of unloosing dissatisfaction against the very social forms arising out of the will to answer the needs of members. This shocked the people who believed that their new society would exemplify the good life. Because a vacuum was left in their spiritual life, there may be a shift toward the Jewish sphere. For filling this vacuum Bitman proposes the establishment in the kibbutz of something like a synagogue—not the traditional synagogue that some *Vatikim* have resurrected in a few kibbutzim, but rather an institution established by a group who reject a blind return to tradition, but who subscribe to a belief based upon some way of understanding God. Bitman's formulation remains purposely vague because he fears that an attempt to arrive at precise understanding might overintellectualize the problem and result in a loss in commitment to the establishment of a center for deepening and extending Jewish culture and practice. Even prayer could be included, but prayer to which a man could relate with agreement. With the development of this center children could participate, eventually bringing in the parents.

Bitman admits, however, that no one within the kibbutz movement is ready to organize and unite around the principle. He justifies his revolutionary proposal by citing William James to the effect that religion is a matter of feeling, acts, and experiences, from which theologies, philosophies, and ecclesiastical organizations may develop. The older generation in the kibbutz came with Jewish memories, while the younger generation has only a cognitive tie to Jewish life. Bitman hoped his proposal, if acted upon, would add the dimension of experience presently absent from the Jewish consciousness of the younger generation. His proposal also aims at assuring the retention of the kibbutz within the boundaries of historical Judaism. Many take issue with his views and consider them pretentious. In addition, there is a fear that the very kibbutz creativity Bitman seeks to encourage would be stifled by the formation of a synagogue structure.

Preoccupation with the synagogue is not the monopoly of Israel

Bitman. For him it is a symbol of the attachment between the kibbutz and historical Judaism. Other have emphasized that the kibbutz must be more Jewish if it hopes to attract the type of immigrant from the Western countries who is seeking values. Research on American immigrants to Israel indicates that those who remain have a strong Jewish or Zionist consciousness—and the kibbutz wants to attract such potential immigrants. Can it succeed if its way of life does not manifest the best of the Jewish heritage? For Western Jews from the Diaspora the synagogue has been an integral part of that heritage, but no kibbutz would establish a synagogue for the sole purpose of attracting new settlers.

What can be done for kibbutz members who need what the synagogue offers, but are unable to support one in the kibbutz? Some hope that by frequenting the synagogue they may become magically endowed with the faith they earnestly seek. Because there have been no synagogues in the kibbutz, the only alternative was private study and prayer, together with family celebration of the Sabbath in one's room. The suggestion of private expression of faith holds little prospect of success. To pray and study privately in a communal society might remove an individual from his community and intensify his sense of alienation. The only alternatives for such an individual would be for him to relinquish his attempt to shift the community in his direction, or to leave his kibbutz and try to build a new one closer to his thinking. Although the kibbutz will honor an individual's personal inclinations to traditional ritual practice, it must operate according to its special genius as a collective.

Moshe Una writes about an encounter with another observant Jew who regarded the kibbutz as an inappropriate form of life for a religious person. Una rejected this view because he sees the religious collective as a necessity in a world where "evil winds are blowing." Una has no intention of suppressing dissent, but he does feel that a religious collective is a powerful defense against the erosion of tradition in our age. The implication for the non-Orthodox kibbutz is that an individual member who is searching for religious faith will be ultimately frustrated unless he succeeds in forming a group around him.

### *Holiness*

Israel Bitman's discovery of the cosmological gap in kibbutz life has a parallel in Yehoshua Manoah's severe criticism of the kibbutz for the absence of "holiness" in its society. When the community was occupied in building the land, elements of holiness could be perceived, but they faded out of sight as the kibbutz became intoxicated by its economic, political, and national activism. Those early years could have prepared the soil for planting within kibbutz society habits and styles of life imbued with "holiness." Bitman's thinking follows the lines of traditional Judaism. He states that there is no holiness in the kibbutz, because they have no prohibitions that would give the Sabbath and the holidays a more clearly defined form. Under the present regime in which "every man may do what is right in his eyes" there is only the dimmest hope for renewal of a sense of holiness in the kibbutz. As understood by Manoah, holiness is intimately associated with the pattern of observance and practice he experienced among Eastern European Jewry. He pleads with the kibbutz for "the magnificent richness of which father's house was full. . . . Where is all that today?" He writes in the style of a traditional Jew describing the Sabbath as a magical queen, Sabbath food with the taste of Eden, and so forth.

> By what means can we drive out the unhallowed greyness in our lives? How can we introduce a little holiness into our dull days?[45]

This despairing cry has echoed back and forth throughout the kibbutz movement, and then faded away. There is a yearning for holiness, but people realize that today father's house is history for them and they must forgo any search for holiness in the Eastern European form. The kibbutz must either accept a life devoid of holiness or else reinterpret the term to fit their new reality. The *Vatikim* are still beguiled by memories of the past. Their experience of Orthodoxy blocks any move in new directions. Whenever the urge to holiness appears, they slip back into the familiar. What will happen to the coming generation when "unhallowed greyness" arouses a craving for means of sanctification? With no evocative past to draw upon and with only a theoretical knowledge of Judaism, the yearning for the holy could yet be productive if it were not choked by the commonplace assumption that Orthodox Judaism is the only medium for communicating holiness. Some *Vatikim* even refuse to permit the use of the word "holiness," except within an Orthodox context. They believe that the concept and the experience are inextricably bound to the world of traditional Judaism and supernatural religion, and should be eliminated from the vocabulary of the kibbutz.

A *Vatik* of strong traditional leanings admitted that religiosity can be other than Orthodoxy. What matters is not the form but the experience of holiness. When asked whether the kibbutz is capable of eliciting this quality in its life, he replied that it may take generations before this can be achieved, but the potential exists.

> Within kibbutz society there are scattered sparks of holiness. Because they are scattered their influence is small. These sparks in kibbutz life should be concentrated and kindled so that they might light the way for the seekers of the good, the beautiful, the exalted, the spiritual, the moral.[46]

This statement contains the tacit admission that holiness is not exclusively confined to Sabbaths and festivals, although their importance is not to be denied within the total picture. It can be argued that holiness can only occur within the supernatural context of traditional Judaism and is inseparably linked to "the holy other," whose recognition is often held to be essential for an experience of the sacred. An alternative kibbutz concept of holiness has been proposed by Avraham Aderet of Ayelet Ha-Shahar, who declares that it is: "the attempt of man to attach his passing life to concepts and values, and if possible to some form of existence above and beyond his life."[47] Aderet is referring to kibbutz society and its values, for he claims that a man who believes in the kibbutz way of equality and cooperation and strives to manifest these values in his daily life has entered the sphere of holiness. For Aderet the kibbutz is a transcendental but not supernatural society. This view has received a measure of confirmation from Rabbi Adin Steinsaltz, who believes that the kibbutz will eventually decline in numbers and strength, but when this happens "the religious moment" of those who remain will be immeasurably reinforced. Because a greater measure of faith and belief would be required to live in a disintegrating society, those who remain will have strong religious sensibilities. He further believes that the future decline of the kibbutz would infuse a religious spirit into Israeli society at large, though not necessarily in any specifically Jewish form. Rabbi Steinsaltz's gloomy forecast, correct or not, contains the unusual admission (for an Orthodox Jew) that the kibbutz possesses a religious spirit. Can this spirit endure without an accompanying perception of the need for a system of sacred objects and ideas? The early settler who remained in the kibbutz had a sacred tie to it. Should the kibbutz crumble, it might revert to the selectivity of its early years and restore a sphere of holiness that is lacking among the many who live there through inertia.

## Tradition in the Kibbutz or a Kibbutz Tradition

The Israeli press from time to time publishes articles that point toward the so-called return to religion in the kibbutzim. The dedication of a kibbutz synagogue for *Vatikim* or the occasional traditional prayer service for a particular holiday usually prompt such articles, which often touch off debates in the internal kibbutz press on the desirability of this apparent trend. In their nostalgia for tradition, some members wrote that the kibbutz was guilty of disservice to its youth by its failure to include more traditional customs in its holiday observances, thereby estranging young people from their heritage. In the letters and articles that followed, it was clarified that the kibbutz has no such intention, but rather faces the perplexing problem of deciding what elements of Jewish tradition it finds acceptable. The basic principle—very difficult to manifest in practice—is that the kibbutz must create a holiday tradition that will faithfully express its own way of life. Only then will it succeed in transmitting this tradition to coming generations. Because tradition has conservative overtones, many people in the kibbutz are convinced that it is essentially static, forgetting that the Orthodox tradition has undergone change as well, with each generation adding another tier to the structure. In confronting the Jewish heritage the kibbutz is compelled to be watchful lest it slip into a conservative stance by restoring traditional practices, without thinking through the reason for doing so. It can be argued that the kibbutz, by moving in this direction, would surrender the right to form a holiday of its own. Its partial success in evolving new approaches to Hanukkah, Passover, and Shavuot would regress by a return to traditional uses. The creative urge would be stifled—tragic indeed for the future of kibbutz Jewish culture. Development of a dynamic holiday tradition with discernible roots "taking" in the soil of the kibbutz may be expected to involve many generations. Why discourage this evolution? The retort is that a distinctly kibbutz form of tradition would become provincial and would isolate the kibbutz from the rest of world Jewry. For example, by using traditional forms of candle blessings, the tie remains intact. Although this view undoubtedly has some supporters and can be seen in actual practice in some kibbutzim, the following position is closer to the kibbutz spirit:

> How is a folk tradition shaped and how is the festival of a people formed? Certainly not in one day and not by the "eminent men of the generation" who impose the desirable patterns from above. A Shulhan Arukh is always the end of a process, a photo

of reality as it developed among the people in different parts of the world. Therefore, local, independent creativity need not be considered as provincial, but rather as one among many contributions to the formation of tradition. . . . None of us know in advance what part of our cultural creativity will "take," what will become, in the course of time, the property of the people or what will pass and be forgotten. But this does not release us from the obligation to experiment diligently and repeatedly and find the proper expression for our life experience which conforms to our basic outlook, our way of life and feelings.[48]

This statement also answers the accusations against the kibbutz that it chooses the easy elements of tradition, rejecting the demands that are "inconvenient." But what is convenient in line with the reasoning of the above quote is chosen precisely because it fits one's spirit and regime of life during this historical period, and not for reasons of comfort. Once this principle becomes firmly implanted in the consciousness of the kibbutz, cultural creativity can advance without furtive and guilty glances over the shoulder. A familiar example of the manner in which the kibbutz dipped into the cultural pool of tradition for the satisfaction of its intellectual and emotional wants is in the use it made of the prophetic tradition. The kibbutz "discovered" that the prophets were generally underplayed in traditional Judaism and gave them a new prominence in their scheme. They were successful in reviving the prophets because they followed a flexible standard in extracting from the tradition what Zvi Raanan of Hazorea calls "the inner truth." The key to this expression is given by another writer of the Ha-Kibbutz ha-Artzi, who declares that there must be a continual search for values of the Jewish heritage that will be acceptable to the mind and heart—for historical experience has taught that whatever the Jewish people observed in their soul, they practiced in life. This generality is not very helpful in analyzing the actual practice of the kibbutz—but it is a valuable source documenting the kibbutz approach to Judaism. Once considered the absolute monopoly of Orthodoxy, it is now widely understood that the Jewish heritage is the inheritance of all Jews, and the kibbutz has an obligation, however selectively, to live by this heritage.

The selectivity practiced by the kibbutz in its confrontation with tradition bears a superficial resemblance to the approach of Reform Judaism. Both movements in many ways depart from *halakhah*. This freedom to pick freely and choose might easily obscure some basic differences between the movements. Reform has assumed for itself a wider sphere of influence, encompassing the entire Jewish people, for whom it accepts an ultimate responsibility. Whatever changes it introduces, whether in practice or thought, are aimed beyond their own members. In this respect Reform Judaism differs markedly from the kibbutz, which adapts the tradition for its own needs alone, and has no pretensions to be an example to the Jewish world.

This point explains the relative lack of hostility of Orthodoxy toward kibbutz experimentation with tradition. Because it relinquishes all claims to be heir and interpreter of tradition the kibbutz is not seen as a competitor—as are Reform and Conservative Judaism. The kibbutz Passover Haggadah, for example, did not emerge as a competitor to the traditional Haggadah. Should there be some "fallout" from their Haggadah, and Jews outside the kibbutz see fit to make use of it, there would be no protest, for there was never an intention that it have a universal Jewish application.

Another point of difference between the kibbutz and Reform and Conservative Judaism is in their use of community functionaries. Reform and Conservative Judaism have a paid full-time clergy, a professional class responsible for explaining, interpreting, teaching, and, when necessary, adapting the tradition. The layman in Reform and Conservative Judaism remains mute in areas within the professional competence of the rabbi, and while the participation and involvement of the laity is encouraged, the rabbi represents authority. In the kibbutz, the situation is almost completely reversed. It has no professional body with a direct responsibility for problems arising out of the Jewish cultural needs of the kibbutz. In fact, very few people at all deal with the subject, for such problems are peripheral to kibbutz society. The people engaged in preparations for a holiday do so on a voluntary basis, acting pragmatically and experimentally because, unlike rabbis, they are not steeped in knowledge of the tradition. Whatever arises out of holiday practice in the Kibbutz is therefore a layman's culture, evolved naturally and organically. Consequently, the tradition, while respected, is not treated as sacrosanct, but as a flexible mold giving shape to the living and ever-changing content of kibbutz life. The way holidays are observed in a particular kibbutz does indeed provide a fairly faithful reflection of the prevailing spirit in that kibbutz and can be an important instrument for measuring that society's social health.

By seeking some means of fertile intermixture between tradition and its own life process, the kibbutz preserves a freedom to discover its own appropriate answer to questions that emerge out of its existence. The flurry around the so-called return to religion has acted as a diversion, falsely leading some to believe that tradition was about to become a new standard for measuring the value and authenticity of kibbutz life. No matter how deeply tradition may make inroads into the kibbutz, it will always remain secondary to the internal beat of kibbutz life. Although the kibbutz may certainly listen to tradition, it will not be dictated to by it. The conditions for a fruitful dialogue between the kibbutz and the heritage of the past were more effective when the *Vatikim* possessed some knowledge of tradition. Although the second and third generations often continue kibbutz traditions that were set by the elders, their ability to cope creatively with the Jewish heritage may be severely taxed by their widespread illiteracy in that sphere. The intended result could be a new conservatism, a static attachment to the holiday practices of the kibbutz past.

In the context of this problem the question of Jewish education in the kibbutz assumes a new urgency. Adults who wish to enhance their knowledge of Judaism can do so through participation in regional seminars, adult education courses, or private reading. But experience has shown that these study groups usually attract the older generation. Young people educated in the kibbutz school system rarely show active interest in studying Judaism. The root of the problem therefore remains in the kibbutz elementary and high schools, which teach Jewish history and the Bible, but generally ignore postbiblical literature. Very few articles on the subject of Jewish education in the kibbutz are available, and those which are tend to dwell on the errors of the past. What to teach now or in the future was hardly ever discussed, except in a very general sense. As kibbutz schools organize themselves for the Israel of the 1980s, the role played by humanistic studies, such as Judaism, is not likely to increase in view of the heavy emphasis on science and technology demanded by the economy of kibbutz society. Besides this particular drawback there is a shortage of qualified teachers of Judaism with little hope for an infusion of new blood. The ideal solution would be for the kibbutz to send its own men and women to the university for higher studies in Judaism. If a call were made in the kibbutz movement for youngsters to choose the teaching of Judaism as a profession the response would probably be very meager. The entire subject remains peripheral. Because the future looks unpromising, with no new and young teachers in sight, efforts have begun on a small scale to shore up the existing structure by instituting study groups in postbiblical literature for kibbutz teachers. In January 1970 the Inter-Kibbutz Education Committee initiated such a study group that met once a month in Tel Aviv for the duration of the school year. Its aim was both to increase knowledge and to suggest effective teaching methods.

In the light of the serious drawbacks confronting the kibbutzniks who seek to introduce more Jewish knowledge into the kibbutz, doubt has been expressed whether the kibbutz can play any significant Jewish role outside its own province. The entire subject interests few kibbutz members. Although occasional remarks have been made at movement-wide conventions on the need for the kibbutz to begin thinking more seriously about its role in the Jewish world, and the role of Judaism in its own world, no kibbutz movement has deemed it necessary to devote time at any of its official conferences to this question. If the kibbutz movement should some day decide that it must play an active role not only in defense, economics, and politics, but also in Judaism, it has outstanding social and spiritual resources. Of course, the rejoinder to any possible kibbutz activism within the Jewish world is that, although the kibbutz was created to serve the Jewish people, its service was not meant to include the renewal of Jewish culture. What did occur culturally in the kibbutz was an incidental byproduct of kibbutz life and not a purposeful act. Most of the missions the kibbutz has assumed were not part of some clearly defined aim, but arose in response to new problems faced by Jewish settlement in Israel.

It is traditional that the kibbutz should provide leadership in areas vital to the survival of the Jewish people, and therefore the Israeli army has a proportionately large number of high-ranking army officers coming from kibbutz ranks. In the past the kibbutz undertook national tasks that no one else was prepared or able to perform, but which today are under the jurisdiction of Israeli government agencies. Its pioneering duties have dwindled over the years and now the kibbutz is searching for new ones. The French sociologist George Friedman believes that a new field for the kibbutz could be to attempt to exemplify to advanced industrial societies the application of technological progress to the service of man, to his physical and moral development, to his happiness. "Here is a new frontier to be peacefully conquered, defended and maintained."[49]

Another new frontier for the kibbutz is being proposed by Stanley Meron of Ma'ayan Tzvi, who calls for the kibbutz to be a pioneer of Judaism. By assuming this broader role the kibbutz would also be serving itself, for aid to the larger society would stimulate the kibbutz and open up hidden sources of power.

> May the kibbutz movement which is called upon to implement Zionism concretely, succeed in creating a Jewish world concept and a Jewish way of life which would be able to unite the entire people.[50]

Exactly how this will come about we cannot envisage, but Meron suggests possible initial acts that may bring the required momentum in their wake. The first step must be to study, so that the kibbutz might absorb more deeply those values of Judaism, such as justice and community, which are vital for its proper functioning. These two values already exist in the kibbutz, but they can lose substance unless effectively reinforced from generation to generation. By utilizing the insights of the Jewish past the kibbutz could energize its cooperative way of life and initiate interaction, opening the way to an exchange of experience. The kibbutz could disclose its discoveries to Jewish society at large, sharing what it has learned through adapting principles to new and changing circumstances.

The new set of instruments and circumstances that the kibbutz created within the Jewish world are its communal and cooperative institutions and form of life. Until recent years Jews lacked the option offered to Christians who sought a communal society. With the advent of the kibbutz, Jewish life has been enriched by the addition of a life-style previously unknown within the Jewish heritage. Now sincere Jews have an additional means of realizing their commitment to the Jewish people or to Judaism, through the introduction of a new social form. As the first Jewish communal society of modern times, the kibbutz opens new avenues for the mysterious flights of the spirit for which the Jewish people so deeply crave and yearn.

# 6
# *Equality*

A sudden smile appeared upon the gentle lips of the strong Yaacob Yitzhak. "It is hard to be a Jew," he said. Then he looked back at the table and asked: "Who has cut my initials into the wood?" No one knew. "And why furthermore are the two letters Yod* cut into the wood one above the other and not next to each other?"

"Very naturally, because two Yods next to each other signify the name of God," someone said.

"In that case," Yaacob Yitzhak announced, "I will now tell you a final story. . . .

"The way it is when two men drink to each other's health and each feels equal to the other and neither of them considers himself superior, that is a matter which I experienced when I began to learn the alphabet. In the book before me I saw the letter Yod, which is so very like a mere point. I asked the teacher: 'What kind of a little point is that?' 'That is the letter Yod,' said he. 'And does that little point,' I asked, 'always stand alone or can two of them stand together?' 'Two of them may stand together,' said he. 'But how does one read them then?' I asked again. 'When two Yods stand together,' said he, 'that signifies the name of God, Blessed be He!' Soon thereupon I saw that at the end of each verse of Holy Scripture there stands two points, one above the other. I did not yet know that these are the points of separation. I considered each of these two points to be the letter Yod. 'Here,' I said to my teacher, 'there is printed constantly the name of God, Blessed be He.' 'Not at all,' the teacher replied. Mark my words. When two Yods [Jews] stand beside each other it signifies the name of God; but when one stands above the other it does not signify the name of God."

—Martin Buber, *For the Sake of Heaven*

---

*Yod is the name of the tenth letter of the Hebrew alphabet. In Yiddish it also means "a Jew," from the Hebrew *Yehudi* (German: *Jude*). Two Yods placed side by side are frequently used as a symbol for the name of God. The initials of Yaacob Yitzhak's name would have been two Yods placed side by side.

## The Faith in Equality

In the numerous articles appearing in kibbutz and nonkibbutz literature on the basic values of kibbutz society, there is general agreement among all writers of whatever movement, school, or persuasion that equality is the cornerstone of kibbutz life and the essence of the kibbutz idea. All the institutions, the social, economic, and cultural forms that have arisen within the kibbutz constitute a commentary on this principle.

To trace the origins and development of the concept of equality in the kibbutz is beyond the scope of this brief section, which intends only to survey the major problems confronted by the kibbutz in implementing this cardinal principle and in evaluating the position of equality within Jewish tradition. An introductory discussion of the significance and spirit of equality should help clarify this difficult, complex, and problematic idea. The initial difficulty one faces in trying to comprehend kibbutz adherence to this principle is its fanciful and almost fictitious quality. Known as a very practical society, the kibbutz nevertheless adopted an idea which runs counter to knowledge. Any experience of human beings is sufficient to disclose the physical, spiritual, and intellectual inequalities among them. Life appears to dictate inequality, with the bright and inventive, upon whom society depends, benefiting from prestige and material advantage. A clear-eyed gaze upon reality would lead most people to deny the validity of equality as a viable idea. But belief in equality is a faith and consequently is based upon an unseen, nonobservable, and unprovable factor—the common humanity of mankind. It is a hidden factor and, unlike inequality, not directly observable. Only through faith in its existence can it be discerned.

Equality is the qualifier of major events in kibbutz life and its standard for judgment when questions of economic distribution arise. Later the material problems that arise out of the kibbutz pledge to activate this principle will come up for discussion. Spiritually, the belief in equality and the concomitant commitment to its practice has had a salutary effect on the relations between members having wide ranges of talent and capabilities. Esteem and worth are usually apportioned in nonkibbutz society according to an individual's material or professional achievements. In the kibbutz, the belief in equality serves as a balance against the decisive weight often given in the nonkibbutz world to substantive accomplishment. An individual in the kibbutz can gain the appreciation and admiration of his peers on the strength of his personality and character as well as on the success of his achievements. He must produce, but he is not judged entirely by this capability. Equality thereby adds another dimension to the appraisal of man, releasing him from the bonds of "achievement."

In this sense the kibbutz attempts to build a society that is not based upon functional divisions, but rather upon the belief that an individual's sincere efforts, even if unsuccessful, entitle him to the approbation of his equals (if not in talent, at least in humanity). By partially releasing its members from the tyranny of economic performance as the single standard for self-definition, the kibbutz has protected its members from being transformed into "means" and has preserved their human rank as goals. Indeed, one of the warning signals of the decline of equality in a kibbutz is a shift in the criteria for evaluating fellow members. Where esteem is gained only because of efficiency, that kibbutz has denied the core of equality and accepted the fundamentals of meritocracy.

This mode of personal evaluation, still dominant in the kibbutz, is called a "religious romantic idealization" by Crane Brinton in his article "Equality" in the *Encyclopedia of the Social Sciences*. He does not consider intellectual justification necessary for this concept, for in his view the belief in equality is a "given psychological fact . . . never felt very strongly except by some uncommonly sensitive spirits." With sharp insight he remarks that "it is an agreeable emotion, for its realization promises peace."

> When discussion reveals disagreements at the very root of morality, rational moral argument must give way to the persuasive methods of preacher and prophet. At this level, to adopt a moral position is to make an ultimate choice—i.e., one in its nature beyond the limits of rational justification, where appeals must necessarily be to the sympathetic emotions.[31]

The existence of the kibbutz is the counterargument to the aristocratic morality, which values man only on the basis of his special talents and achievements. As believers in the intrinsic worth and dignity of the human personality, the kibbutz takes pride in its interpersonal relationships. In discussing their own society, members were heard to remark: "We are more humane" (in comparison to the "outside"). This statement was often made in the full realization that an economic price had to be paid for this moral stance. In the moral vision the opportunities and rewards of life do not rightfully belong to the one who is in a position by birth, accident, or ability to control the flow of goods, services, and powers toward himself.

The nobility and moral grandeur of the egalitarian idea would be denied by few, but even its supporters are likely to shrug their shoulders in despair at the prospect of even partial implementation. Some people left their kibbutzim not because of dissatisfaction with the principle of equality, but because of the innumerable obstacles in the path to its realization resulting from the normal pettiness and cupidity of human beings. *Vatikim* now admit that they had a naive conception of human nature—as if it were clay in the hands of the potter, which under proper environmental conditions could be molded into any shape desired. Human resistance to the majesty of great ideas is often a keen blow to sensitive people whose devotion to principles occasionally hardens their hearts, making them incapable of forgiving their fellowmen for unwillingness to make every sacrifice for the sake of an abstraction. As one former Orthodox kibbutznik put it: socialism is a wonderful principle, but people aren't equal to it.

Living in a kibbutz, on a close day-to-day basis, puts a severe strain on belief in human equality. Each day this postulate must be reborn in the kibbutznik; otherwise he might easily slip into an untroubled contempt for the frailties of his fellows. "Sometimes ideology helps," remarked a member who was born and raised in a kibbutz. Equality, therefore, remains an elusive goal, out of reach, but sincerely pursued.

> The important thing, however, is not that it should be completely attained, but that it should be sincerely sought. What matters to the health of a society is the objective towards which its face is set, and to suggest that it is immaterial in which direction it moves because the goal must always elude it, is not scientific, but irrational. It is like using the impossibility of absolute cleanliness as a pretext for rolling in a manure heap, or denying the importance of honesty because no one can be wholly honest.[52]

These remarks were directed by R. H. Tawney at his British contemporaries who believed that equality might strike a blow at liberty. They also have relevance to the contemporary situation in the kibbutz and in Israel society. A common criticism against the kibbutz heard from urban Israelis is that it has failed to achieve equality. The objection is similar to the argument against adherence to religion—i.e., that if one is unable to be orthodoxly religious, religion should be rejected altogether. The kibbutz is a natural target for such views, for a spiritual movement rooted in principle and values will inevitably be charged with laxness or hypocrisy by individuals who permit themselves the luxury of unrelenting criticism. Whoever decides to live by a more difficult standard must accept the inevitable censure of those who make fewer demands upon themselves. Yet within the kibbutz itself, one hears some muttering against the gradual debasement of equality. Although equality is considered by some social scientists to be one of the kibbutz values that have been creatively modified, there is still a body of opinion in the kibbutz that believes that this value has been seriously compromised. Whatever the justice of this view, it indicates a despair and "failure of nerve" within a segment of kibbutz society. As the only social body in contemporary Jewish life that is dedicated to the realization of the principle of equality—albeit on a miniature scale—it would be tragic were the kibbutz to conclude that its experiment had failed. The Jewish heritage would be the ultimate loser, for by focusing itself upon this principle the kibbutz has added another tier to Judaism and struck a blow against the commonplace assumption that only the past may be a source of religious values.

## Equality in the Jewish Tradition

In the Jewish tradition, as in Christianity, equality existed only as a potential. In actuality, these two religions, despite their affirmation of human equality before God, condoned many social, economic, and political inequalities. Louis Finkelstein, in his article "Human Equality in the Jewish Tradition According to Biblical and Rabbinic Tradition," labors valiantly to discover in tradition even a hint of the notion that all men are created equal, finally concluding that only the belief in immortality can serve as the ultimate symbol of human equality. Indeed, in Judaism all men are to be buried in the same simple way, with no distinction between rich and poor. According to Finkelstein equality in Judaism is not a question of rights. "All human beings are equal in their obligations to God. All men are equal therefore in their relation to God, possessing no rights, only duties. Man has come to earth to fulfil his Creator's purposes. Nevertheless, human rights are asserted in the Bible and Talmud, deriving from the premise that God loves justice. Therefore, artificial inequalities, unless necessary for the fulfillment of a transcendent purpose set by God, are abhorrent to Him as a violation of His will."[53] Traditional Judaism only attempted to mitigate man-made inequalities, not eradicate them. Indeed, denunciations of the callous rich are found throughout prophetic literature, the wealthy and the wicked being used as synonymous terms. Those biblical institutions which contained the seeds of social reform—equal division of the land (Leviticus 25) and the jubilee year, where land once sold would return to its original owners—were never carried out.

With the rise of socialist movements in the nineteenth and twentieth centuries, egalitarian ideals penetrated Jewish circles. Devoid of ideological weaponry for its defense, traditional Judaism was unable to ward off the invasion of these ideas. As young Jews abandoned traditional Judaism for socialism, some Orthodox spokesmen attempted to defend tradition by asserting a socialist bias in Judaism. This could be done only by taking great liberties, as was realized by Rav Kook, who courageously faced the fact that the "ambition to build a just society on egalitarian principles without public ownership of property finds no real echo in the written or oral Torah—which does not anchor itself in egalitarian ideas."[54] Rav Kook, profoundly impressed by the dedication to the ideal of a just society in the kibbutz movement, was troubled by the absence of a similar dedication among traditional Jews. He resolved this problem by applying the principle of generality—i.e., that Judaism "is more general and therefore more unified." Other cultural groups, not so universal as Judaism, are able to develop their more limited cultures to a fuller extent, cultivating and amplifying a particular segment to a greater degree than is possible in Judaism. He believed, however, that every positive achievement in human culture is immanent in Jewish culture. In the future these scattered, dispersed, and undeveloped spiritual components will be assembled and inserted into their proper place. The kibbutz movement could be conceived of as an agent in this process, gathering the faintly glowing sparks of egalitarian ideals now dispersed throughout distant spheres of Jewish tradition and igniting them. When Rav Kook visited Bet Alfa in the 1920s (as related by a former member of that kibbutz now living in Ramat Yohanan), he asked the kibbutz to build a synagogue, even if no one attended it. The synagogue was to serve as a retreat and a physical reminder, a provision against their overdedication to the social ideal at the expense of losing consciousness of the cosmic dimension. Rav Kook's attempt to Judaize egalitarian ideas passed unnoticed in kibbutz circles. For them equality and Judaism remained as disparate as ever, despite the effort to include them within one system.

The kibbutz today is the sole Jewish group committed to equality as a fundamental social principle. How successfully has it fared in manifesting this ideal in its daily round? The pursuit of that question could serve as an instructive guide in observing the development of a new kibbutz *halakhah* emerging from that principle.

> The kibbutz does not boast of justice, honesty, ethics, love, brotherhood. The kibbutz boasts of equality and cooperation. If there two are realized, the rest follow.[55]

This statement was made by a veteran settler of Sha'ar Ha-Golan (Ha-Kibbutz ha-Artzi). When interviewed, he spoke pessimistically of the decline of equality in the kibbutz as a result of population expansion, the rise in the standard of living, the demands of members, and the affluence of the surrounding society. A simple egalitarianism was suitable for those early, uncomplicated days, when the kibbutz population was more homogeneous in age and attitude, work was less specialized and more easily rotated, and the economic standard was so low that egalitarian sharing was almost an economic necessity. The simplicities of the founding years now belong to ancient history, when not only the same housing and food were provided (principles that are in application today as well) but even similar clothing. Garments were not marked. Each member received from the laundry whatever was available and clean, no matter what the size or fit. But this rough approach was short-lived. Today the drive toward individuality has put an end to this method.

## Obstacles

Not unlike the principle of Sabbath rest, which becomes inordinately complex in practice, equality, as the "absolute" of kibbutz life, became progressively more intricate when put to the test of experience. Moshe Una has declared that equality will always remain a sought-for value rather than a realized one—primarily because it harbors innate obstacles to its realization. Equality cannot be objectively rated or gauged in the very areas where it should be decisive, such as personal capabilities and personal needs. In addition, when attempts are made to manifest the principle through the equal division of goods, equality is distorted. Other principles of significance to kibbutz life may often conflict with equality, as for example, human freedom, which avows the right of man not to be subjugated to others and to develop his personality. In the early beginning of the kibbutz, members deliberately restricted their freedom out of belief that this was ultimately the most heroic sacrifice they could perform. A veteran of Ramat Yochanan related how she would undertake the most burdensome and (to her) repellent tasks out of conviction that she must submerge her individuality for the general good. Today, a balance is being sought between the potentially contradictory principles of equality and freedom, for the ideal of equality could easily become a negative principle, awakening envy and greed among members who feel deprived in comparison with others. This negativity, a result of a mechanical approach to equality by which all members receive the same no matter what their needs, has had the unwanted and harmful result of suppressing talent (in the name of equality) and blocking individual and communal enrichment in art and science.

The kibbutz has learned, after fifty and more years of experience, that such factors must be given proper consideration if equality is to continue as its loftiest value. A mechanical application will fail to suffice and can undermine the very principle itself.

The principle "from each according to his abilities, to each according to his needs" is effective as long as a kibbutznik indeed provides his kibbutz with the full fruit of his abilities. Most members are loyally giving their best, though no objective standards exist for determining whether a man is in fact contributing the maximum. What is to be done, however, when a member is clearly failing to deliver? Should the provision of his needs be dependent upon his contributions?

> The provision of needs is not conditioned by the placing of capabilities at the disposal of the kibbutz. . . . This is the principle of non-conditionality, the most basic principle in our lives. As much as this principle appears anarchic, it is the reality of our lives, and the kibbutz is not possible otherwise. . . . Provision of a member's needs is sacred as long as other members are provided for. No one may be punished by a withdrawal of needs, nor anyone rewarded by receiving more than his needs.[56]

Opposition to this basic tenet of kibbutz life occasionally crops up in the kibbutz. There is no argument about a member who, though his capabilities are clearly limited, is making a determined effort to bear the communal burden. Members are angered by individuals who openly exploit their kibbutz, forcing them to carry an additional and unnecessary burden. In the *Iggeret* of October 26, 1961, a member of Degania Alef proposed a revision of the accepted kibbutz interpretation of equality. Since many members were now more interested in receiving than in giving, equality should be related to effort. The less the endeavor, the less the provision of needs. A reply appeared in a later issue of *Iggeret* that, while admitting that there was occasional exploitation, warned that any change in this doctrine would signal the abolition of the kibbutz. Besides, what possible criteria exist for measuring genuine capability? The clinching argument against a merit system in the kibbutz was based upon a moral and doctrinal proposition—that the use of material sanctions reveals lack of faith in the ability of the kibbutz to raise the moral level of its members. In addition, even though the kibbutz generally is aware of the capabilities of most of its members, a mistake could conceivably be made, and one injustice would outweigh all other confirmed and verified instances of evasion of work.

After the period when all clothing was held in common, a new system was instituted. Individual garments were provided by the kibbutz. A step had been taken away from mechanical equality to a more qualitative equality, when garments began to be distributed at a small kibbutz clothing shop. Eventually this system gave way to another. In most kibbutzim, members now receive a cash allowance for purchase of clothing at private shops in the city. This step was taken to preserve equality for it was discovered that some members were more aggressive than others or friendlier with the person on duty at the shop, and therefore able to wangle better merchandise. With a flat cash sum available, everyone can buy what he wants without being dependent on the tastes of the kibbutz buyer.

This system has now been extended to include budgets for a significant number of items, and a personal spending allowance. In effect the general sum amounts to a salary received by each member to be spent according to his wishes. This approach removes the dronelike monotony of communal consumption, allowing each member to budget his funds according to individual preference. The all-inclusive sum remains very small however, because the kibbutz realizes that it cannot have a life of equality without some limitations upon the consumer demands of the individual. In other words, equality requires a more modest style of life than that of the consumer-oriented society surrounding the kibbutz.

The issue of collective organization of consumption is a lively point of discussion. Supporters of a general budget for each member, which permits him freedom of choice, claim that the individual's needs and perferences and not the dictates of his kibbutz should be the decisive factor. Opponents state that, in any event, most persons' wants are determined by their culture, by the economic level of their society, and by the advertising industry. The kibbutz will have to find a middle way between the blandishments of a consumer society and the mild asceticism necessary to ensure the survival of an egalitarian mode of life.

Another strain of egalitarianism is the rise of specialized professionals whose type of work often accords them privileges not available to most. In those idyllic days when a more rudimentary agriculture was the mainstay of kibbutz life, jobs and posts could be rotated easily among members to avoid the creation of a class of specialists. With the introduction of highly mechanized equipment into agriculture and the expansion of regional kibbutz industries, there have arisen small groups of people whose expertise requires a heavy investment in study and training. This may entail certain privileges, such as a personal car granted by a regional industrial complex, which can be exploited for private trips with the family. This is a serious problem, impeding the effective implementation of egalitarian principles, and it is dealt with differently throughout the movements. Some kibbutzim leave the question of private use of an automobile to the kibbutz conscience of the member. Some indeed abuse this privilege, others do not. Some kibbutzim are stricter, requiring members who use automobiles received from outside sources to turn in the keys to the motor pool on Friday afternoons. On the Sabbath the vehicles remain unused, and are returned to their drivers for work on Sunday mornings. Whoever wishes to take a trip on the Sabbath must follow the standard kibbutz procedure of ordering a vehicle from the motor pool and paying the standard price per kilometer.

Another potentially privileged group, as yet small in number, is the academicians—the term usually referring to university graduate, often with advanced degrees, who are employed in institutions of higher learning in Israel. They would naturally receive all the benefits of a faculty member at a university—a sabbatical year, travel, grants, funds for books, and facilities for additional study. These grants would not be considered counter to equality since it is now recognized that an academician has a right to these privileges to ensure his professional advancement and they are therefore his needs. A decade or so ago, this would have been unacceptable. The kibbutz was wary of intellectuals—even though it had a substantial number of them in its midst. What it primarily opposed was the use of education for the pursuit of titles, degrees, and status. The practical bent of the kibbutzniks also made them skeptical of studies with no "useful purpose." These reservations carry less weight today, as the kibbutz resigns itself to higher education as a technical and cultural necessity. Besides, many young men and women who applied for permission to go on to advanced study and were refused thereupon abandoned their kibbutz for the city. This has raised another problem posed by egalitarianism.

The pressures in a kibbutz to conform may result in a downward leveling of bright people and their flight from the kibbutz. Steps are being taken to correct this situation and to protect the kibbutz movement against the perils of provincialism. Otherwise, their intellectual youth would feel trapped and try to break away. An extreme view on this matter is held by Adin Steinsaltz, who does not believe the kibbutz movement can absorb intellectuals at all, or produce them, for that matter. The conditions of kibbutz life, he claims, discourage creativity. Even the Orthodox kibbutz movement suffers, for Orthodoxy is an intellectual religion and the kibbutz does not yield intellectuals. Only recently is the kibbutz movement beginning to send its young men and women to universities, where they often gain excellent reputations in faculty circles. Time will indicate whether this new generation of kibbutz students will return to their settlements and contribute to making the kibbutz more culturally diverse, without endangering equality by the creation of a separate class.

> the fundamental idea of the kibbutz . . . is not that all should do the same work . . . but that one will be an engineer, another a professor, another will work in agriculture and a fourth in education—and they will live in one society with the feeling that they are appreciated as human beings, according to their standing in that society and not according to their place of work.[57]

The kibbutz is unable to avoid the formation of different types of elite groups, whether in leadership, management, technology, professions, ideology, or culture. The prevalence of egalitarian patterns, however, has successfully inhibited the emergence of favored groups. Much effort is made to diminish differences. Members who have gained a higher status make a special point of behaving as simply and as inconspicuously as possible. Invidious distinctions are suppressed and deferential behavior ruled out. Within the membership itself, therefore, the kibbutz has successfully avoided the kind of offensive class differences that might generate a destructive social tension.

The egalitarian ethic is under further attack from another, external source that has managed considerably to thin out the secondary egalitarian principle of self-labor. With the arrival of large numbers of unskilled immigrants to Israel in 1950s, a call went out to the kibbutz movement from the Israeli government to hire as many of these workers as possible. Reluctantly this was done. Today many kibbutzim are striving to rid themselves of hired workers because of the effect it has on the members. With hired help available to kibbutz members, they often slip into becoming work managers, advising and looking on as others do their work—a secularized version of the *Shabbes goy* of Orthodox Judaism. Unless this wound is closed, there is a real danger that the kibbutz will become a landed estate, existing on the labor of others. Suffering from a severe shortage of workers, some kibbutzim have reluctantly taken on hired help in the hope that an improvement in the growth of their population will evantually permit them to release their employees. This would have to be done during a period of economic expansion or boom, to prevent these workers from becoming unemployed.

In the era when kibbutz life had few material amenities, there was one radio in the dining room for all the members. In the course of time, a radio was distributed to each member or family, though not without protest. Defenders of kibbutz ideology declared that members would isolate themselves in their rooms, drift apart from each other, and eventually lose their feeling for social solidarity. However, there was no resisting the trend. Television has now arrived, accompanied by the same problems. In the long run every family will have a set. In a few kibbutzim TV sets have been placed in the dining room, social club, or neighborhood shelters. The kibbutz movement is aware of the possible effect of TV. Representatives of three movements met in 1968 to consider the anticipated consequences. Because televisions's visual impact is more magnetic than radio, there was apprehension that TV would tend to isolate members in their rooms and draw them away from the public functions so necessary for the cultivation of the communal spirit.

Anxiety that the general assembly might be weakened because of the allure of TV is an expression of a legitimate concern for the future of a key institution in the kibbutz egalitarian system. Direct democracy and rotation of leaders are the political expressions of egalitarianism. Deterioration of this institution poses serious problems for the kibbutz.

> The wish of the kibbutz is to achieve equality in all respects, including power of decision and power to influence decisions. Such equality cannot be achieved if participation is passive and confined to electing management and to voting. Taking part in the general meeting without an all-round participation in kibbutz life does not in itself secure equality. Kibbutz democracy, therefore, is not based on constitutional rules, but is a result of the will of the members to identify with it [the kibbbutz].[58]

In his article on kibbutz democracy, the source of the above quotation, Menahem Rosner analyzes the causes underlying the apathy toward general assembly meetings so prevalent in many kibbutzim today, and makes concrete suggestions for correcting the deterioration of this vital institution. One of the requisite conditions for successful achievement of democracy is equality of living conditions for kibbutz officials and other members of society. There should be no privileges to make it advantageous to hold office for long periods. "The supposition is, therefore, that there is a correlation between the equality of all members and the changeover of officials." The issue is an extremely complex one, and the successful functioning of kibbutz democracy depends upon the harmonious meshing of a number of disparate components. Rosner believes that, despite the decline in participation, the authority of the general assembly remains paramount. Any decrease in this authority can be attributed to a general decline in the intensity of kibbutz values.

This brief review of the changes in the principle of equality during the short period of its functioning in kibbutz life discloses the tension generated between the demands of this ideal and the claims of human self-interest. By seeking to activate this ideal— with the difficult demands it makes on its adherents—while striving to satisfy the multifaceted needs of its members, the kibbutz inaugurated a new, vigorous, and bold quest in the evolution of Jewish ethics. The development of an egalitarian *halakhah* is completely innovative in Jewish life—a unique contribution of kibbutz society. By making man and morality the center of this new and democratic *halakhah* the kibbutz has redirected Jewish tradition toward the concern for man, from which it had veered in the past centuries of defensive battle for survival.

# 7
# *Ritual and Culture*

> Holidays cannot be concocted. . . . It is possible to reformulate or revise them, but not to create something out of nothing. The holiday is a group creation in which a large and varied body of forces take an active part: religion, tradition, history, art, nature, etc. Just as good poetry cannot be composed on demand . . . so is it impossible to have a custom-made holiday or festival ceremonial. Genuine festivities are from the heart and come to the world in a holy spirit, and if this is not present, of what value is advice from afar? My one suggestion is this: Celebrate your father's festivals and add to them something of yourself, according to your taste and your energy. The basic principle is that whatever you do be done in faith, out of a living emotion and a spiritual need. And do not become too sophisticated. Our fathers never grew weary of their Sabbaths and festivals, even though they observed them during their lives in one form. They always found new savor in them. And do you know why? Because they were not jaded and the blessings of the holidays dwelt within them.
> —Haim Nahman Bialik, A Letter to a Friend, 1930, Bar Mitzvah Collection, 1967

## *The Kibbutz as a Creator of Ritual*

In articles and literary statements written by *Vatikim* about holidays and festivals, the prominent figure of Haim Nahman Bialik appears with regularity. For that generation he was "master and teacher," a secular rabbi. One of his *responsa* appears as the opening quotation of this chapter. His famous call for a life guided by the yoke of commandments went unheeded, as did his appeal that holidays and festivals of the Jewish people not to be allowed to drift into anarchy. Among the non-Orthodox communities of Israel, only the kibbutz has paid more than lip service to Bialik's pleas.

What accounts for the attraction between the kibbutz and the festivals? Why has only the kibbutz tapped the resources of Jewish tradition while other non-Orthodox Jews have either refrained from ceremonial action or resorted to the familiar practices of the synagogue?

The literary evidence of the *Vatikim* does not disclose an immediate affinity between the holidays and their contemporary kibbutz practitioners. The promethean "Religion of Pioneering" sanctified daily life to the point of obscuring the boundaries between sacred and profane. Engaged in the physically trying tasks of conquering the soil, the *Vatikim* had little time for observance of holidays and festivals. Besides, they were not prepared to abide by the customs of their father's house, feeling that it would be unbecoming—even reactionary—to live a holiday by the standards of the rejected society of European Jewry, especially when the old culture was ineradicably connected to the repudiated religious tradition.

In the enthusiasm and naiveté of youth, the settlers believed they possessed the requisite capabilities for pioneering a new cultural creation. But if tilling the soil was extremely difficult for them, it proved to be easier than cultural pioneering. The rebels discovered that they had exchanged one set of chains for another, replacing cultural tyranny with emptiness. If anything, emptiness proved to be more dangerous than the chains that bound them to the past. As men of tomorrow the *Vatikim* overlooked the integral role of the past in the fashioning of a future. They wanted to be born anew, without a past, a tradition, or a history. But this desire was inevitably frustrated. Not only was it a psychological impossibility to erase those formative years, but the natural organic development of the kibbutz thrust the *Vatikim* into a confrontation with problems that defied solution other than through the medium of holiday observance.

The kibbutz made the belated discovery that it could not continue without ritual forms once it ceased to live as a youth-movement camp and became a settled, fixed community with cultural roots in the very soil it cultivated. But what rituals? And how were they to be performed? The kibbutz was confronted with a problem faced by all societies in which traditional religious forms cease to have a hold on men. Could rituals be instituted that would be a faithful reflection of the group values? Today the kibbutz is still grappling with this issue, because its own values are undergoing modification and its rituals are beginning to lag. In its search for appropriate ritual forms the kibbutz is, in a sense, a precursor of modern society, which lacks meaningful rituals. The rituals of lodges, fraternities, or small social groups are no replacement for the communal cohesiveness that religious ritual can exercise upon a society.

Orthodox Jews undoubtedly consider kibbutz holiday ritual to be impoverished, but if it acts as a means for expressing the real beliefs of its participants, it can fulfill the function of successful rituals, which can be understood as a pattern of group behavior, prescribed by custom or authority for observance on particular occasions. The success or failure of ritual is no mere game for the kibbutz movement but a matter of extreme urgency. Ceremony is more than a group cement for the kibbutz. Without suitable ritual expression for its values, kibbutz society could undergo a severe crisis in morale.

In the beginning, among the main values of kibbutz life were agriculture and settlement of the land. Appropriate ceremonies soon appeared to give expression to these purposes. Though they were not new, they were original. By identifying with the biblical and post-biblical past when Jewish farmers tilled the soil, and by an emotional receptiveness to its contact with the soil, the kibbutz created a number of agricultural festivals for which it is justly famous. The Omer of Passover and Bikkurim (the first fruits) of Shavuot are the two most outstanding examples of the interaction among the kibbutz, the land, and the Jewish heritage that led to fitting and timely rituals.

Why has the kibbutz become a creator of holiday ritual—a phenomenon with no parallel anywhere else in Israel? The human components of kibbutz society play no small part in this. Had all those who set foot in the kibbutz stayed, it would have become a movement of immense proportions. But most did not, and those who remained constituted a small but determined group, conscious to an extreme of their society's image. The ritual they generated reminded them that they were a special group who must struggle for their future. The ritually united group is a powerfully cohesive group—provided that the ritual still continues to express the real beliefs and to fulfill the basic needs of the participants. Every enactment of ritual reinforces the group as to the reason for its existence, its distinctive character, and its basic purpose.

Once the rebellion against Orthodoxy began to wear off and the "Religion of Pioneering" slackened, the kibbutz discovered itself in a cultural vacuum. As David Maletz states, "We were left naked

... only with ourselves, cut off from the tie with tradition and the culture of generations." Within a brief span of time the realization dawned upon them that their newly emerging set of social and ideological relations required cultural statements from the past in order to find adequate and comprehensible representation in the present. The new culture found some form of relationship to the old to be indispensable. These are the two parallel streams in the ongoing development of kibbutz culture—the stream of the Jewish heritage and the stream of life—both connected by tributaries that feed and infuse each other with new and different nutrients.

> There is no way of separating the social sphere from the cultural sphere. . . . Culture maintains itself from the social relations between man and his neighbor and between man and the community. . . . culture has its revelations through the social climate, customs, ceremonies, and those relationships which make up the stable foundaton of life's continuous flow.[59]

Did "life's continuous flow" lead the kibbutz to more extended ritualism? Whoever knows how to listen to what is occurring in the depths of kibbutz life realizes that within it there is a yearning for deep and stable cultural values and a way of life based upon them. Two basic reasons have been suggested for this longing. One is that communities created by people who seek to form a new and different society require firm social and cultural foundations. Holiday ceremonials are a key factor in providing the requisite stability for the new society in process. But even this desired stability is in motion as a result of the flux of human relationships. Because the community is building its life cooperatively, individual problems within the kibbutz become the responsibility of the community at large, often transforming a private problem into a public issue. When an individual in a kibbutz has cultural needs that the kibbutz has left unsatisfied, he may alert the public. If he is endowed with drive and determination, he stands an excellent chance of turning his private needs into public ones. Because of the unstinting efforts of a small number of people who invested their energy in the creation and perpetuation of holidays, there now exists the present kibbutz tradition. Admittedly, even the most zealous would have been doomed to frustration had the soil not been fertile for their creative innovations in those early days. Had the public been intransigent or indifferent, no will, however resolute, could have penetrated the corporate consciousness of the community and added to it the holiday dimension. A communal will now exists for the continuity of holidays in the kibbutz, and the generation that initiated kibbutz festival customs has transferred responsibility for their practice to the second and third generations.

What is available to the kibbutz members who undertake to assure a satisfactory holiday in their kibbutz? As a rule, the cultural committee chairman is ultimately responsible, but in many kibbutzim special subcommittees are appointed for each holiday because by kibbutz standards only a team working cooperatively can ensure a proper holiday.

To ensure a steady flow of traditional and contemporary holiday material, the kibbutz movements have joined to form the Inter-Kibbutz Committee on Holidays and Festivals. This committee, staffed by representatives of three movements (the Orthodox kibbutz movement is not included), regularly prints pamphlets and booklets. It also offers advice and guidance to cultural committee chairmen or to the chairmen of special holiday committees who are new at their job and seek professional help. In their advisory capacity, members of the Inter-Kibbutz Committee often tour kibbutzim to observe physical conditions that may have an effect on the shape of holiday practice, and to impress upon the kibbutz the ultimate significance of the holiday calendar for the future of the movement. Of course, the Inter-Kibbutz Committee has no authority to prescribe holiday practice, but may only recommend according to past practice and custom. In essence it is conservative, making no attempt to determine new values or decide what should be permitted or forbidden. Behind this caution lurks the fear of creating an authority that might easily stifle creativity in individual kibbutzim by pronouncing judgments in favor of or against a custom that may be current in certain kibbutzim.

The fear of imposition has proved unfounded. Most kibbutzim tend to adopt the material of the Inter-Kibbutz Committee since they often lack the resources for producing their own. Since the Tel Aviv office reproduces the practices of other kibbutzim, the simplest thing for a harried cultural committee chairman to do is to imitate accepted custom. Inadvertently, and as a consequence of the cultural and spiritual conditions in many kibbutzim, the Inter-Kibbutz Committee on Holidays and Festivals has become an authority. In 1970 they published, for the first time, a small booklet (very much like a Passover Haggadah in appearance) containing the bare frame of a ceremony for Rosh Ha-Shanah. It was adopted by many kibbutzim because, confused about Rosh Ha-Shanah, they were eager to use the ceremony put at their disposal.

The availability of a receptive audience for its publications transformed this committee into an authority, not in a legal sense but as a body accepted by its constituents as a dependable and reliable source for guidance and leadership.

## Problems of Holiday Practice

In conversation with kibbutz members who are active in the holiday sphere there was heard, parallel to pride of achievement, an insistent undercurrent of dissatisfaction with the low prestige that problems of holiday practice, and of Jewish culture in general, have in the councils of the movements. Although movement-wide conferences have been held on a broad range of subjects, at no point has any movement (the Orthodox kibbutz excepted) seen fit to convene an assembly to discuss the place of holidays in kibbutz life.

> The holiday in the kibbutz is a free growth, best comparable to folklore. The entire system of holiday practice is voluntary, non-obligatory and based on goodwill. The entire matter is so free that no one can be rebuked, because involvement is voluntary. Yet every year somehow things get done. Despite instability the basics remain the same.[60]

Some hold this system to be chaotic, others consider it the glory of the kibbutz and warn about dire consequences should the free growth become stunted and kibbutz culture cease to be run by amateurs. Professionalism is steadily creeping into every niche of kibbutz life following upon the discovery that job rotation is a viable social principle, but an economic failure. Little profit can be expected from branches run by men and women who never remain on the job long enough to acquire the necessary expertise. Members of a particular branch are sent out for study and refresher courses to keep in touch with the constant stream of knowledge being introduced into their field. But in the cultural committee, whose activities leave a strong imprint on the social morale of kibbutz, chairmen rotate. As a result, the cultural committee chairman does not learn from his mistakes and whoever follows him commits the same errors. Today the principle has already taken root that the chairman be granted a few free days per week for full dedication to this duties. Will the increased professionalism and specialization of kibbutz life reach the cultural realm as well? Will "professional Jews" begin to arise in the kibbutz? Asher Maniv of Maayan Tzvi raises the warning signals against turning cultural committee chairmanship into a permanent post. He declares that we are not professionals and we must not become professionals. The entire value of cultural activity is in its being a joint creation emerging out of our way of life.

Despite the seeming anarchy of amateurism, a move in the direction of more permanent staff for cultural affairs could be disastrous for the future progress of kibbutz culture. However, developments are moving the kibbutz in the direction that Asher Maniv considers undesirable. Although against the formation of a professional class, the late Mattityahu Shelem of Ramat Yohanan, formerly an unquestioned leader in matters of holidays and festivals, reluctantly concluded that the kibbutz has little recourse other than the appointment of persons to be responsible for kibbutz holidays.

Shelem regrets the near impossibility of creating a spiritual atmosphere in the kibbutz dining room—a task that would probably try the patience of the most proficient professional and is much to demand of an amateur. The kibbutz may therefore have no choice but to appoint individuals who would make the cultural, religious, and artistic life of the community their personal concern. In the kibbutz of today such serious matters can no longer be left even to inspired amateurs. Aryeh Ben-Gurion of Bet ha-Shittah, an active member of the Inter-Kibbutz Committee and a prolific editor of publications on the holidays, describes the job of a cultural committee chairman as the most arduous in the kibbutz. To leave it in the hands of amateurs would be a serious error, especially in the light of his appeal to all cultural committee chairmen that they read and think, and not just act as technicians. Reading and thought demand time—more time than is available in a few days pulled out of a working week.

A careful reading of the following statement by Zvi Ra'anan of Ha-Zorea, which constitutes a basic platform of Jewish cultural aims for cultural committee chairmen, should provide sufficient argument for deciding whether amateurism or specialization is what the future holds for the kibbutz:

> How can we revive in the heart of a generation living at the end of the twentieth century a cultural heritage which has absorbed a large measure of Jewish religious faith and a petrified tradition, which in the course of time has lost its vitality for the majority of the people? How may we distinguish between this heritage and this tradition? How may we remove this heritage from the hands of those who declare themselves to be its only genuine bearers? How may we connect our magnificent heritage with the present and the future? How may we associate ourselves with the cultural development of the modern world . . . without detaching ourselves from earlier strata of our culture? How may we create in the younger generations the rich associative world of our national heritage, from the Bible, by way of the *Midrash* and *Aggadah* to Bialik, without turning all of it into a required subject at school, rejected because it has little in common with them and the spiritual life of our time?[61]

It is therefore indispensable, Ra'anan concludes, to think clearly about the spiritual and intellectual structure of modern man and the place that the religious belief and ceremony of our heritage have in this structure. How many people in the kibbutz are capable of fulfilling the mandate set forth by Zvi Ra'anan?

What are the problems connected with the practice of a holiday in a kibbutz? A major barrier recognized by almost every prominent leader in this realm is the shift in the cultural tastes of the kibbutz public. Internally, a more diversified, heterogeneous population and, externally, the growth and development of a large and profitable entertainment industry in Israel have influenced kibbutz culture and, consequently, kibbutz holidays. In the past the basic ingredient of kibbutz cultural life was ponderous—lectures, ideological groups, serious political discussions, literary evenings, classical concerts, and efforts to re-create a holiday pattern. Today there is only a residue of this, and the characteristic intellectual tension of the kibbutz has given way to a predominately light style, with the weekly movie assuming the role once held by the more serious activities. Not that there is no serious cultural and intellectual life left in the kibbutz. What has taken shape is the formation of dual cultural levels—the popular and the serious, with the latter in a secondary, peripheral position compared to the earlier years, when participative cultural activity was more widespread.

Today passive enjoyment prevails. The young people have identified with the stream of popular entertainment flooding Israel's society. They often experience difficulty in wrenching themselves loose from the simplifications of popular culture to enter into the seriousness of purpose required for discerning the values and conceptual systems inherent in holiday ceremonies. These complaints against kibbutz youth on this count were made by *Vatikim* who do not usually disavow the second and third generations. Just as joy and mourning cannot be mixed, so serious ceremonies cannot be combined with entertainment. This understanding has yet to take root and until it does, a holiday in the kibbutz can never hope to attain or approach the reverence and awe that the synagogue occasionally preserves. Also, in a more heterogeneous population the strong identification that formerly existed between individuals and the kibbutz no longer contributes to the hold that kibbutz ritual has on people.

> Children grow up with a blasé attitude toward everything. . . . Grownups have become so accustomed to dynamic change that they scarcely notice novelty. . . . No wonder ritual today is neither appreciated nor practised, for ritual flourishes in an atmosphere of childlike awe before the sublimity of life. The sophistication of many so-called moderns prevents them from expressing their deepest and loftiest emotions. Most noticeably lacking is the capacity of modern industrialized man to experience and to express gratitude and to enjoy the simple pleasures.[62]

Kibbutz literature on the holidays is a commentary on the above statement. However sincere the efforts to impart a reverential atmosphere, they must contend with a kibbutz public that is too sophisticated and too secular, lacking the simple directness that would permit it to celebrate and obtain release from the everyday. Ceremonies are distinguished by a relatively passive community participation. This passivity has no effect upon the critical stance individuals may take toward the form of the ceremony, its content and execution. In many ways synagogue practice is far less exacting. The ritual will repeat itself even if the congregation is dissatisfied or bored. In the kibbutz, however, there is no sacred institution, such as the synagogue, to preserve and protect the traditions of the past. To mold a tradition is to struggle against the low boredom—tolerance—level for ceremonies that have to be constantly repeated if they are to become traditional ceremonies. Nevertheless, a kibbutz tradition has at least been created for Passover.

Kibbutz youth who often complain of boredom usually resist any change in the ceremony that wearies them. M. Shelem, the composer of the Omer ceremony, after performing it in the same way for twenty-five years, suggested a "sabbatical year," but his proposal was rejected by youth, who apparently perferred the same ceremony. Shelem wrote innumerable articles on kibbutz holidays, drew up ceremonies and composed songs, and felt a profound sense of responsibility toward the perverse and contradictory public he served. In his articles and in his personal conversation he vacillated between pessimism and optimism. Although quite aware of all the deficiencies of the kibbutz as a holiday congregation, he declared that every year each holiday is eagerly anticipated by the community, which demands an impressive and convincing ceremony. Yet the holiday cannot meet the community's expectations if only a small fraction of its people help in the preparations while the community at large remains passive. Shelem repeatedly stressed the dangers of passivity to the future of kibbutz holidays. As he put it, a man cannot come to a holiday as an empty vessel. When a kibbutz community only waits for a Passover meal, the holiday is destroyed. To convince the community to increase its consciousness of the holidays is an uphill struggle. In addition to technical performance of ritual, increased participation requires an attentiveness and identification with the holiday's values. This can only be achieved in an atmosphere of concentration—of *kavanah*. In the light of the mutuality required for an authentic holiday experience, the complaints of some of the public are a counterbalance to the views of such men as Shelem. The most common complaint is boredom—induced not by the nature of the material itself, which is often composed of readings from classical Jewish literature, traditional music, etc., but by the amateurish way the selections are read, the poorly prepared dances, the ill-rehearsed sketches. In brief, the lack of professionalism can result in a dull and unattractive ceremony.

This illustrates the dilemma of "bought" culture in the kibbutz, which may be more professional, but nullifies the kibbutz value of independent creativity. The kibbutz could train its own professionals unless it fears the organization of a separate caste, a quasiclergy that will take over responsibility for the artistic and spiritual success of holidays. The present situation is frustrating not only to thoughtful and sensitive members of the kibbutz congregation, but also to the initiators, creators, and practitioners who are more than technicians, and are searching for holiday rituals that have a spiritual tenor. In sum, few cultural tasks can equal in difficulty those that are faced in forming, shaping, and casting a Jewish holiday in a kibbutz.

Despite the grumbling and dissatisfaction, no one has suggested that the kibbutz solve this recurrent problem by disposing of communal holiday ceremonies, abandoning responsibility for their observance, or relegating their active performance to the individual families. Then the complaints might cease, for each family would be able to determine its own cultural or religious standard and live by it, releasing the kibbutz from a burdensome yoke. Indeed, in one kibbutz, the team responsible for the weekly *Kabbalat Shabbat* were so furious at the inattention of the members that they threatened to cancel the *Shabbat* ceremony altogether. It was only a warning signal to caution the community, but it created a clamor within the kibbutz, and succeeded in obtaining the desired promises of good behavior, proving that attachment to holidays runs deep in the kibbutz. Mattityahu Shelem, who said that if Passover celebrations were threatened it would be the equivalent of "failing to provide food," considers it unthinkable that the kibbutz would relinquish its holidays despite the discontent that accompanies their yearly observance.

Were the holidays to fall victim to the increasing trend toward privacy in kibbutz life, the community would become not unlike a village, with each family celebrating, or not celebrating, according to its own understanding. This would be in accord with traditional patterns of Jewish life, in which the family has served as the basic cultural unit and a child's experience of holidays in his home has often engraved lifelong memories. There is no scarcity of books and articles in Israel, Europe, and America that describe the warm, enveloping spirit of the holidays in small Eastern European Jewish towns. Bella Chagall's *Burning Lights* is paradigmatic. This type of literature appears in kibbutz journals as well, often before major holidays, when *Vatikim* of Eastern European origin become nostalgic for the lost richness of the home they left in rebellious haste.

It would be false to deny the profound impressions that a holiday makes on a sensitive child brought up in a home of high cultural and spiritual standards. These experiences supplied the source material for the literature that wrapped much Eastern European Jewry in an aura of gentle and sublime holiness, even though many families practiced the holidays perfunctorily and lifelessly, as evidenced by their abandonment of observance once they were distant from the Eastern European environment and settled outside the influence of shtetl mores. Because the kibbutz accepts responsibility for the cultural and spiritual growth of its members, it is unwilling to forgo communal observances even with all the resultant problems. The kibbutz leadership relizes full well that the average member would be bewildered if left to his own resources on holidays, and could end up playing cards. But since the kibbutz uses a common demoniator for holiday practice, it leaves its more sophisticated members dissatisfied. Perhaps there is no other recourse for the kibbutz, though some try to satisfy their more intellectual members through ceremonies devised for smaller and sophisticated groups.

The rich and expansive literature on the intimacy and warmth of holidays in "my father's home" has no equivalent in kibbutz literature. Only two generations of youth have experienced holidays in the kibbutz. Before the appearance of an appropriate literature more time must elapse, and a more articulate generation must arise. Perhaps maturity or advancing age will encourage reflection, but future kibbutz authors will doubtlessly write about their holidays with less fervor than their European forebears. Whatever impressions a communal ceremony might make, the intimacy of the home probes greater depths.

Until literary echoes begin resounding, the pulse of the community has to be measured by eliciting the members' reactions to a particular ceremony. A consensus will influence the editing or revising of ceremonies. In certain kibbutzim traditional blessing and the name of God appear in their Passover Haggadot because the community does not object. In other communities such a step would provoke considerable resistance, therefore blessings are omitted. In principle, a delicate balance is sought between the people and the leadership through an exchange of attitudes and views. At all times the dialogue must be governed by the famous rabbinic dictum: One does not impose decrees upon the public that it would be unable to fulfill. This is practiced to a fuller degree by the kibbutz than it probably was by its rabbinic originators, whose literature reflects a continuous war between the rabbis and the Jewish masses when their conduct was not in conformity with the idealistic views of the leadership. The rabbis sought every means to elevate the lives and values of the people and cannot be conceived of as "embodying the values of the folk" in themselves. In the kibbutz the "folk" receive full attention, so that efforts to shape their values will not encounter stubborn resistance. Slow, gradual, almost imperceptible changes can be wrought in the community's position toward the holiday's through an ongoing process of cross fertilization between the ideas of the whole group and the creatively productive figures from their ranks.

## *The Nature Festival*

An example of the drift in community attitude toward holidays appears in the modifications and reinterpretations already introduced into the nature festivals. The kibbutz has justly earned a reputation for restoring the ancient nature festivals of the Jewish people. Because of the centrality of agriculture in the kibbutz scheme and the romantic attachment to the land characteristic of Zionism, the agricultural festivals were a natural growth for their time and place.

A few Jews had settled as farmers in different parts of the world, but only in Eretz Israel was the Jewish world rewarded by a return to the harvest festivals of antiquity. The *Vatikim* believed they were restoring to the realm of the present the ancient biblical agricultural festivals that had been interrupted for generations. By this huge leap backward the Bible would gain a new immediacy for the young Jews now tilling the soil of their forefathers. Whether this biblicalism is reactionary or progressive is not at issue, for though the commemoration of the nature festivals required a long look back into the past, it was accompanied by a forward outburst of energy that contributed immeasurably to the molding of both kibbutz and Israeli culture.

The nature festivals no longer command the central position they once attained, but have slipped into a slow, steady decline. On Shavuot this is especially noticeable. In the Diaspora this holiday was dedicated primarily to Mattan Torah, commemoration of the revelation of the Torah at Sinai, while Shavuot as Hag Ha-Bikkurin, Festival of the First Fruits, was underplayed. Understandably, Mattan Torah was completely absent from the festival as it initially emerged out of the kibbutz and agriculture still remains its foundation stone. But this, too, is beginning to give way to the historical focus. Most commonly the shift in emphasis is attributed to the increased mechanization of agriculture. But this view is shortsighted, for what has indeed occurred is a basic revision in the kibbutz community's relationship to agriculture. Shavuot no longer has its former significance because agriculture is now sharing with industry its prior position in the kibbutz economy. The number of people occupied in agriculture is steadily being reduced as kibbutz industry moves forward to the position of major employer. The members who work in education or the services also have minimal contact with the soil. The developing kibbutz economy has become diversified, with agriculture by no means the largest branch. It is also likely that the younger generation may be temperamentally unsuited to a nature festival. Bruno Bettelheim calls kibbutz youth "emotionally flat." If he is right, then the nature festivals must suffer, for they demand from their practitioners an almost romantic sentimentality toward the land and its soil. The kibbutz Sabra is more sober than his parents, and this sobriety dampens the powerful emotional impressions and sensations that a nature festival elicits from its participants.

Now that nature festivals have begun to recede, the public discussions of recent years on kibbutz "paganism" are pointless. Nevertheless, a review of the question can clarify the nature of kibbutz ritual. Kibbutz journals have published statements warning the kibbutz public of the paganism inherent in nature festivals. It is noteworthy that the authors of these admonitions were of German-Jewish origin. The specter of Nazism hovered over them, threatening to scuttle the discussion before it could be judged on its merits.

The use of the term "paganism" in conjunction with kibbutz nature festivals naturally angered those who were responsible for devising them. "Paganism" is not a term to be used indiscriminately, because in its ancient Middle Eastern and European forms it consisted of more than a simple, mindless animism, having developed an imaginative mythopoetic approach to life together with an extensively rich and lavish literature. If the kibbutz was accused of this, then clearly the verdict had to be—innocent. Ancient paganism, with its pantheon of gods and its mythic approach to natural phenomena, is light years away from the mentality of a kibbutznik offering the first fruits of his harvest during the Feast of Weeks.*

The *Vatikim* responsible for the nature festivals did not declare themselves *apikorsim* and nonbelievers in order to embrace a belief in nature as a god or as an object of worship. The use of Nazi paganism as a stick to beat kibbutz nature festivals may have originated as a reaction to mythology used by the Nazis for the

---

*For an excellent description of ancient paganism, see H. and H. A. Frankfort, John A. Wilson, Thornhild Jacobsen, *Before Philosophy* (Penguin Books, 1949: original edition, University of Chicago Press, 1946).

propagation of their blood-and-soil teachings. German paganism was a weapon in the Nazi revolt against universal Jewish and Christian values. It is farfetched to hint at an analogy between the Nazi rejection of historical monotheistic religion and the rebellion of a few Eastern European Jews, some of whom simply longed for contact with nature as an escape from the rigors of their enclosed existence within the four walls of the academy. When they arrived in the kibbutz and worked its soil they resumed the traditions of their biblical ancestors by relating to nature as an object and not a subject. This automatically releases them from the pagan collar. Their tie to the land was national and historic—not mystical. In the kibbutz, nature is subservient to a higher power. In the Bible that power was God; for the kibbutz it is man.

"Multiply and replenish the earth and subdue it" (Genesis 1: 28) could easily have served as the motto for the first kibbutzniks, for as humanists tilling the land, paganism in any form would have been deeply abhorrent to them. Their real achievement lay in the restoration, for a time, of an intimate bond with the natural world that existed among Jews in antiquity. In the Diaspora the ritual of the natural year had been replaced by historical ritual, which succeeded in severing any connection with myth. The kibbutz ritual therefore follows the pattern of traditional Jewish rituals as described by Gershon Scholem:

> The history recollected (in the three pilgrimage festivals) was not regarded as mythical history, enacted in another dimension of time, but is the real history of the Jewish people. This history-saturated ritual was not accompanied by magical action. Rites of remembrance produce no effect. They conjure up identification of the pious with the experience of the founding generation which received the Revelation. The ritual of Rabbinic Judaism transforms nothing, and is strangely sober and dry about rites of remembrance with which a Jew calls to mind his unique historical identity. The ritualism of Rabbinic Judaism lacks the ecstatic, orgiastic element present in mythic rituals. It is astonishing that ritual which rejected all cosmic implications should have asserted itself for so many generations.[63]

The entrance of kabbalistic thought into rabbinic Judaism did eventually have the effect of imparting cosmic implications to Jewish ritual and with it a dread that any ritual deviation, no matter how slight, would constitute a sin against God, who stands in desperate need of exact and punctilious ritual performance. Once the deity becomes dependent upon ritual acts, these acts assume cosmic significance of such proportions that any change becomes menacing enough to be opposed at any price. But even prior to the introduction and dissemination of kabbalistic thought to the masses, the ritualism of rabbinic Judaism remained firm—an "astonishing phenomenon," according the Gershon Scholem. A partial answer to the puzzle of Jewish ritualistic vitality—despite its divorce from the "mother of ritual" (the myths that are represented in the drama of ritual)—is in its all-pervasive character.

Kibbutz rituals, like those of rabbinic Judaism, are sober and dry, but unlike rabbinic Judaism, they are sporadic, for kibbutz ritual does not absorb life itself into a continuous stream of ritual but, instead, extracts ritual acts from life's flow at particular climaxes and turning points. Rabbinic Judaism makes ritual a daily event, while the kibbutz limits its ritual actions to holidays or celebrations of special events in the history of the community, thereby creating an episodic ritual.

## The Origins of Kibbutz Ritual

When the religion of pioneering was at its zenith, ritual was deemed unnecessary, but after the restoration of holidays, when their social and intellectual content became depleted, a slow move began toward a renewal of that sense of holiness which had sustained the kibbutz in its preritualistic beginnings. But now this feeling had to be achieved through institutions and forms just as the holiness in their parents' home in Eastern Europe had been mediated through ritual.

> We are breaking our heads trying to find an expression of holiness for secular man. Perhaps some day we will find a way to arouse awe, a sense of self-examination. We have not reached that yet.[64]

The Sabbath and the holidays are proved and tested channels for transporting Jewish man to the realm of holiness. They are evocative moments for seekers of the sacred, which explains, to some extent, the reawakening of interest in their place within kibbutz society.

The origin of the bewilderment and groping about the question of holidays is in a yearning for patterns . . . for providence, for . . . holiness—yearnings for God. And these yearnings of the public are very tragic for they have no outlet.[65]

This, however, was not David Maletz's final and conclusive word, for he was apparently dismayed by his own statements, and began searching for sources of holiness within kibbutz life that could overlap those traditional ritual forms which had been bearers of holiness within Eastern European Jewish life. God's command, which had sustained the sacred for Eastern European Jewry, no longer had obedient followers. An equivalent to God's command must be derived from kibbutz life, which is built on the commandments between man and his neighbor. Maletz believes that the kibbutz cannot exist forever solely on this category of commandments, for the stability of the ethical *mitzvot* are dependent to some degree on commandments between man and God. Although the kibbutz lacks cosmic *mitzvot*, as traditionally understood, there is no reason it cannot develop *mitzvot* for expressing a relationship "between man and his place in the universe." Such mitzvot should not be shrugged aside as theoretical and impractical.

For us this point, the importance of man's position in the universe, is decisive for its results in the formation of cultural values.[66]

This statement can be derived from Maletz's past. He had experienced the rich cultural life of Eastern European Jewry that had an eminently religious content because of the *mitzvot* between man and God, such as prayer, study, Sabbath, holidays, and so forth. To expect the kibbutz to find equivalents is utopian at this state of its evolution, although there is always the possibility that a generation may arise at a point in kibbutz history when a particular confluence of historical, social, political, and economic events will foster the very type of *mitzvot* Maletz proposes. His significance to that future generation lies in the legitimacy he bestows upon them. In the kibbutz past they would be able to find theoretical precedents for their deviations from generally accepted kibbutz norms. This is the ultimate importance of some men in the kibbutz whose views seem completely unrepresentative of the kibbutz movement. Some day, their ideas may begin to react with new or different human materials. The result may be just a minor reaction—or an explosion.

The holiness that welled from the springs of Eastern European

Jewish life was an effect of a cause that no longer functions in the kibbutz, and Maletz suggests an alternative source for generating a sensitivity to the sacred. Because the kibbutz is a combination of an ideal and daily living, it adds a savor to living (the Hebrew phrase *ta'am b'haim* can also be translated as "significance to life"). This savor, or significance, has the force of holiness.

> We lack the force of an absolute commandment, but from the depths of the kevutzah something is perhaps beginning to take shape which is essentially the origin of the absolute commandment. The origin is in a religious feeling and in the pulsing life of the kevutzah, empowered and irradiated by that feeling, which itself draws from that great idea of communal creativity, the *yahad* (union, or oneness).[67]

This oneness is not the mystic union of a believer with his God, but of a man with his kibbutz, or more precisely with the living souls in his kibbutz. *Yahad* allows the kibbutz to struggle through those gray, sometimes ugly days when vision is clouded. But then there come outbursts of spiritual elation, both in public and in seclusion. No one can trace them, but they are felt in every beat of the communal heart. Then, says Maletz, one can feel the throbbing pulse of life's meaning.

Once life is grasped as significant, the next and natural step is to bless and sanctify it. Maletz does not state the type of blessing a man should utter. Perhaps he may silently bless in his heart. Maletz leans heavily upon the *yahad* as the prime source for the holiness he believes so essential for the vitalization of the kibbutz holiday. But does the *yahad* exist today as he envisages it, or is his vision only a memory? A *Vatik* of Ramat Yohanan remarked that a corporate soul was born during those few moments of union, but that *yahad* remained a fleeting, transitory experience with little practical consequence in the daily life of the kibbutz.

Today social heterogeneity and the generation gap have made *yahad* a still rarer occurrence, though attempts to revive it may be feasible through the medium of smaller groups. The kibbutz is aware that if this cohesive force should disappear it would be deprived of a creative power that it can ill afford to lose, if communal life is to remain genuinely cooperative and not disperse completely into family nuclei. But even if this were to occur, the very existence of an entity called *yahad* could act as a spur to future generations to resist social fragmentation of the kibbutz. When Martin Buber remarked that *yahad* was the Sinai of the future, he gambled, along with David Maletz, on the potential for holiness of communal life. More than the three generations living today will have to elapse before a kibbutz tradition of holiness takes shape. "Remember that four hundred years passed between Ezra and Hillel." Because a number of kibbutz ideas, such as socialism and equality, are new to Jewish life, they have to be firmly entrenched in the kibbutz way of life before appropriate rituals can be created for them. But as may be surmised, dissatisfaction with the current pattern of kibbutz ritual is widespread among sensitive people. These laments are often accompanied by a thinly disguised admiration of Orthodoxy, whose celebration of the Sabbath and holidays is supposedly overflowing with qualities denied to the kibbutz. Some look toward Orthodoxy ("we are envious of religious Jews"), but despair of reaching the spiritual heights attributed to traditional Jews. Orthodox Jews themselves are often skeptical, sometimes contemptuous of kibbutz holidays. One kibbutznik with Orthodox inclinations goes so far as to describe kibbutz holidays as a profanation of sacredness. No one, not even the most committed, is satisfied. This discontent may rescue the kibbutz holiday.

As against the spiritual self-flagellation so popular in the kibbutz, the views of Ze'ev Gazit of Ein Dor (Ha-Kibbutz ha-Artzi) on kibbutz holidays are a refreshing contrast. Unlike most respondents, who were hesitant and doubted that a Jewish holiday could be observed secularly, he was self-assured. He interprets secular as observance of a festival in an atheistic fashion, the honest and sincere step for Jews who, for example, deny that God took Israel out of Egypt or aided modern Israel in the Six-Day War. Yet an atheistic approach does not strip a holiday of holiness. "Only a superficial rationalism ignores such phenomena in societies."[68] In the midst of the tumultuous confusion surrounding the entire subject of holidays, there was a refreshing note in the opinions of a believer in the value and significance of the kibbutz holiday. The rejoinder to the Ze'ev Gazit outlook appeared in a statement of Professor Zvi Werblowsky of the Hebrew University:

> The secularist is faced with his desire for the impossible—an authentic and legitimate Jewish commitment that disregards the traditional religious sanctions and presuppositions of Jewish existence. Jewish religion is not only characteristic but also constitutive of Jewish existence.

According to Werblowsky, there is a hopelessness to the secularist's desires. Yet the drive to build a kibbutz holiday tradition still continues. But kibbutzniks understand, from the depths of their experience, that to create a kabbalah, a past worth inheriting, is a superhuman task, particularly in an age when factors that generate ritual are practically overwhelmed by the ubiquitous presence of commercial spectator culture.

> But rituals cannot be manufactured. They depend on the existence of genuinely shared common values, and only to the extent to which such values emerge and become part of human reality can we expect the emergence of meaningful, rational rituals.[69]

This occurred with the agricultural festivals, for the early settlers did not mechanically devise their ritual. They believed that it grew naturally and unpretentiously out of the life-style they led in a land whose historical associations impelled them toward the course they took. The joy accompanying their return to antiquity enriched and confirmed reality, spiritualizing their daily life.

The *Vatikim* believed that they were successfully forming a tradition, only to witness its slow dissipation in their lifetime. However, those previously dormant agricultural bases of the holidays will not again be allowed to sink back into their earlier inertness, but will instead become part of the kibbutz kabbalah that one generation bequeaths to another. The observance of this kabbalah also includes rituals of traditional Judaism that have become part of the kibbutz tradition. In many kibbutzim, for example, no bread is eaten during Passover, not because of belief in divine fiat, but because the community has commanded itself to do so. This self-command arises out of a number of factors: the dawning realization that rebellion for its own sake is futile, the desire to inculcate social and national values, the search for a spiritual outlet, and the need for a cultural tool to animate powers of creativity. Passover is the only holiday whose roots in kibbutz soil are so deep that it has become a tradition. When asked if he were willing to participate in a traditional Seder, a young man formerly from Gal-Ed replied: "I am satisfied with the Kibbutz Haggadah." This remark was significant, for this young man has strong religious leanings and would not prefer the kibbutz Haggadah had it not satisfactorily replaced the traditional text.

But only Passover has earned the appellation "tradition." The rest of the holidays are still in search of appropriate kibbutz forms. Although the general tenor of the literature on the subject continues to be bravely optimistic, pessimistic notes do appear from time to time. Recently, the chairman of the Inter-Kibbutz Committee on Holidays and Festivals saw fit to write an article of grave importance for the future of the kibbutz tradition in process.

> There is cause for pessimism if our generation fails to mold ceremonies for the holidays, as was done with the Passover Seder. . . . Time is working against us. Many years ago holidays were revived in the kibbutz. It was a creative period. There was joy, a unitary bond. Today holidays are "executed." We are impassive. . . . There is no identification between the individual and the festival. The holiday is improvised . . . light, sometimes even insulting. We do not feel that we will be able to preserve the gains achieved some years ago. . . . During the creative period of the holiday a different relationship existed. The festival was an expression of values. Now there is fatigue . . . our spirit is empty, the public deaf, lacking in sensitivity. The conclusion: to raise the subject in the agenda of our society, before creative artists, educators, parents. We must also enrich our knowledge of sources—in Bible, *aggadah*, poetry, custom. . . . If we do not attend to the holiday, either emptiness or religion will seize control.[70]

During the 1930s and 1940s there was a creative outbust of holiday song, dance, and art in the kibbutz movement. Artists outside the movement also contributed their talents, building up a stock on which the kibbutz has been drawing ever since. Aryeh Ben-Gurion does not believe the kibbutz can live off its cultural savings account without incurring a deterioration of value—therefore he appeals passionately for a revival of that golden age. On this troubled note we shall now observe the place of the holiday in kibbutz life.

# 8
# *Holidays and Rites of Passage*

> It is through ritual movement, gesture, song, and dance that man keeps in touch with the source of creativity. Ritual appeared along with myth in man's development and springs from the same source. In ritual, men "act out" the reveries and hopes of the tribe. Ritual humanizes space as myth humanizes time.
> —Harvey Cox, *The Feast of Fools*

## Rosh Ha-Shanah

"Both Rosh Ha-Shanah and Yom Kippur . . . are different from other Jewish festivals in that they bear no relation to nature nor to any historic event in the Jewish past. They are concerned only with the life of the individual, with his religious feelings and innermost probings."[71] This comment by Haim Schauss on the Jewish festivals condenses the problem of the Day of Awe for the kibbutz movement. The holidays and festivals of the Jewish year have taken on new life, but not the solemn days of Rosh Ha-Shanah and Yom Kippur and the four minor fasts. There is little chance of the last being restored to the kibbutz calendar year, but the High Holy Days, and particularly Rosh Ha-Shanah, are beginning to make their presence felt once more, after a lengthy exile of almost half a century.

In 1971, the Inter-Kibbutz Committee on Holidays circulated among the kibbutzim a booklet it had drawn up for use on Rosh Ha-Shanah. An analysis of the contents of these booklets will reveal that, although there may have been a minor revival of Rosh Ha-Shanah on the kibbutz scene, it can no longer deservedly be designated as a Day of Awe. Moreover, Yom Kippur, the holiest day of the year in traditional Judaism, the *Shabbat Shabbaton*, the Sabbath of Sabbaths, does not exist for most kibbutzim.

Unlike the pilgrimage festivals or Purim and Hanukkah, the High Holy Days cannot be connected to any event in the historical past or related to the cycles of nature. In the idiom current in the kibbutz, both Rosh Ha-Shanah and Yom Kippur, particularly the latter, are completely "religious," and therefore resist adoption. Religious elements exist in Passover, Shavuot, and Hanukkah, but they are intertwined with agricultural and national themes that can be extracted without doing irreparable damage to the fabric of the holiday. Indeed, in some instances the emphasis on the nonreligious elements serves to widen and expand the breadth and scope of a holiday such as Hanukkah, which had become narrowly reduced in its content. Rosh Ha-Shanah and Yom Kippur lack any natural and national qualities, and until recently seemed consigned to spiritual exile. Yet these holy days, despite the limbo to which they had been consigned, are now proving that the persuasiveness and persistence of their messages can touch even the nonreligious kibbutzim.

In the weekly bulletins of the Ihud, comments and letters began to appear as early as the 1950s, decrying the absence of Rosh Ha-Shanah from kibbutz society. Voicing the fear of spiritual invalidism, particularly among the children, these statements were little more than a helpless complaint. They were probably written by individuals who had had the experience of Rosh Ha-Shanah in their youth, gladly abandoned it, and then had second thoughts as they saw their children growing up and maturing without knowing anything of their parents' experience. Answers came swiftly to the periodicals, all of which can be summarized in the following way: Rosh Ha-Shanah as developed in the synagogue over the centuries as a day of awe, of fear and trembling, has been left behind irretrievably. There is no chance of reliving the kind of emotional experience the believer had known. Once this fact is accepted by people serenely, they can cease their self-recrimination and realistically endeavor to confront the problem of Rosh Ha-Shanah in all its complexity.

The arrival of the New Year in the 1970s is noted in several ways. The building of synagogues in some of the older kibbutzim is noteworthy, but it is no indication of a trend. High Holy Day prayer in a kibbutz attracts only a few, though some come with their children to observe, or to hear the shofar blast. At the other extreme, many kibbutzim mark Rosh Ha-Shanah by devoting the day to a review of the past year in the world, in Israel, and in the kibbutz. This is usually done as part of an evening program, which may be both serious and light: a lecture or symposium on a subject such as the "kibbutz in Israeli Society." This is sometimes followed by a short film or slide show locally produced, showing personalities and events from the past year in the kibbutz.

This one illustration does not exhaust the possibilities for cultural committee members who face the question each year: What is to be done on Rosh Ha-Shanah? The focal theme in many kibbutzim, whatever its variations, remains unchanging: the key incidents of the past year as they touched upon and influenced life in the kibbutz, and as they may affect the coming year. Rosh Ha-Shanah has therefore become a day of evaluation not for the individual, but for the kibbutz. The form of presentation, whether it is a symposium, lecture, sober opening session of the year's general meetings, film or slide show, should not be allowed to mask the inner dynamics of this type of Rosh Ha-Shanah. The kibbutz is judging itself. There is none of the solemnity or earnest seriousness of synagogue rites, but a concern with serious principle remains. The collective, on occasion, feels duty-bound to review its past.

An unusual combination of the old and new occurred in the late 1960s at Hatzerim, a young kibbutz near Beersheba. Due to the persistence of one member, an abridged prayer service was held for the High Holy Days. When a notice announcing services was pinned on a bulletin board, no one signed up—apparently out of embarrassment—though a number turned individually to the organizer. Once the fear of public reproach had been overcome, the number of participants rose precipitously. No conclusions can be derived from this isolated episode, especially since this particular kibbutz was founded by members of Tzofim, the Israeli scout movement, and may not reflect the feelings of most kibbutz-born youth. However, in addition to prayer, Hatzerim had its first general assembly of the year 1967 on the second night of Rosh Ha-Shanah, confining the meeting to a minimum of practical affairs. Instead, most of the meeting was devoted to a discussion of "the essence of our relationship to the land of Israel." The evening concluded with a *heshbon nefesh*, a self-evaluation of the kibbutz way of life.

Some kibbutzim have sought to explore a middle way, an intermediate path between the synagogue and the yearly review of events. The September 1967 edition of *Yedi'on* (the monthly inter-kibbutz bulletin on cultural affairs and programs) carried a list of thirty-six kibbutzim that have compiled and edited booklets or programs for Rosh Ha-Shanah evening. These works are composed

*Holidays and Rites of Passage* 145

of readings and songs drawn from ancient and contemporary Jewish literature.

What is the content of such programs? If Rosh Ha-Shanah has none of the "adaptive" characteristics of other holidays, how can it possibly experience even a miniature revival? A number of booklets, including the latest Inter-Kibbutz version, and the maximalist version of Mishmar ha-Sharon and Ginnegar,[72] indicate that when will and emotion are unable to resist the current, the intellect finds answers to the most glaring of contradictions. Certainly the kibbutz recognizes that human necessity sometimes compromises even the most ideal, aesthetic, and intellectually satisfying principles. Something similar appears to have occurred with Rosh Ha-Shanah, whose probing into the human soul has touched upon sensitive and unexplored regions of the individual and collective kibbutz psyche.

Unlike revisions of prayer books that appear in the United States, no introductions are written for kibbutz ceremonial material to explain the assumptions that underlie the choice of selections. Only the Rosh Ha-Shanah booklet of Bet ha-Shittah, while having no explanatory introduction, contains some remarks of elucidation from another source. The content of this Rosh Ha-Shanah booklet is explained in the following terms:

> In Tishri (the first Hebrew month of the year) the world was created. The holiday of reviewed experience. Man and creation, man and soil. The central motif—encouragement of the belief in man and in the work of his hands. A striving for completeness.[73]

This set of beliefs is only tangentially related to the traditional mood of Rosh Ha-Shanah. Yet the material appearing in the Bet ha-Shittah program, which is the basis of the Inter-Kibbutz booklet, is in the main composed of traditional sources. Tradition, though flexible, could not provide the editors with suitable material in praise of man and his works. Whenever this theme appears, it is carried by modern Hebrew writers.

A summary of the Inter-Kibbutz pamphlet and the program of Mishmar ha-Sharon will reveal some of their underlying assumptions and perplexities.

After beginning with short poems of the New Year or quotations from the Bible and Mishnah, the major feature of Rosh Ha-Shanah—the blowing of the shofar—is quickly broached. This act can be interpreted in a number of ways, but the kibbutz has exploited the messianic national theme of the shofar verses in the traditional *Mussaf* (additional) service of Rosh Ha-Shanah.

> Sound the great shofar for our freedom;
> Raise the signal to bring our exiles together;
> Draw our scattered people together from among the nations;
> Assemble our dispersed from the uttermost parts of the earth;
> Bring us to Zion
> Thy city singing, to Jerusalem Thy sanctuary
> With everlasting joy.[74]

Significantly, the sections of the shofar verses that are omitted dwell upon the blasts of the ram's horn at the revelation at Sinai. In Mishmar ha-Sharon, an explanation by Maimonides on the meaning of the shofar is appended. It is completely religious in tone, pointing out that the shofar is intended to awaken men from their torpor, so that they might investigate their deeds, repent, and remember their Creator. This is typical of the way in which the kibbutz finds a rationale for using religious passages. No matter how often a quotation may mention God, it is permissible, provided that God is not petitioned or praised.

This view of the kibbutz about the nonreligious use of religious sources helps to explain why the libraries of Israel do not catalog kibbutz Passover Haggadot as liturgy. In library card catalogs, kibbutz Haggadot do not appear with the same number as traditional ones. God may be described as He appears in traditional prayer texts, and this is not considered dishonest by kibbutz secularists, because they feel that we should be familiar with our ancestors' experience of Rosh Ha-Shanah. Nevertheless, what a difference remains between declaring "all secrets and countless mysteries from the beginning of time are open to Thee. There is no forgetting before Thy throne of glory; there is not a thing hidden from Thine eye," which is said at Mishmar ha-Sharon, and proclaiming God's greatness. Inevitably the fine distinctions kibbutz members are forced to make begin to wear very thin. Religious experience will not stand or fall by the inclusion or exclusion of a specific verbal formula. The word game is part of the kibbutz battle with Orthodoxy and with its own confusions. Trapped by Orthodox thought patterns, the kibbutz does not realize that prayer can be more than petition or praise. The kibbutzniks are not convincing when they deny that their references to an uplifting, elevating, or ascension of the spirit are a form of prayer.

A section from the Bible is read, but not from the traditional portions of the binding of Isaac or of Hannah's prayer for a child. The opening verses of the Book of Genesis are read, followed by the section from chapter 30 of Deuteronomy on the blessing and the curse, concluding with the call "you shall choose life." Proper homage is paid to the binding of Isaac through the inclusion of a number of short *midrashim* on the subject. The decision to read Genesis and Deuteronomy can be attributed to the theme of birth and creation that is part of the Rosh Ha-Shanah liturgy.

Appearing as a supplement to the selection from Genesis is Psalm 104, Borkhi Nafshi, read in the synagogue on Saturday afternoons between Sukkot and Passover. This reading starts, traditionally, on the Sabbath when the Book of Genesis is begun. Psalm 104 is closely connected in spirit to Genesis, for its major theme is creation and the grandeur of nature.

The portion from Deuteronomy seems appropriate to the spirit of the day that points to the opportunity of renewed choice between blessing and curse. Biblically, of course, the choice was between acceptance of God's covenant or its rejection, but for the kibbutzim the choice between blessing and curse can be reinterpreted with little difficulty. Whether these selections will become set readings, or will be replaced by others every few years, is as yet too early to determine.

While it is not expected that Rosh Ha-Shanah as a Day of Judgment will appeal to the kibbutz, a short prayer of Rabbi Elimelech seeking ethical and moral purity has been inserted in the Inter-Kibbutz ceremony. This lovely prayer contains an outline of desirable moral qualities to be sought, and of undesirable qualities to be avoided. Concentrated in this prayer are standards for the self-judgment the kibbutz must make from year to year. Failure to live by those standards will bring upon it the "evil decree" of social disintegration, a fate that has befallen a number of kibbutzim unable to marshal the moral power to moderate pettiness, quarrels, friction, and outright conflict.

Included in almost every example of Rosh Ha-Shanah programs are poems by modern Hebrew writers, some famous and well known for their literary output, others with only a local reputation in the kibbutz movement. They have in common a sensitivity to the surrounding world of nature that escapes the average man. In the kibbutz code of values the significance of nature remains unimpaired. Despite technological advances and mechanization of agriculture, there can be no iron-clad assurances that the land will unfailingly give forth its fruits each year. On Rosh Ha-Shanah, as on Passover, there is a seasonal change, a new climate, and a turn of the agricultural cycle. Implanted in the midst of this changing and transfigured world, some kibbutz ceremonial and emotional expression of the relationship of individual and society to this environment seems inevitable.

Leah Goldberg wrote a poem that seems to have become a Rosh Ha-Shanah classic in the kibbutz:

> Teach me my God to bless and pray
> The secret of a fading leaf, the glow of ripe fruit
> Of this freedom, to see, to feel,
> To breath, to know, to hope, to fail
>
> Teach our lips blessing, song and praise
> As your span renews itself morning and night
> Lest my day become as it was in the past
> Lest my day become ordinary and mundane.[75]

In Bet ha-Shittah a brief ceremony is introduced, marking the end of one agricultural cycle and the beginning of another. On Rosh Ha-Shanah day, the first furrow is plowed in anticipation of the new season for seeding winter crops. The New Year beginning on the first of Tishri is, therefore, Rosh Ha-Shanah not only for kibbutz society and the individual living within it, but for the nature cycle. Throughout the ceremonial material for Rosh Ha-Shanah nature is described as essentially harmonious and cooperative, but dependent upon the good will of man for the continuity of its beneficence. An "ecological" *midrash* is quoted to excellent effect in this regard.

> When the Holy One blessed be He created the first man, He took him and showed him all the trees of the Garden of Eden and said to him: "See how lovely and worthy are My creations. Give thought not to spoil or destroy My world, for if you spoil it, no one will be able to repair it after you."[76]

Inserted within the broadly traditional themes—the shofar blast heralding a return from exile, the New Year as a day of assessment of the relationship between man and man, man and the society, man and his environment—there exists a motif found only in the kibbutz Rosh Ha-Shanah ceremony. The accomplishments of the

## Holidays and Rites of Passage    149

kibbutz movement have sustained the optimistic ideology its members brought with them that glorified man as a unique creature progressively developing in the direction of a fuller and more spiritual humanity. Some of the pessimistic philosophies of modern thought, defiling man and demeaning him, have had little effect on the optimism of the kibbutz. Because of its partial success in building a new society, the kibbutz retains the optimism of men of affairs who have seen the work of their hands produce perceptible and salutary results. The god has yet to fail—at least in the kibbutz—so man is not yet tarnished to the same degree as he is in the West.

This may partially explain the poems glorifying man that appear in the Inter-Kibbutz booklet. Man, the acme of creation, appears at the conclusion of the Bible reading for the day. Instead of following the more ambiguous, ambivalent, and realistic path laid out by tradition—depicting man as capable of the greatest evil as well as greatest good—the kibbutz treatment of Rosh Ha-Shanah portrays a one-sided being. Reluctance to use the traditional vocabulary of sin and transgression may explain this oversimplification of the human condition, for certainly kibbutz society is well aware of the weakness and human frailties to which its members are heir.

> For my soul is still a straining bird
> I have not sold her to a golden calf
> For I yet believe in man as well
> In his spirit, his bold spirit.[77]

A cornerstone of the kibbutz social structure is its faith in man. Mutual trust and belief are basic requirements of a cooperative society. Were this faith to give way to suspicion, the entire social edifice would crack and crumble. Believing in man, therefore, becomes for the kibbutz an ontological necessity. The kibbutz as a human enterprise is grounded in an optimism that is in constant need of reinforcement. Without confidence in his spirit, hope in man becomes an emotional impossibility.

Towards the conclusion of the ceremony there is a section extracted in part from the Mussaf service of Yom Kippur. It is the prayer recited by the high priest after sending the scapegoat out into the desert and having come out of the Temple "in perfect health." Below is the entire prayer as it appears in the traditional Yom Kippur liturgy, and in the form developed by the Inter-Kibbutz program.

May it be Thy will, Lord our God and God of our fathers, that the forthcoming year shall be for Thy people, the house of Israel, a year of abundant prosperity; a year of generous decrees declared by Thee; a year of grain, wine and oil; a year of attainment and success; a year of meeting in the sanctuary; a year of enjoyable living; a year of dew, rain and warmth; a year of delicious fruits; a year of atonement for all our iniquities; a year wherein Thou wilt bless our food and drink; a year of business transactions; a year of attending our sanctuary; a year of plenty and delight; a year wherein Thou wilt bless our offspring and the fruit of our land; a year wherein Thou wilt bless our coming and going; a year wherein Thou wilt save our community; a year wherein Thou wilt be merciful toward us; a year wherein Thou wilt open Thy goodly treasure for us; a year wherein Thy people, the house of Israel, will not be in need of one another's aid nor the support of another people, for Thou will bless the products of their own hands.[78]

May it be that the forthcoming year shall be for Thy people, the house of Israel, a year of abundant prosperity, a year of generous decrees; a year of grain, wine and oil; a year of attainment and success, a year of enjoyable living, a year of dew and rain, a year of delicious fruits; a year wherein Thou wilt bless our food and drink; a year of plenty and delight; a year wherein Thou wilt bless our offspring and the fruit of our land; a year wherein Thou wilt subject our enemies; a year of peace and serenity; a year wherein Thou wilt lead us with head erect to our land; a year wherein Thy people, the house of Israel, will not be in need of one another's aid nor the support of another people, for Thou wilt bless the products of their own hands.[79]

Although these words are not uttered in a kibbutz synagogue, and direct petitionary appeals have been modified, they still remain a prayer. Unacceptable fragments have been eliminated from the original and a few verses added—which puts in doubt the standard kibbutz view that they are not revising prayers. Their retort would be that they are not addressing God and therefore are not praying, as witness the exclusion of the name of God except when it would be an offense to Hebrew syntax. All the omissions which appear in the kibbutz version of this prayer are consistent with its professed denials. The only questionable absurd omission is the reference to a year of business transactions. Here socialist piety has closed everyone's eyes to the reality of the multifarious business transactions in which kibbutz society engages daily, whether in the sale of agricultural or dairy produce, or of manufactured items. The absence of business transactions within the kibbutz itself fails to justify ignoring the growing involvement of the kibbutz in the business and commerce of Israeli society. The mental vestiges of the supposed contamination by contact with business have led to the curious phenomenon of the kibbutz playing the saint where it has no legitimate basis for doing so.

The written material on Rosh Ha-Shanah is a valuable guide to the spirit in which the kibbutz is now approaching that day. It fails, however, to measure the spirit evoked during the ceremony itself, which even under the best of circumstances would be far removed from the atmosphere generated in a traditional or even a liberal synagogue. For instance, at Ramat Yohanan a meal is served outdoors on Rosh Ha-Shanah evening, with rows of benches set up on a large illuminated lawn. At one side there is a small platform for the readers and choir. The festive atmosphere engendered makes it impossible to create a solemn or serious atmosphere—if that is sought at all. The choir and readers, shuttling on and off the platform, contribute to the mood of informality. The prevailing good spirits produce a Rosh Ha-Shanah observance entirely at odds with the traditional one. Moreover, the kibbutz tradition of informality is a formidable obstacle to the evocation of a day of awe. Until the High Holy Days are accepted as solemn moments in progression through life, the kibbutz will miss their implications for its society.

## *Yom Kippur*

The "Solemn Days" returned for a brief moment to the life of Kibbutz Ramat Yohanan on Yom Kippur. No synagogue service was held, but a serious and earnest program was conducted on the eve of this holiday.

An early meal was served out of respect for the day that has been the holiest in the Jewish calendar, but that until recently was so totally ignored in some kibbutzim that members were recruited for special tasks requiring large numbers of people. Now the era of uncompromising heresy against tradition is over. The program for the eve of Yom Kippur began in Ramat Yohanan at approximately nine o'clock and lasted for about three quarters of an hour. It was attended mostly by the middle-aged and elderly. As I experienced it, it was almost too solemn. By the standards of traditional Judaism, little happens. Many Orthodox Jews might say that it would be preferable to disregard the day completely rather than observe it in such an imperfect way. Nonetheless, it is worthwhile to ask what was behind even this limited return to Yom Kippur.

In 1964 *Yedi'on* initiated a debate on the subject of Yom Kippur. Under the heading "Why is there no observance of Yom Kippur in the kibbutzim of Ha-Kibbutz ha-Artzi," Zvi Ra'anan of Ha-Zorea presented the case against the gradual infiltration of Yom Kippur programs particularly into Ihud kibbutzim.[80] He objected to the type of programs that consisted of lectures or talks on Yom Kippur in Jewish tradition, Jewish martyrology, the binding of Isaac, the *mitzvot* between man and his neighbor, the self-evaluation of kibbutz life, or a memorial service. These subjects are usually accompanied by a record or tape of Bruch's Kol Nidre and selected melodies from the Yom Kippur liturgy.

In common with their Orthodox antagonists, many Ha-Kibbutz ha-Artzi members reject the possibility that Yom Kippur can be practiced in a manner other than its present form in the synagogue. There can be no objection to hearing records of Yom Kippur melodies or conversing on the *mitzvot* between man and his neighbor, but what relation do these activities have to the historical Yom Kippur? Apparently, the opposition to these programs originates from an apprehension that the introduction of Yom Kippur programs into the kibbutz is an opening through which the "religious" content of the day, concealed under the guise of folklore, will inevitably enter. According to this view, Yom Kippur is beyond the power of reinterpretation by even the most gifted sophist. In short, it is not just a day devoted to communion with ethical niceties, but is also richly, profoundly, and existentially a day of communion between man and God. For the kibbutz movement to reenact, through its Yom Kippur programs, a day of such profoundly religious significance, is to dishonor the Jewish tradition. Only the believer can seek and succeed in having the kind of experience that Yom Kippur can grant.

In this line of argument Zvi Ra'anan launches into an attack on those kibbutzniks who would introduce Yom Kippur into the kibbutz for nationalistic reasons, and who argue that if the majority of the Jewish people, including nonbelievers, attend synagogue on

Yom Kippur, the kibbutz is obliged to mark the day out of a sense of national solidarity. But the kibbutz, of all groups, should be the last to follow the majority blindly. During the most fruitful years of pioneering, it was assailed by many critics as a heretical body arrogantly striking at Jewish tradition. Had the kibbutz heeded its opponents, it would never have achieved any of its unique accomplishments.

To blur ideological distinctions would be of no service to democracy and would not advance social harmony and unity. The kibbutz has sought to lead and should adopt only those principles and practices of others that are worthy of emulation. Why then reinstate Yom Kippur out of a sense of solidarity with Jews who ordinarily never attend synagogue other than on the High Holy Days? In such a context their motivations are suspect and their commitment to Yom Kippur little more than vague, superficial sentimentality. "We, as an ideological movement, should not permit such Jews to lead us."[81]

In the counterarguments marshaled by members of the Ihud, the anticipated use was made of proofs that Yom Kippur is not purely religious, but has secular-national aspects. This approach is part of a campaign of self-persuasion, for only under the banner of secularism or nationalism will the kibbutz be capable of bearing Yom Kippur. The soul seeks its rationalizations. Only Yitzhak Maor of Ashdod Yaakov Ihud, while making use of the national-solidarity-humanistic argument, succeeded in putting his finger on those vague, intangible, inarticulate human quests for understanding, meaning, and self-transcendence.

> Not only can these holidays [during Tishri] be interwoven into kibbutz life, but they must, if we are to achieve the spiritual elevation of man and of Kibbutz society.[82]

Maor admits that a traditional Yom Kippur cannot be introduced into the kibbutz, but he believes that the day is not alien to the kibbutz spirit and if properly absorbed, could be a genuine blessing. In the kibbutz the constant contact engendered by living in a small society creates inevitable frictions. A day for reconciliation and appeasement could be of significant social benefit. The common objection against the prayer form of Yom Kippur is met by Maor through an extension of the word prayer to include the diversity of human experiences that direct mankind toward the transcendent, and in this he would include music or poetry, for example. Maor's discussion of the question of Yom Kippur is unique in its hint of the numen glowing faintly in the background. But in the light of the human and spiritual components of kibbutz society, it must remain in the dim background. The foreground is to be reserved for the national-historic or universal components of Yom Kippur.

At Geva one Yom Kippur eve began with a paraphrase of the introductory section to Kol Nidre:

> With God's [*Makom*] consent
> And the consent of this community
> We come together to begin and try to
> Observe this holiday, Yom Kippur,
> And to begin and try to redeem ourselves
> From our confusion about this day.[83]

The late Yaacov Raz, who opened the evening, later wrote provocatively that of all the holidays Yom Kippur should be the closest to the spirit of the kibbutz. He understands the reasons that the kibbutz repudiates the day, but once the movement outgrows this untoward rejection, it will be able to embrace the day with little hesitation. Raz conceives of the kibbutz as a communal brotherhood, or a cooperative community whose basic principle is the betterment of its way of life by refinement of the relations between man and his neighbor. The singular combination of the individual and the collective brought about by Yom Kippur makes it especially appropriate for the kibbutz. Theodor H. Gaster writes:

> When the community declared in the statutory confessions of the day, "we have robbed," "we have slandered," "we have committed adultery," it was their collective conscience that was speaking, and what they were acknowledging were not merely individual misdeeds, but collective defilement of their character as a "holy nation and a Kingdom of priests."[84]

To a community for whom a healthy collective conscience is a vital necessity, Yom Kippur is the ideal and the most important of all the holidays. It is indeed strange that this day should be rejected by those in greatest need of it.

At Ein Ha-Shofet, of Ha-Kibbutz ha-Artzi, founded by Americans and named in honor of Justice Brandeis, home discussion groups were held on Yom Kippur eve in the middle 1960s. The experiment at Ein Ha-Shofet attracted wide interest because of its adherence to the principle of Yom Kippur as a day of self-evaluation. "The central problem is our life—the interaction between the individual and the kibbutz collective. In other words, how can we learn to live together in the same society?"

The aim was to institute a dialogue in the hope that clearer understanding of kibbutz life would reduce tension and limit aggression. All the generations were represented. Material for preparatory reading was compiled and distributed to the participants. The literary sources were as disparate as Rav Soleveichik, Ahad Ha-Am, Agnon, Buber, Marx, and Lenin. In addition to the Yom Kippur theme of self-criticism and reevaluation, the question of how kibbutzniks could reinforce their tie with Jewish tradition was raised. At Ein Ha-Shofet such talk became a functional Yom Kippur ritual. At Ramat Yohanan the ritual was a theoretical and abstract exercise in the yearly study of themes and concepts of Yom Kippur. This experiment was unique in the kibbutz movement. According to its major initiator, Y. Ron-Polani, a meeting of the kibbutz membership was called, at which a few individuals decided that the hour had arrived for the kibbutz to mark Yom Kippur. Despite some difference of opinion plans were made for a number of changes in the customary order at Ramat Yohanan on the day before Yom Kippur. All labor was to cease by 2:00 P.M. The dining room would be empty.

Yom Kippur programs at Ramat Yohanan began in 1965. In the first two years the evening was primarily explanatory, devoted to the content of the day and its relevance to kibbutz society. The next step was to choose the subjects that would serve as pivotal ideas for the coming yearly programs. "We selected the subjects out of the heritage of our people that have a tie to the characteristic content of this holiday."[85] The major responsibility for collecting, assembling, and presenting such material for Yom Kippur was delegated to Y. Ron-Polani, now retired from his position as principal of the local high school. From 1967 onward the subjects were the concept of responsibility in man's life; the readiness for personal sacrifice for values sacred to man (this program followed the Six-Day War); self-evaluation and repentance; the *mitzvot* between man and his neighbor.

The format was similar to most kibbutz holiday programs—alternating readings and songs. What differentiated Yom Kippur practice from the other holidays is that children did not participate, and the absence of dancing or of any other dramatic arts. The elements that involve the entire community and particularly the youth—food, children, dance or drama—are all conspicuously absent on Yom Kippur. As a result the program attracts only the serious youth and the elders. The solemnity of the program has a limited appeal to a younger generation brought up on joyous holidays. In addition, the sudden observance of Yom Kippur after a hiatus of decades may have raised questions in the minds of young people who had been taught by example to ignore Yom Kippur and then suddenly were confronted with its reappearance. This abrupt turnabout by the *Vatikim* could lead to a mild cynicism among the younger people. Also, the younger generation tends to relate to holidays as social events, generally ignoring content and message. In these circumstances there is little wonder that Yom Kippur lacks the status of other kibbutz holidays and appeals only to a minority. This fact has not been lost on the initiators of the ceremony.

> Can we permit this (preparing the Yom Kippur ceremony) to be a matter for a few amateurs or for a few responsible individuals? If the community does not have the will to be constant—what will be the fate of this day? In kibbutz society nothing is more difficult than crystallizing an atmosphere and mode of life for every festival which would be honored and recognized by the entire kibbutz society, or at least the great majority. . . .
> A special effort must be made to right the situation.[86]

Although no one has actually sabotaged the day, cooperation is not always available. The kibbutz choir, which performs at all public ceremonials when its services are required, refused to sing for Yom Kippur evening, although it had appeared on Rosh Ha-Shanah. Whatever the reasons, whether they be shame, embarrassment, or ideological opposition to the day (the least likely cause), the choir's refusal and the accusations of coercion made against the early scheduling of the pre–Yom Kippur meal sparked a lively controversy. In addition, the Yom Kippur committee had sought, through a questionnaire, to elicit responses from members on reactions to the first programs. A summary review of the evening dedicated to the subject to repentance indicated that the program contained little material likely to arouse opposition on its own merits. Actually, it was the celebration of Yom Kippur day itself that touched a tender nerve.

The Kol Nidre evening on repentance began with a reading from Leviticus, declaring the tenth day of the seventh month as a day of affliction, followed by a reading on repentance by Professor S. H.

Bergman of the Hebrew University. A record of Kol Nidre was then played. Afterwards there was a sermonette on Rabbi Akiva's statement from Pirke Avot that everything is anticipated but permission is given, a story about Rabbi Shneur Zalman of Lyady, founder of the Lubavitcher movement, and an excerpt from Martin Buber's writings. Kibbutz sources were introduced through quotations from conversations of young people on a number of random Jewish themes. In conclusion, notable writers such as Shai Agnon, Haim Guri, and Avraham Shlonsky were quoted in support of a return to the Jewish heritage. The concluding "blessing" summed up the central idea of the evening—*Teshuvah* (repentance and return) to the Jewish heritage.

> And also we who have awakened in the last number of years to the need of giving our own expression to Yom Kippur evening— is this not a sign of continuity, of the way to repentance [return] to the sacred heritage of our people? The way to repentance, as we said, is not easy. The way to a return to the people's heritage is not of one piece.[87]

The general impression of the evening was that of a lengthy sermon or lecture punctuated by Yom Kippur music. The readings were performed by several people. There was general agreement that the format was too abstract and theoretical and given to an excess of moralizing. As a beginning however, it remained a bold attempt to break out of the conditioning occasioned by childhood experiences and of years of neglect. The *Vatikim* are only too aware that Yom Kippur was never intended to be a scholarly review of great ideas, but was primarily an emotional experience in which ideas were commingled with feeling.

> We are in no position to say we have achieved a spiritually elevating experience, which we are endeavoring to do. We are still indeed very distant from that. A great number of people in our kibbutz have reservations about any attempt to revive Yom Kippur in our society. It is also doubtful if many who attend the assembly bring with them more than passive agreement and a large degree of curiosity. Therefore, what has been fixed in the meantime, as a beginning, is only a sort of external framework.[88]

Ron-Polani's experiment with Yom Kippur was discontinued in the beginning of the 1970s.

What is to be within that external framework in addition to a spiritually elevating experience? Opinion in the kibbutz seems to be moving toward an acceptance of certain "digestible" elements of Yom Kippur. Is it possible, however, to speak of a uniquely kibbutz approach to the spirit of the day that would distinguish it from Yom Kippur elsewhere? Although it is perhaps premature to point to more than the obvious external differences, one theme repeats itself within kibbutz custom and literature on Yom Kippur—the recurrent necessity for a collective *heshbon nefesh*, a self-examination, evaluation, and joint stock-taking of the collective conscience of the community, as well as the personal conscience of the individual. In a kibbutz the interdependence of the collective and the individual requires a periodic renewal and rededication to values that is possible only through a holiday as permeated with ethical values as is Yom Kippur.

> If the Kibbutz cannot achieve a collective *heshbon nefesh*, what then is the significance of its being a kibbutz society?[89]

This opinion, voiced by Amram Ha-Yisraeli, a teacher from Givat Haim (Ihud), sums up the sense of difference he believes Yom Kippur should have in the kibbutz. But before this aim can come even close to implementation, the day must gain a new acceptance in kibbutz society.

## *Sukkot*

> Sukkot . . . was at one time [in antiquity] considered the greatest Jewish festival. . . . Though Sukkot officially had the same status as Pesach and Shavuot, it played a much greater role in the life of the people than did the other two agricultural festivals; and when people said "The Festival" without any other specifications, the great autumn festival, Sukkot, was meant. In the older books of the Bible which tell of the life of the people in the time of the independent Jewish Kingdom, the only festival given considerable attention is Sukkot. Sukkot, then, was apparently the main festival of the Jews of those times.[90]

As the Jewish people lost their ties with agriculture upon their dispersion from ancient Israel, Sukkot lost its centrality in the holiday cycle and moved toward the periphery. For an increasingly urban people, Sukkot as the agricultural Festival of Ingathering assumed less and less importance while the historical motif of the

Festival of Booths took on greater significance. The harvest theme was retained, however, in the decoration of the Sukkah with fruits and vegetables hung from the sides of the booth or from the beams of its open roof. Although tenaciously observed over the centuries, celebration of Sukkot has suffered visibly from the conditions of modern life and, of the three seasonal festivals that punctuate the Jewish year, possesses the least contemporary relevance for the modern Jew. The agricultural themes of Passover and Shavuot have been overshadowed by ideological elements of supreme importance in the theological-historical posture of Judaism—the Exodus and the Revelation at Sinai. Both of these concepts are conceived as continuous experiences in the life of Judaism. Dwelling in booths, however, is difficult to recognize as such, especially when the historicity of that event is doubtful.

Oddly enough, Sukkot was barely acknowledged in kibbutz society until the last decade, and in many kibbutzim was either ignored or observed in a perfunctory manner. Now that the kibbutz has concluded that all major holidays should be given some measure of observance, there has been a slow revival of Sukkot celebrations and the quest of a Sukkot tradition has begun to take on momentum. As is sometimes the case in such instances it was the children who sparked this revival, for in many kibbutzim Sukkot amounted to little more than a children's holiday, with booths built in the children's homes, but not for the adult population. This was a curious phenomenon indeed, for Sukkot arrives at the conclusion of an agriculturally critical season. In Ramat Yohanan the apple- and pear-picking season concludes about then with the fruit already in, the cotton harvested, and the citrus fruit season just beginning.

One of the causes for disregarding Sukkot was the stress laid upon Shavuot as the primary agricultural festival of the year. Sukkot was considered an unnecessary repetition of Shavuot. But now that no holiday of the year can be left uncultivated, Sukkot is arising as an agricultural parallel to Shavuot. Another possible explanation for the rise of Sukkot, based primarily upon verbal rather than documented sources, is the decline of Shavuot and its principal ceremony of Bikkurim—the presentation of the first fruits. The kibbutz has been groping for some form of ceremonial expression on Shavuot for the ideal of Mattan Torah, and this may be an indicator not of the emergence of Mattan Torah as a parallel to Bikkurim, but as a substitute for it, resulting from the attenuation of the immediacy of Bikkurim. This ceremony is not likely to be eliminated as the historic-religious motif of Shavuot assumes greater importance among some of the kibbutzim; both themes will probably be given ritual representation, but the agricultural motif of Shavuot will find in Sukkot another outlet for symbolization.

A number of themes appear during the week-long holiday of Sukkot. All of them are given concrete expression in the festivities at Ramat Yohanan, along with the addition of a new motif. Sukkot as the Festival of Booths is celebrated on the first evening of the festival, and the entire kibbutz eats its evening meal in a huge Sukkah built parallel to the dining room. A Sukkah of the size that will seat close to 600 people requires close to a week's work to construct. Before the meal a short ceremony is held, based upon the customary round of readings, dances, and songs for the holiday. After the meal the dancing begins, lasting until the late hours of the night. During the intermediate days of the holiday, there are no special ceremonies or programs, but on the last day of Sukkot the kibbutz conducts a ceremony that includes three themes of the Sukkot season.

In recent years, a water festival—Hag ha-Mayim—is held on the last day of the holiday, and includes the Festival of Ingathering and a passing salute to Simhat Torah—Rejoicing in the Torah. The Water Festival takes place in and around the illuminated swimming pool, which has had special jets installed for producing fountainlike sprays of water. Floating platforms are constructed, serving as stages for the dancers and readers. Members and their guests spread blankets on the lawns surrounding the pool.

The ceremony itself revolves around the two major themes of Water and Ingathering. Sukkot signals the end of the dry season and the beginning of the late autumn and winter rains upon which Israel's agriculture is completely dependent. The Water Festival is a kibbutz version of two practices of traditional Judaism—one retained today in the synagogue, the other having disappeared with the destruction of the Temple. In the synagogue services for the last day of Sukkot, the prayer for rain was introduced into the Amidah and is repeated until Passover, when it is replaced by prayers for dew until the next Sukkot. While the Temple stood, there was a ceremony for rainfall on each day of the festival. Known as the Water Libation *(Nissuakh ha-Mayim)*, it was performed by a priest who was presented with a golden flagon of water from the neighboring pool of Siloam. The water was then poured into a silver container, whose spout was trained upon the altar. In a country such as Israel, with limited water resources, the water festival had a direct immediacy and significance. Although the kibbutz could not possibly subscribe to the magical intent of the ancient Water Libation ceremony, its own contemporary ceremony, with jets of water spilling upon the surface of the pool, stirs the primal consciousness of man's dependence upon natural forces.

The Festival of Ingathering was represented through exhibitions of the produce of each major agricultural branch of the kibbutz. In addition to the display of agricultural yields and dairy and poultry products, Ramat Yohanan included in its Ingathering an exhibition of the latest output of its prospering plastics factory, Palram. The inclusion of an industrial plant among exhibitions generally devoted to agriculture is an interesting innovation, an unspoken prayer not only for good rains, in season, but also for economic stability, heavy orders, and plant expansion. The introduction of an industrial component into Sukkot as the Festival of Ingathering has added a uniquely contemporary dimension to the holiday.

In many kibbutz holidays the children are featured in the ceremonies. On the last day of Sukkot, traditional Simhat Torah flags were given to them in their kindergartens and children's homes. At the very end of the evening, before the smaller children were taken off to sleep, the youngsters marched around the pool waving their flags. This was intended to suggest the traditional *hakafot* of Simhat Torah.

Some local customs worthy of mention are from Ein Shemer and Bet ha-Shittah. In the former kibbutz, part of Sukkot was dedicated to a literary ingathering. In other words, members of the kibbutz who have written stories, poems, or articles, as yet unpublished, have their works read on this holiday. In the latter kibbutz, the traditional *arba'at haminim*—palm branch, citron, myrtle, and willow—are distributed to every family with the addition of a fifth plant—a sabra, the prickly pear of the cactus plant. This adds a contemporary touch, since the sabra had become symbolic of the character of the modern Israeli. It is also consonant with midrashic explanations of the four traditional varieties, which have often been homiletically interpreted as representations of physiological and character traits. The palm branch, for example, is treated as a symbol of backbone. So the sabra has become the character symbol of Israeli-born youth—tough and prickly on the outside, soft, tender, and sweet at the core.

The pioneers of the Water Festival were two kibbutzim in the

Jordan Valley, Massada and Sha'ar ha-Golan. In the collection of Sukkot ceremonies published by the Inter-Kibbutz Festival Committee, the form of observance and the thought underlying the festival was described by a member of Massada.

> As we approach preparation for the holiday we see before us a way to integrate past tradition with the setting of our contemporary life.... This program may be executed only beside a pool of water such as a swimming pool, reservoir, fish pond, lake or stream.... We sought to commemorate in this ceremony portions of the ancient ceremony. According to the *aggadah*, the ceremony was replete with torch processions, song and dance. Therefore, we open the ceremony with a trumpet blast followed by a crossing of the water with torches and the lighting of a large beacon. The holiday is declared and rows of torches move in the direction of the beacon towards a special arch to receive the "high priest," who arrives accompanied by a procession of dancers, singers, musicians and torch bearers. In his hands are two jars for water and wine. He then performs the Water Libation ceremony. The ceremony concludes with a torch dance performed by one dancer. According to the *aggadah*, Rabban Gamliel would juggle burning torches. The ceremony concludes with the "high priest" and his retinue entering a boat decorated with flowers and greenery and crossing the pool.[91]

Of the different themes of Sukkot, the Water Festival has become the major one at Ramat Yohanan and sets the mood of the holiday even more than the giant Sukkah constructed for the evening meal of the first day. The evening hour and the setting—the abundant use of flowers and fruits for decoration, the colorfully lit surroundings, the vivacious dancing of the young people, the readings from biblical and other ancient Jewish literature, all culminating in fountains of wind-blown water spraying over the pool and dousing the onlookers—contribute to the formation of a happy and joyous holiday spirit difficult to duplicate on any other festival. As a "new" holiday, the Water Festival restores some of the sparkle Sukkot had during Second Temple days, when it was among the most beautiful of Jewish festivals. It is premature to determine whether this ceremony will eventually become a kibbutz tradition, but the kibbutz Water Festival has certainly restored some of the luster to a ceremony of which it was said: "He who has not witnessed Simhat Bet ha-Shoevah has not seen festivity."

## Hanukkah

> Hanukkah is observed for eight days, beginning with the twenty-fifth day of the month of Kislev. It is not one of the great Jewish festivals and bears no aura of sanctity. No special ceremonials have been built around it.[92]

This remark appears at the beginning of the chapter on Hanukkah in Haim Schauss's work, *The Jewish Festivals*. After historical presentations and analysis, he concludes his chapter with statements that will serve as the guideline for this section:

> With the spread of the Zionist sentiment the importance of Hanukkah increased in Jewish life. The close of the past century and the beginning of this century saw a new epoch in the history of Hanukkah. The festival emerged from the mistiness in which it had been obscured for two thousand years, during which it existed as a semi-holiday. . . . It is observed now also in those Jewish circles where the religious festivals play an important role. Hanukkah is rapidly becoming one of the greatest of Jewish festivals.[93]

Published in 1938, ten years before the creation of the State of Israel and one year before the outbreak of World War II, Schauss's book prophetically grasped the development of Hanukkah into a major festival. Increase in Zionist sentiment is behind the popularity of Hanukkah, a holiday renewed not only by the kibbutz movement, but by the entire Jewish community of Israel. Hanukkah and Purim, with a low degree of religiosity and a high degree of folk and carnival spirit, have become major holidays in Israel. In traditional Judaism both these holidays have been considered appropriate for children, but hardly worth the serious consideration of adults. While children still retain a significant part in Hanukkah celebrations, adults play the major role because the message of the day has a direct bearing upon the life and past experience of the adult community. The Jewish community, both in pre–World War II and in pre-State days, was locked in a struggle against foreign domination that made its identification with Hanukkah understandable. The question posed by traditional Judaism—Why Hanukkah?—found ready answers.

Traditional Judaism, which has long been ambivalent about Hanukkah (Judah the Prince, the redactor of the Mishnah, would have eliminated it had he the power to do so), answered the question "Why Hanukkah?" by ascribing the day's significance to a miracle. Among miracles, that of Hanukkah is relatively minor compared to the miracle of the Exodus. The burning of candles for eight days lacks the metaphysical and historical dimension of the Passover miracles. In any event the holiday had a minor status, so that any reevaluation of the historical reality of the supposed miraculous events would have little effect on its relevance for many Jews.

It is not a coincidence that the official symbol of the State of Israel is the candelabrum of the ancient Temple of Jerusalem. The heroism of the Maccabees and their determination physically to resist their enemies has always been a guiding light to Israel. For most Israelis the answer to "Why Hanukkah?" is as clear as the lights of the candles lit on that holiday all over the country.

The revival of Hanukkah began outside of Israel, in the Hebrew day schools of Eastern Europe at the beginning of the twentieth century. Songs, plays, and stories were written in honor of the rediscovered national holiday. It was in Israel, however, that Hanukkah came into its own, as educational bodies and communal institutions nurtured it by instituting new ceremonies, such as torch races and a mass pilgrimage to the grave of the Hasmoneans in their home village of Modi'in. A Hanukkah menorah is often prominently placed on the roof of public institutions or the tallest building of a kibbutz, usually its silo.

Hanukkah has by now become firmly established as a national holiday of Israel. A large menorah has been installed on the roof of the Knesset building in Jerusalem, where it is lit every evening of the festival with the number of lights corresponding to the number of days that the holiday has progressed. Aside from this official notice of the day and celebrations held in schools, there is no ceremony for any of the adult community seeking some manner of observance. Families light Hanukkah candles in their homes or give gifts to their children. This is the extent of Hanukkah celebrations in urban Israel—with the addition of private parties that generally bear little relation to the day, but are rather opportunities for a social get-together.

The kibbutz, however, has ideal conditions for celebrating national and folk holidays, and Hanukkah in the kibbutz overflows with social and ceremonial activities. Generally following the theory that a contemporary Hanukkah should be constituted of historical, folkloristic, and socializing elements, many kibbutzim have created a variety of activities for most of the eight days of the holiday. Hanukkah is rich in motifs that can be ceremonially introduced without any danger of clashing with kibbutz values, as illustrated by M. Shelem's arrangement of the underlying principles of the holiday.

(a) The principle of folk heroism, the struggle for national liberation. The victory of the spirit of the few over the numerical strength of the many—a motif which was reinforced through events of our day.
(b) The principle of the symbolism of light—the light of heroism and of belief.
(c) The social principle of folk gaiety, entertainment and mirth.[94]

The symbol of light is made very tangible and plays a central role in kibbutz celebrations. Candles are lit in the homes, the communal dining room, on the menorah on top of the granary, and in lantern processions led by the children. Ramat Yohanan follows the School of Shammai, lighting all eight candles at once on the first evening of the holiday, when its major ceremony is held. Each candle is made symbolically representative of a significant value in the life of the kibbutz and of the Jewish people, and is dedicated to that value. During the candle lighting Hanukkah songs are sung by the choir or the community. The different kibbutz movements may attach values to the candles in close harmony with their own ideological stance, and meanings and symbolism may change somewhat every few years, as new circumstances warrant it. After the Six-Day War, for example, the light of a united Jerusalem made its appearance.

The candle-lighting rituals disclose the paucity of traditional material available for ceremonial use of Hanukkah. Except for the hymn "Rock of Ages," the musical accompaniment to Hanukkah is of relatively recent, non-Orthodox origin. Even Handel has been recruited, for one of his melodies from the oratorio *Judas Maccabeus* has become a popular addition to the Hanukkah repertoire. Because of Hanukkah's semi-holiday status and the ambivalent relationship traditional Jewry had toward it, the kibbutz was forced to use modern Hebrew literary material for its ceremonies. The customary biblical reading was replaced by a noncanonical source. In this instance the apocryphal Book of Maccabees provided the verses needed for furnishing historical legitimization. While the use of a selection from the Book of Maccabees for Hanukkah ceremonies hardly canonizes the apocryphal work, it does succeed in reinstating this book, previously lost to the Jewish people, into a rank more befitting its historical importance.

Manifold meanings are attached to the eight candles of the candelabrum. Examples from two kibbutz movements, the Ihud and Ha-Kibbutz ha-Artzi, should provide an insight to the approach of kibbutzim in these movements to the celebration of the festival. In Yizrael of the Ihud, their candles were at one time given the following meanings: the light of the Maccabees, the light of Massada (the last fortress to hold out against the Romans in the great revolt of 66–70 CE), the light of the Holocaust and the Rebellion (the reference is to the ghetto rebellions against the Germans during World War II, particularly the Warsaw Ghetto uprising), the light of the revival of the State, the light of labor, the light of faith, the light of ingathering of the exiles, the light of the Sinai victory.

In a weekly bulletin of Ha-Kibbutz ha-Artzi, *Ha-Shavua*, the following suggestions were made for kibbutzim seeking authentic symbolism: the light of the Maccabees, the light of Shomer (a small Jewish self-defense force in Israel of the pre– and post–World War I period), the light of the reclaimers of the valley (the Yizrael Valley, one of the first areas to be extensively settled by kibbutzim), the light of the Histadrut, the light of the Haganah, Palmah, and the Israeli army, the light of the kibbutz, the light of the new immigrant, the light of the generations of children. While there is a certain amount of overlapping between the two ceremonies cited, the symbolisms of Ha-Kibbutz ha-Artzi are almost consistently contemporary. By being persistently up to date the symbolisms used by Ha-Kibbutz ha-Artzi do not repeat or duplicate themes that appear in other holidays as well. Hanukkah, in other words, was a relatively empty barrel, so that pouring new wine into it hardly necessitated emptying much old. The choice of symbolism by Ha-Kibbutz ha-Artzi is consistent with their image of the contemporary Jewish holiday—a day dedicated to the ceremonial embodiment of the national and social values of the Jewish people.

After all eight candles were lit on the first evening of the holiday, Ramat Yohanan changed the ritual of the House of Hillel by emptying the candelabrum and adding a new candle on each of the eight evenings. A common custom is to rotate the lighting, with a different school class performing the ceremony on the successive evenings. After the serious symbolism of the first evening, folk gaiety and entertainment occupy most of the remaining days of the holiday. Few kibbutzim can afford to have a special program for each evening, but most succeed in organizing at least a few. At Ramat

Yohanan in 1970, the first Friday night of the eight-day period was set aside for a party. A menorah-making competition was held, and there were games and contests, and an intimate and joyous atmosphere. Traditional potato pancakes were in abundance. A few days were set aside for a film festival—in this instance, of works by Ingmar Bergman. A number of members were unhappy about the choice of films—gloomy and depressingly inappropriate to the joyous festival. That particular Hanukkah week's program should not be considered typical. Closer in spirit to Hanukkah was an evening set aside for members to recall and retell tales of courage and valor they had witnessed. These stories were then collected, edited, and eventually published as a booklet. The second theme, light, was treated literally. Members were asked to recall stories about light, and a collection was published by the kibbutz. Of all the holidays continuing for at least a week—Passover, Sukkot, and Hanukkah—it is the last that generally has the fullest round of activities and programs. This is particularly puzzling in view of the relative absence of forms for celebration. Despite having no tradition to draw upon, this holiday nevertheless took firm root.

## *Purim*

> Purim is . . . in every way a pure folk festival.
> —Theodor Gaster

As a purely folk festival, observed in the kibbutz from its earliest days, Purim would seem made to order for this society. Indeed, no doubts were ever raised about the necessity for celebrating Purim year after year. In the kibbutz literature on holidays there is none of the hesitation and bewilderment with regard to Purim that is so common in the approach to many other holidays. Strictly a joyous and jubilant festival, it would seem that there could be little cause for any uncertainty on the nature of this day. However, even Purim has come under the criticism of a number of *Vatikim*, who believe that the holiday has become debased.

Most of the *Vatikim* recall that in Eastern European Orthodox society Purim was not considered a holiday deserving of the attention of a thoughtful adult. It was believed to be solely a children's holiday. Even the synagogue was permitted to become a center for the raucous noisemaking of the children when the Book of Esther was read during services. Despite all the merrymaking, however, Purim did contain the hint of a serious message of deliverance from the evil plots and designs of an enemy of the Jewish people. Purim, however, is not the only holiday to bear this message, and when it is compared with the two holidays of similar import, Passover and Hanukkah, it loses its luster.

Now recognized as completely unhistorical, the Book of Esther inevitably suffers when contrasted with the nobility and heroism of the characters who figure in Passover and Hanukkah. This probably accounts for the discredit into which the Book of Esther has fallen in the kibbutz, where it was not considered as a worthy example of the Jewish spirit. In the kibbutz Purim, therefore, the Book of Esther appears only as a background for parodies or satirical sketches. In contrast, the Book of Ruth, sometimes dramatized during Shavuot, has been treated with utmost respect and regard.

Being fundamentally earnest people who also knew the art of rejoicing, the *Vatikim* sought for a way to inject some serious content into the festive Purim spirit. In this search the kibbutz was assisted by the city of Tel Aviv, the originator of the famous Adloyada Parade. The name given to the parade is derived from a Purim folk saying—that a man should drink enough wine or alcoholic beverages on Purim *adloyada* (until he does not know) i.e., confuses "blessed is Mordecai and cursed is Haman." Here is one of the few instances when the kibbutz has been influenced by an urban form of celebration. The Tel Aviv municipality spent large sums to build floats and decorations for the parade, manned by the high school youth of the city who invested heavily in the time and effort necessary for its success. Jerusalem held a smaller version. In the 1960s the Adloyada was canceled and has yet to be substantially revived.

While at its peak, the Tel Aviv Purim carnival was distinguished by more than merriment. The choice of subjects for the floats was also dictated by serious interests. The themes were biblical or political and often included satirical representations of public figures. This punctuation of Purim with thoughtful themes influenced the kibbutz to include "heavy" motifs in the light tone of the holiday. For instance, during the British Mandate period, when refugees were being illegally smuggled into the country, the theme of a Purim masquerade party at Ramat Yohanan was a refugee ship. The Purim theme of rescue and deliverance made its appearance, detached from the Book of Esther but linked to the immediate burdens carried by the kibbutz community, for in those days the kibbutz often served as a haven for refugees who successfully slipped through the British net.

Little remains today of that earnest Purim spirit. Only rarely do themes appear that continue in the tradition of intermingling joy with serious intent. In the opinion of some *Vatikim* the move toward a completely carnival spirit deprives Purim of whatever tie it might retain with the traditional past. According to this view, Purim in the kibbutz no longer has anything in common with the Purim of tradition. Not all *Vatikim* are as critical. The second and third generations are responsible for Purim celebrations—and some parents are much more indulgent than others. Each generation should be permitted its own mode of expression, said one *Vatik*. Others come down hard on the young people, castigating them for turning Purim into a masquerade party, with not one spiritually redeeming feature. Perhaps this is an unreasonable demand to make. One holiday, such as Purim, could be set aside solely for complete relief from the momentous and the meaningful, and be devoted to release and relaxation.

At Ramat Yohanan the exciting and vibrant Purim party of 1971 was one of the best that anyone can remember. It was designed and executed by the younger generation, and enormous efforts were invested in planning and decoration. The dining room was transformed into a richly colorful hall, swarming with masquerade costumes of every description. The kibbutz keeps a small storehouse with costumes and cloth for this purpose. That particular year there were three themes—the hippie pad, the English bar, and hasidic villages—held in three different buildings and staffed by a small group of appropriately dressed members who served the many visitors. Later in the evening, everyone congregated in the dining room for additional skits and performances. The hasidic village was run mostly by elderly members who had memories of hasidism and possessed a large repertoire of hasidic melodies and dances. Deference was thereby paid to the traditional past.

Perhaps more of the Jewish folkloristic past could have been added, especially satires based on the Book of Esther. What was particularly impressive was the energy and drive shown by the young people in preparing for the holiday. The question is whether this same drive could be channeled into other festivals as well and in particular those with a somewhat more sober content.

## *Passover*

Of all the festivals, Passover most closely epitomizes the kibbutz approach to the Jewish holidays. The traffic to kibbutzim on the day before Passover is heavy, as thousands of invited guests stream out of the cities to participate in the kibbutz Sedarim, packing kibbutz dining rooms throughout the country with hundreds and, in some cases, over a thousand people. The preparation and effort invested in such a huge communal Seder are enormous, involving dozens of individuals occupied with the organization of the various components—culinary, artistic, ceremonial. In some kibbutzim a number of places are kept open for tourists or new immigrants, whose introduction to the Israeli style of life could find no better means.

As in almost every instance of kibbutz holiday practice, the Seder as known today is a relatively recent innovation. Only in the early 1930s did kibbutzim begin producing the first of the many Haggadot that have made their Seder the unique institution it has become today. Before the advent of this period of creativity the kibbutz Seder was a parody of the traditional ceremony. At this stage in kibbutz development little mention is made of the playfulness of those early years, perhaps because the *Vatikim* may be somewhat ashamed of their youthful shallowness. In the 1970s, however, parody of the Seder would be unacceptable, for it has become, especially in the eyes of the former parodists, a serious ceremony.

This radical reversion of the Seder is a paradigm of the social and spiritual changes the kibbutz has undergone in the short yet intense period of its existence. Passover is, in effect, the only kibbutz holiday that sank such deep roots that it has become a tradition with a recognizable form repeated year after year with few changes. By now the three major federations have produced Haggadot of their own to be used by their member kibbutzim. These Haggadot have not undergone any major revisions in recent years, and represent the essence of the kibbutz position on Passover.

The Passover holiday has become focal to kibbutz life. The effort put into a proper observance of the day exceeds that invested in any other festival. Passover has in effect succeeded where other holidays have faltered or have not yet successfully developed the stability desired by their re-creators. The present position of dominance held by Passover can be traced to a number of factors, among them the simple chronological fact that it was the first festival to be rejuvenated by the kibbutz.

Passover was a festival that came from Europe to Israel with a stock of pleasant, warm, and rich memories. Although there was a general revolt against traditional holidays among the *Vatikim*, Passover apparently suffered least from their rejection of the past.

Childhood and adolescent experiences of the Seder seem to have been sufficiently rewarding to protect this holiday from the repudiation other holidays experienced. Yet, despite its being the first holiday to reappear on the kibbutz scene, and despite the depth to which it penetrated the consciousness of the *Vatikim*, Passover was not destined to immediate and complete acceptance into kibbutz society. With all their affection for and attachment to the traditional Passover Seder, the *Vatikim* were unable to enact it as did their parents. This is evidenced by the creation of hundreds of kibbutz Haggadot. They had to go through a process of confrontation with the traditional Haggadah that was to result in the fairly definitive versions of kibbutz Haggadot in use today.

In their Eastern European countries of origin the *Vatikim* had celebrated Passover while there was still some snow on the ground and nature had not fully revived from its winter doldrums, yet they knew that the holiday went together with the glorious spring of Eretz Yisrael, where prayers for dew had a point of contact with the realities of nature. "Dew" is no longer a pious formula detached from real life, but an actual event. The rapid and effective adoption of Passover as the first major kibbutz holiday would have been less successful were its major themes not in keeping with the circumstances of life in kibbutz society and in the Jewish community at large. For despite agreeable memories of childhood or the stimulation of their new natural surroundings, the *Vatikim* could not have sat at a Seder without some commitment to the basic motif of Passover—as they reinterpreted it.

The Passover Haggadah relates the story of the Exodus from Egypt and the redemption of the Jewish people as a metahistorical event guided throughout by God's will and purpose. The release from slavery and the recovery of freedom, while natural events, were interpreted as supernaturally directed. The redemption from slavery was not merely a release from bondage, but was aimed at leading this unique and chosen people to the foot of Mount Sinai. From that point they were to enter a land promised to them by God, a holy land. This episode in the life of the Jewish people bears a centrality that even the most obdurate heretic could not deny, but he could deny that the Exodus was one of God's miracles. And this is precisely what the kibbutz Haggadot state. The Jewish people gained their freedom, but not through dependence on God's miracles. In the latest Haggadot of the Ihud and Ha-Kibbutz ha-Me'uhad there appears a Midrash, not found in the traditional Haggadah, that characterizes their vision of a Jewish people released not only from Egyptian bondage, but from a passive bondage and dependence upon God's miraculous intervention in human affairs.

> When Israel was standing at the water's edge the tribes were quarreling with each other. One said I will first descend into the sea and another said I will first descend into the sea. The tribe of Benjamin jumped forward and descended into the sea. Then the princes of Judah stoned them. Rav Yehudah said: "This is not how it happened, but instead one said: I am not going to descend into the sea, and another said: I am not going to descend into the sea. Nahshon Ben Amidav jumped forward and was the first to descend into the seas."[95]

This Midrash was well chosen for the kibbutz Haggadah, for it mirrors a kibbutz self-image. They see themselves as the modern descendants of Nahshon Ben Amidav (in modern Hebrew *nahshoni* means "bold, daring"), for they were the first to earn their freedom by boldly leaping into the barren sea of Israel during the second and third decades of this century, while most Jews were apathetic to the Zionist enterprise. The religious message of the Midrash—that God's miraculous splitting of the Red Sea could only have come about after human will and effort had made it possible—could be easily overlooked, and the Midrash reinterpreted to accommodate the *Weltanschauung* of the editors of the kibbutz Haggadah. As this Midrash indicates, the historical circumstances of the Jewish people and of the early Zionist pioneers in the twentieth century were sufficiently parallel to the ancient Exodus that it is no wonder Passover was the first holiday to be revived in the kibbutz. The contemporary state and predicament of Jewish history gave Passover a special urgency. The values of freedom and of national redemption demanded expression. Thus the kibbutz movement began producing and editing its hundreds of Haggadot and composing music for them, thereby successfully instituting Passover as its central holiday.

Today few kibbutzim print their own Haggadah, relying instead on the official version produced by their respective movement. But there has been no basic change in orientation. Whether in the early years of that creative outburst when the kibbutz Haggadot were artistically and graphically simple productions, or in the aesthetically attractive Haggadot of today, the message remains the same—freedom was achieved by natural means and not through supernatural redemption. There was no difficulty in reinterpreting Passover in this context since freedom is a major value of kibbutz life, and no contradiction existed between the significant values of Passover and focal values of kibbutz culture.

The contemporary Haggadot of the three movements have become somewhat stabilized. In this process, some of the material that appeared in the early Haggadot simply fell into disuse. Certain material on the subject of the Exodus taken from modern Hebrew literature lost out to material from traditional sources. In other words, the potency of the classics outweighed and overpowered contemporary creations. In the Haggadot of the Ihud and Ha-Kibbutz ha-Me'uhad only Bialik's poetry retains the place it once held jointly in kibbutz Haggadot with the work of other modern Hebrew poets. Not only the grandeur of his poetry explains his staying power, but also the special relationship between Bialik and many of the Vatikim indicated in earlier sections of this work.

During the initial period of its rejuvenation, kibbutz Haggadot served as the repository of themes that had no echo in the traditional Haggadah. Whatever events occurred in the Jewish world that seemed appropriate to Passover would be noted in kibbutz Haggadot. The Arab riots of the 1930s, the sudden expansion of border kibbutzim prior to World War II, the first news of the Holocaust, the grim realization of the fate of European Jewry, the struggle for independence, the rise of the Jewish state—all these themes appeared in Haggadot close to the time of their occurrence. Passover functioned as a ceremonial outlet by means of which the kibbutz members identified themselves with the struggle of their people for freedom.

After the establishment of the State of Israel many of the pre-state themes fell by the wayside. Israel's Independence Day was established in proximity to the Day of the Holocaust as well as a Memorial Day for soldiers and civilians who fell in Israel's struggle for freedom and independence. These new holidays and days of memorial emptied the kibbutz Passover of its topical commentary and content, confronting the editors of Haggadot with a new problem—how to restore the timelessness of Passover without returning to the form of the traditional Haggadah.

In 1952, the Ihud convened a conference of Haggadah editors. The process described above was already beginning, and the editors admitted their bewilderment.

> In our confusion we are digging through the dust of remote generations. Perhaps out of the depths there will arise a clear, authentic holiday, a custom that speaks to the heart, a refreshed form.[96]

As one of the participants so aptly stated, the time had arrived to produce Haggadot that express the beliefs and moral structure of their society. These beliefs could be gathered from meetings of editors who not only exchanged opinions but compared the many Haggadot produced by different kibbutzim over the years. To no one's surprise, the differences were minor, justifying the eventual production of unified Haggadot for each movement that would summarize the general consensus of the kibbutzim scattered throughout the country.

What implications emerged from the many Haggadot of the kibbutz movements? What themes of affirmation and rejection dominate their official Haggadot? Because God's supernatural attributes are denied, entire sections of the traditional Haggadah offering praise to God, as well as the grace after meals, have been omitted. However, not all references to God were struck out, as was done in the early days of the kibbutz movement. Psalms and well-loved songs such as "Who Knows One?" from the traditional Haggadah are read and sung at the table. Biblical sections, particularly from the Book of Exodus, are woven together to form a narrative outline of the Exodus from Egypt. Mention of God in the kibbutz Haggadah is inevitable, but at no point is He praised or offered thanksgiving.

The editors of the kibbutz Haggadot are unwilling to return to the traditional form because they do not believe that traditional formulas of blessing or prayers of praise and thanksgiving can be methaphorically reinterpreted. Honesty and integrity require the omission of such sections. But they do not think it is hypocritical to read biblical sections or sing songs at the table that testify to the dominantly religious coloration of Jewish culture. The folkloristic bias of *Vatikim* of Eastern European origin allows them to overlook the contents of a section in the Haggadah that has become a folksong. Once the Jewish people have sanctified a selection, it is admitted into the kibbutz Passover canon. The best example is "V'he Sheh Amdah," whose verses appear to be in contradiction to their principle of omitting all reference to supernatural miracles.

> This is the promise which has stood by our forefathers and stands by us. For neither once, nor twice, nor three times was our destruction planned; in every generation they rise against us, and in every generation God delivers us from their hands.[97]

Its inclusion in the Haggadah of the Ihud and Ha-Kibbutz ha-

Me'uhad is explained as a concession to the folk origin of its accompanying melody. However, the grace after meals could not be consistently included even if there were many folk melodies surrounding it. The origin of this fine distinction could perhaps be traced not only to the mystic belief of some Eastern European Jews in the sanctity of the creative products of the Jewish people, but also to an anti-rabbinical bias, attributing to the rabbinical class the imposition of set and rigid forms that subdued the free spirit of creativity inherent in the people.

The major aim of the Haggadah of whatever persuasion is to relate the story of the Exodus from Egypt. The kibbutz feels, however, that its approach is an improvement on the traditional version, because it has made the retelling of the Exodus the focus of its Haggadot. By devaluing God's role in the Exodus, the figure of Moses appears as leader of the people. The puzzling omission of Moses from the traditional Haggadah has been rectified by the inclusion of narratively connected biblical verses portraying Moses as a shepherd, as the representative of his people confronting Pharaoh, and at the head of the "mixed multitude" leaving Egypt. There is no hint of hero worship in the kibbutz Haggadot, and although Moses' character can barely be developed in the short space of a Haggadah, at no point is he deified.

Another major theme is the coming of spring. Of this there is no trace whatever in the traditional Haggadah. In the kibbutz Haggadot spring serves as a short opening motif before giving way to the narration of the Exodus. Selections from the Song of Songs interweave with selections from medieval Hebrew poetry on the cessation of the winter rains and the beginning of dew. The first Haggadot to introduce this motif used the works of modern Hebrew writers, but as in the case with the recounting of Exodus, classical and ancient texts, such as the Song of Songs, outweighed and outshone modern writers. As a result, the opening pages of kibbutz Haggadot have been swept clean of twentieth-century Hebrew writers, except for the Haggadah of Ha-Kibbutz ha-Artzi, which retains one poem, on dew, by Abraham Shlonsky.

A final theme, only barely hinted at in the traditional text but expanded in the kibbutz Haggadah, is the ingathering of the exiles. The concluding cry of the Seder—"Next year in Jerusalem!"—has been considerably enlarged by interposing poems by Yehuda Ha-Levi and selections from Amos and Isaiah, all centering on the return of the Jewish people to their ancestral land.

This brief summary of the structure and sources of the kibbutz Haggadah points at the purpose motivating the editors, who were searching for an alternative mode of observing Passover outside the synagogue. Yet, as even the most cursory perusal of a kibbutz Haggadah will indicate, they kept close to Jewish sources, skillfully weaving them into a new Haggadah by adhering to the central historical theme of redemption from slavery, while introducing new motifs firmly constructed on a solid underpinning of traditional sources.

In the course of the development of the kibbutz Haggadot the editors were in general agreement on the underlying theological approach and on the basic structure. There were a few points, however, that always remained controversial—the four questions, and the few verses beginning "Pour out your wrath upon the nations." The latter problem was solved in the same way by Ha-Kibbutz ha-Artzi and Ha-Kibbutz ha-Me'uhad—by simply eliminating the offending section, although not without a measure of ambivalence. The Ihud retains this verse in its Haggadah, but during the Seder at Ramat Yohanan it is skipped, for the approach of the Ihud is that no kibbutz is obligated to read the verses, but can follow its own practice.

The Ihud shows a similar attitude toward the four cups, though in a reverse direction. Because many kibbutzim use different symbolisms for the four cups the editors decided to eliminate them altogether from the Ihud Haggadah, with each kibbutz using the ceremony it considers best. Consideration for local custom is physically evident in the Ihud Haggadah, which has three punched holes on the back edge for the convenience of kibbutzim that wish to insert their own versions of a particular ceremony, such as the four cups. In the Haggadah of Ha-Kibbutz ha-Me'uhad the four cups are drunk as symbols of major themes within the Haggadah itself. The cups are named, in the order of their sequence, the cup of spring, the cup of freedom, the cup of independence, and the cup of ingathering of the exiles. Ha-Kibbutz ha-Artzi has the cup of deliverance, the cup of redemption, the cup of consolation, and the cup of blessing for the children. This kibbutz movement, despite its former political radicalism, proved conservative indeed in editing its Haggadah, which still retains more traces of the pre- and early-State years than do the other kibbutz Haggadot. The song of the partisans and references to the Holocaust are still retained, even though Memorial Day and the Day of the Holocaust proclaimed by the state are completely dedicated to these themes. There are also more quotations from modern Hebrew poets in their Haggadah. The four questions, which are completely traditional in the Haggadot of the other movements, have a uniquely kibbutz formula in the Haggadah of Ha-Kibbutz ha-Artzi.

> On all other nights we eat both leavened bread and matzot
> On this night only matzot
> On all other nights children and parents eat separately
> On this night we eat together
> On all other nights we eat hastily
> On this night we eat leisurely and keep vigil
> On all other nights we talk of mundane matters
> On this night we relate the full story of the Exodus from Egypt.[98]

The Haggadot of the other movements reinstituted the fully traditional questions only after the 1960s. Up to 1965 the Ihud had three traditional questions and a fourth of their own invention: "On other nights we speak of mundane matters but on this night we all speak of the oppression of our people and their redemption." Ha-Kibbutz ha-Me'uhad had only presented the question, but provided no answers—until 1961, when the traditional formula was fully included. So except for Ha-Kibbutz ha-Artzi, the kibbutz federations have witnessed, in the lifetime of most of their founders, a complete turnabout in their relationship to the four questions. When kibbutz Haggadot first appeared, their editors considered the traditional questions to be completely pointless, favoring questions that they considered significant and relevant, thereby deserving serious and considered replies.

On the eve of World War II the four questions were used as a vehicle for summing up the dominant atmosphere and spirit of that tense period, when Nazi persecutions moved into high gear, Arab riots and guerrilla warfare were a constant threat, new kibbutz settlements of the "wall and tower" type had been established in key strategic points, illegal immigration was just beginning, and the Jewish community was apprehensive about the outbreak of global war. In the 1939 Haggadah of Kibbutz Tel Yosef there appeared an appropriate series of questions and answers.

> How are these days different from all other days? On all other days there is both an aspiration for peace and for war in the world. In these days the entire world is moving towards war. On all other days some of the tribes of Israel live peacefully while

others are persecuted. In these days every tribe is being destroyed. During all the years of building the homeland we were acquainted with periods of expansion and of restrictive decrees. In these days they seek to uproot everything. What will be the answer to all our enemies and those who would banish us?[99]

After the founding of the State of Israel, many Haggadot included the question appearing in the Ein Harod 1950 Haggadah: "How is this night different this year? We are free men in the State of Israel and the gates are open to those who are returning from exile."

The period of revision of the four questions is generally over for the kibbutz. Today children recite or chant the same series of questions repeated by Jewish children all over the world. Formerly, the serious type of topical questions had been asked by an adolescent or a young man, and they demanded a solemn and weighty reply. No longer. The four questions have once more become the province of small children. The charm of children's voices proved more festive than the earnest speeches that topical questions once provoked. Today, second and third graders sing the four questions in the traditional melody and the reply is sung by the entire community, in unison. This made a powerful impression during the Seder at Ramat Yohanan, as the squeaky voices of some twenty children were responded to by the rich swell of several hundred adult voices.

Participation in a kibbutz Seder, despite the inconveniences of lukewarm food and crowded conditions, substantiates the remark of a *Vatik* that "Passover in a kibbutz is steeped in the light and spirit of Judaism." The food is tasty, but not of the highest standard, so there could be no suspicion that culinary motivations are predominant. David Maletz, whose commitment to the kibbutz has always been tempered by blunt criticism of its failings, writes of his astonishment at the amount of labor and expense put into a kibbutz Seder. In no case can this be explained away merely as preparation for a festive party. For days before the holiday the atmosphere in the kibbutz of "kosher for Pesach" is not too distant from what he knew in the traditional Jewish home. This bustling preparation is as integral a part of the holiday as the celebration itself. At Ramat Yohanan the preparations for Passover occupy scores of people and electrify the atmosphere in anticipation of the day itself. Gift packages of alcoholic beverages, or juice, according to choice, cakes and candies are distributed to all families. The preschool children hold their own Seder, for they are considered too small to attend the adult ceremony. The children bake their own matzot and prepare their own grape juice.

All this prepares the setting for the Seder itself, which is conducted by a series of readers, accompanied by the kibbutz choir. The entire Haggadah is finished before the serving of the meal, with traditional and modern songs coming later. Having finished eating, a number of members sit in the center of the dining room, gather a sizable crowd around them, and begin a singing marathon that lasts till midnight. There is no songbook. All the songs are sung spontaneously. Dancing follows.

More than any other holiday in the year, Passover captures the essence of kibbutz communal Judaism. The traditional Seder is a family celebration, limited to its small circle with additional guests. The kibbutz Seder is for the extended kibbutz family and, while the small nuclear families sit near each other, the Seder binds together hundreds of individuals into a communal body. The children singing the four questions have their parents, but when they ask the four questions and are answered by the entire community, they are "our children" and not only "my children." No words can convey that unique sensation.

In retrospect, the Seder is a satisfactory experience if the Haggadah is carefully followed during the ceremony. The kibbutz simplification of the traditional Haggadah makes the Exodus from Egypt clearer and more striking, while enough of the folkloristic material is retained to ensure that the Seder does not turn into a dry literary recitation.

On the evening of the day following the Seder, the Omer ceremony is performed. At one time this ceremony was practiced independently, but of late it has become an appendage to Passover. The word *omer* means "sheaf." In biblical and postbiblical times, up to the destruction of the Second Temple, the first sheaf of grain, usually barley, was brought to the Temple priest the morning after having been cut at sunset, on Passover day. Fifty days were then counted (the "counting of the Omer"), the fiftieth day being Shavuot. Once the temple no longer stood, the bringing of the Omer was discontinued but the custom of counting still remained, practiced to this day in traditional synagogues, where it is a petition for the restoration of the Temple service.

There is little difficulty understanding the reasons behind the renewal of this festival by the kibbutz. Scores of kibbutzim had adopted an Omer ceremony to deepen the attachment of the young agricultural pioneers to land and soil, reinforce the tie of the young kibbutznik to his ancient past, and strengthen his identification with the Jewish farmers of antiquity. As long as agriculture remained a significant value in the kibbutz, the Omer ceremony captured the enthusiasm of the kibbutz movement and became a unique attraction of its holiday year. In the 1970s, however, one reads of kibbutzim that have canceled the Omer or perform it with the utmost difficulty. Without the authority of tradition the Omer lacks the ancestral roots of a Jewish holiday practiced by the generations. The leap of the kibbutz back into biblical custom traversed a vacuum of close to two thousand years. The Omer might nevertheless have struck roots had farming remained focal, but even so, the technological revolution in agriculture might have destroyed one of the major sources of the Omer—a direct, unhindered, and immediate tie between the farmer and his soil. In the kibbutz ceremony shortly to be described, a scythe is wielded by the men cutting the grain. A few years ago some young people suggested that the scythe be replaced by a combine. The land no longer has a special quality—national, historical, mystic—but is an object most efficiently manipulated by a machine.

When the kibbutz Omer was at its height, one of its initiators described it thus:

> According to all the sources before us it is not only a religious ceremony but also a Hebrew spring festival, which has no nature rites but is conditioned by a way of life and customs of a people rooted in its land. Realistically and symbolically this festival fits well into the spring, the time of the first harvest and into . . . Passover as a symbol of blooming and rebirth.[100]

Omer in the kibbutz is the artistic creation of a few men who composed the words and music for the ceremony. There are today three basic versions of this ceremony—of Ein Harod, Ramat Yohanan, and Heftzi-bah—all having in common the basic ceremonial structure of songs, dances, and Bible readings. The time of performance varies. Some kibbutzim observe the Omer before the Passover Seder begins so that they may be able to wave the first sheaf during the Seder. Others wait until twilight of the first day of Passover.

At Ramat Yohanan the participants, members of the kibbutz and invited guests, gather in the center of the kibbutz before beginning the procession to the nearby field set aside for the ceremony. The younger children are dressed in simple peasant-style costumes with wreaths of flowers strung through their hair. High school youth and young adults with some talent as dancers join the procession. The boys and the men are dressed in blue shirts and black slacks, some carrying decorated scythes, while the girls and the young women dress in an affected style intended to be reminiscent of biblical times. Leading the procession is a decorated tractor pulling a wagon containing the large straw basket later to be filled with offerings of flowers and the first sheaves cut by harvesters.

The ceremony takes place on a raised platform flanked on three sides by waist-high grain. A choir and small orchestra are off to the side. As the day ends the ceremony begins with a trumpet call. Intermixed with singing, dancing, and readings, the high point arrives as a small crew of harvesters line up to begin cutting the grain with their long-handled scythes. Behind each harvester stands a woman to gather the fallen grain. Once a small patch has been cut, the harvesters with the grain in hand ascend the platform for the sheaf-waving dance. Afterwards the grain is thrown into the large basket that had meanwhile been placed in the center of the platform. This is the high point of the Omer and takes place at sunset, just as the fields begin to glow lightly with the fading colors of the day. After a brief concluding section the ceremony is over, and participants and onlookers disperse. According to printed versions of the ceremony, its conclusion calls for horseback riders and torch processions, but these were not in evidence at the Ramat Yohanan Omer of 1971.

What of the future of Omer? Has it taken root as a holiday or already become artificial? At Ramat Yohanan, three generations have participated in this ceremony, and a tradition of over thirty years exists. But there are no guarantors of the future, for the kibbutz is in a state of constant flux, and once the *Vatikim* pass off the stage, the generation that received the ceremony will probably make changes fitting to its own spirit. By the third generation fewer members of the kibbutz will be working in agriculture. Although the kibbutz is placed in a rural setting, its members have become, in a sense, urbanized, having lost the direct, almost naive relationship to nature and the soil that characterized the first years on the land. Once this attachment weakens, ceremonies glorifying the change of seasons, or nature's fecundity, have to be artificially imposed, since they do not emerge out of personal experience, as with the *Vatikim*. The Omer then becomes a vestige, though a significantly valuable one. Its continuity, even in an attenuated form, can assure some kind of connection, however tenuous, between man and the natural environment in which he lives.

Passover and the Omer in the kibbutz are instructive illustrations of the power of the past. But more than tradition is behind the persistence of Passover and the hesitation about Omer. When all is said and done, Passover is a bearer of powerful ideas and concepts, fortified and reinforced by centuries of historical experience, joined with contemporary needs and reality. The Omer, for all its artistic vitality, remains peripheral to the central questions rising out of the depths of man's soul.

## *Holocaust Day*

Holocaust Day is marked throughout Israel one week before Independence Day. Memorial ceremonies for the Jews of Europe exterminated by Nazism are conducted under national auspices, with the major ceremony held at the amphitheater of Kibbutz Lohamey ha-Getta'ot (ghetto fighters), a kibbutz founded by survivors of the Warsaw Ghetto and other ghetto uprisings against the Germans. This solemn commemoration, designated by the Knesset in keeping with Israel's role as a refuge and new homeland for survivors of the Holocaust, is chronologically connected with the outbreak of the Warsaw Ghetto, the largest of ghetto resistance movements. That doomed uprising broke out on Passover, in 1943. Emotional ties to the Jews of Europe are too powerful to permit a minor memorial addition to Passover in honor of the six million. The catastrophe that overtook Jewry rent the fabric of Jewish life throughout the world. Although superficially Jewry appears unified by the memory of the bestialities of Nazism, in actuality the Jewish world has been beset by a turmoil of emotions. The Holocaust reinforced the national instinct for survival, but it has laid open to melancholy doubt the religious constituent of Jewish identity. After Auschwitz such reaction could have been expected. The inner turbulence of Israeli Jewry has yet to surface completely on Holocaust Day, the contemporary Tisha B'Av. Serious questioning has hardly touched the surface in explaining the meaning of the Holocaust. The wounds have not yet healed, and a generation has not yet arisen that is sufficiently distant from the events to place them in any adequate perspective.

The people responsible for planning and executing a memorial ceremony for Holocaust Day have at their disposal booklets published by the Inter-Kibbutz Committee on Holidays. Unlike other days marked by the kibbutz, Holocaust Day has no unique ceremonial form in the kibbutz. The relevant material is taken from the archives of institutes dedicated to collecting, editing, and publishing the documentary source materials. The suggested ceremonies appearing in the book were not composed by members of the Inter-Kibbutz Committee, although proposals do appear for appropriate arrangement of the memorial ritual.

At Ramat Yohanan the program is held on the eve of the day. It takes place after the smaller children are put to bed. On the afternoon of that day every member finds in his mailbox a large memorial candle and a small pin with the word "remember" stamped on it. Members are asked to burn the candle in their homes and wear the pin. In the dining room photographs are hung of the Jewish ghettos of Eastern Europe, concentration camps, and other scenes that perpetuate the mournful memories. However melancholy the mood created by this pictorial evidence of Jewish suffering, a note of heroism tempers the depression. Other pictures that are included emphasize the courageous battles of the doomed ghetto fighters. Indeed, the full name of the Holocaust Day in Israel is "the Day of the Holocaust and the Revolt."

The members slowly begin to filter into the dining room for the ceremony, their voices muted and spells of silence filling the air. A stage is erected with a background depicting in abstract form the quality of life and death in the ghettos and camps. The readers are flanked by a large eternal light, whose flames shoot out into the enveloping silence of the hall. The ceremony is brief—no more than half an hour. Children participate as well, reading from the notes and diaries of their dead unknown friends and brothers who failed to reach adolescence or adulthood. It is difficult to remain calm or controlled. The evening concludes with "El Maleh Rahamim" (God of Compassion), whose tragic and dramatic chant sums up the mood and temper of the service. The charged emotional content of the ceremony has a powerful effect. The members silently leave the dining room and disperse to their rooms.

The number of younger people present is not inordinately large. Elderly people, who remember, are deeply affected by poems and readings such as "Mein shtetle brennt" (my town is going up in flames). For the native-born generation the Holocaust Day ceremonies become more problematical. Young kibbutzim in general have experienced difficulty with observance of Holocaust Day. But whatever their difficulties, the younger kibbutzim perservered with this ritual of remembrance, which apparently did have an effect on the native-born generation. When young soldiers who fought in the Six-Day War were asked where they derived the strength and courage to fight so bravely, more than a few replied that they were determined to prevent another Holocaust. The pathos of Holocaust Day had silently penetrated into a generation where it lay dormant, but ready to block the repetition of another tragedy for the Jewish people. Said a kibbutz soldier:

> The Jewish aspect of the war applied to each one of us. Something in our education has made us very conscious of this Jewish tragedy. . . . It's true people believed that we would be exterminated if we lost the war. They were afraid. We got this idea—or inherited it—from the concentration camps. It's a concrete idea for anyone who has grown up in Israel, even if he personally didn't experience Hitler's persecution, but only heard or read about it. Genocide—it's a feasible notion. There are means to do it. This is the lesson of the gas chambers.[101]

### *Israel's Independence Day*

The standard English texts on Jewish holidays and festivals—the works by Schauss and Gaster—omit Israeli Independence Day from their table of contents. For Schauss this omission is understandable, for his book was published (in the English version) in 1938. Gaster's book came out in 1952, and although he makes mention of the likelihood of the rebirth of holidays and festivals in Israel, no mention is made of the new holiday celebrating Israel's independence. The omission can be attributed to the character of this new holiday, which was declared a civic, national holiday for the citizens of the State of Israel, but was never proclaimed a Jewish religious holiday by Israel's ecclesiastical authorities. Since then Israel has experienced more wars, and an awareness of the state's existence has penetrated more deeply into the consciousness of Jews throughout the world. An Israeli Independence Day parade in New York City's Fifth Avenue is a public, mass manifestation of sentiments for Israel. The Reform movement in America has adopted Israeli Independence Day as a religious holiday, fashioning a brief service especially composed for that day, which begins with a special candle blessing. Because of the affinity Jews have for the State of Israel, its Independence Day verges on becoming a religious holiday, although the step of making such a declaration has been taken by only a few.

Outside of the Reform movement in America and Israel no organized religious group has declared this day as a religious festival of the Jewish year. In Israeli synagogues and in many synagogues in the Diaspora a prayer is said on Sabbaths and holidays for God's blessing upon the State of Israel. Only the Orthodox kibbutz movement has produced a separate prayer book for Israeli Independence Day. A number of Orthodox rabbis have raised the day to the status of a quasi holiday by permitting haircuts. (In the period of fifty days between Passover and Shavuot, which is considered a mourning period in traditional Judaism, no haircuts or marriages are permitted, except for Lag B'Omer, the thirty-third day of that span.) Israeli Independence Day occurs before Shavuot, so the few rabbis who permit haircuts have thereby quietly acquiesced to the inclusion of this civic holiday in the calendar of religious festivals. The question is whether this initial step, hesitatingly taken by only a few individuals, will eventually result in the sanctification of Independence Day in synagogue rites and rituals. In general, however, the Orthodox rabbinate has approached Independence Day with the utmost caution and apprehension.

Up to the year 1969 the major event of Independence Day was the military parade held annually in one or another of the major cities of Israel. Tel Aviv and Haifa were the sites of the parade in the majority of instances and onlookers came from all over Israel. When the military march was discontinued, Independence Day lost the major attraction it had to offer the public. But even before the parades were discontinued, there was comment on the lack of joy in the Independence Day celebrations organized and run by the large municipalities and small communities. The fabled dancing in the streets was limited to public school youth.

Only once, in 1947, when the United Nations voted in favor of partition of Palestine between Jews and Arabs, did the population spontaneously dance in the streets. When the final vote was in, not only children but also adults in pajamas—for it was nighttime in Israel when the voting took place in New York—poured out into the streets and danced for hours. This has never been repeated. Once Independence Day became institutionalized, the fervor was drained out of it, despite many attempts to inject a livelier spirit. Indeed, the press provides a yearly measure of Independence Day articles on the theme "Why doesn't the Israeli know how to rejoice?" The popular celebrations are so often not only dull and stale, but are also shrinking numerically, as more of the urban middle class retreat into their new apartments for private celebrations. Where large crowds do congregate, it is generally for mass parties or entertainment.

What of the kibbutz movement? Has it succeeded in fashioning out of Independence Day a holiday that gives even partial expression or representation to the meaning of Israel? The military parade may have raised morale or demonstrated Israel's power to her neighbors, but it could hardly signify the importance of Israel to its citizens, to the Jews of the Diaspora, or to Jewish history and thought. Because of the centrality of the yearly demonstration of military hardware, the holiday remained underdeveloped. The kibbutz movement, as a collective society, has an inherent advantage over the fragmented city. Nevertheless, it has also failed to find a satisfactory form for celebrating Independence Day. Writing in 1966, Zvi Ra'anan of Hazorea states:

> We in the kibbutz movement, who have a different social character and are a collective society bearing social values, and generally know how to fashion our holidays—we too have not yet achieved that form which fits Independence Day and which can satisfy our personal and general desires and our educational needs. . . . During an extended period Independence Day stood in the light of the direct personal experience of the generation of the [1948] war and therefore its focus was the memorial evening for the fallen soldiers, which had a tone of mourning . . . the festive speech with its pathos of "we came and we fought" and stories of "those days.". . .
>
> In addition we had a picnic or fair for children. If we are honest with ourselves we'll openly admit that we are dissatisfied with that form of the holiday.[102]

Although this description is not typical of the entire kibbutz movement (except for the picnic, which almost every kibbutz has adopted), he is justified in pointing out that the generation that fought in the 1948 War of Independence shaped the holiday, particularly in kibbutzim that supplied the majority of the troops for the Palmah, a crack unit in the 1948 war. The tendency to reminisce and relive those heroic days opened Independence Day in the kibbutz to the danger of becoming a cliquish holiday for a small coterie of war veterans. Although not denigrating the value of memorials or popular picnics and fairs, Ra'anan suggests that the core of Independence Day be a serious ceremony, that will artistically and experientially signify "the deep reflective content of the holiday." Although the kibbutz movement may not have adopted the exact themes suggested by Zvi Ra'anan, it has arrived at his conclusion. In 1971 the Inter-Kibbutz Committee on Holidays published for the first time a "Haggadah" for Israeli Independence Day, compiled on the basis of the Haggadah prepared and used for some years at Kibbutz Givat Brenner. This booklet of readings and songs is heavily laden with old-fashioned Zionism.

The production and promulgation of this Haggadah can be understood against the background of the profound impact of the establishment of the State of Israel. Arising shortly upon the conclusion of World War II, when the horrifying reality of the Holocaust was just beginning to dawn upon the Jewish people, Israel became more than the fulfillment of Zionist prophecy or a homeland for the dispossessed. Its creation came near to being a redemptive act, a second Exodus from Egypt.

> This redemption is no less in its strength, splendor and triumphs, and even in its miracles, than the redemption from Egypt. Why should we not know how to glorify the remembrance of our redemption, to sanctify it and be sanctified by it. . . . Why should we not know how to weave around this day legends and tales which will relate to the coming generations the greatness of our sons—our heroism and our heroes?[103]

Independence Day and Passover have related themes. Independence Day, as a second and more tangible Exodus, has the advantage of being more immediate and real than the ancient Exodus. Passover has the sanctity of tradition behind it, while Independence Day has barely begun to shape ceremonies or practices that date back no more than a few years. Independence Day is still vivid in the memory of many of its celebrants, and therefore alive and compelling. Its future vitality will be tested in the coming decades and centuries when no survivors remain and the day will have been relegated to the historical memory of the Jewish people. But will that 1948 generation succeed in transmitting to future generations the significant events of that seminal period in Jewish history when the State of Israel was born? Will the coming generations be able to relive that experience, as generations of Jews have relived the ancient Exodus? On Passover a Jew can feel as if he had been present as a participant in the Exodus. To be a second Passover, Israeli Independence Day must follow in the successful pedagogical path laid out by its predecessor and find a ritual means of remembering the past. A Haggadah is therefore a natural consequence of the theological intent of Independence Day as a parallel to Passover.

> The first evening should be in the spirit of "and you shall relate it to your sons." . . . . There are many members here who were not in Israel during the War of Independence. It is already history, so we must impart to it the character of "and you shall relate it to your sons."[104]

The Inter-Kibbutz Haggadah, published in 1971, has had to keep pace with the rapid changes in history that occurred since the compilations of the first Haggadah at Givat Brenner. The Givat Brenner Haggadah contains in its selections of literature and music the last sixty years (of Zionist and Israeli history), beginning with Herzl, going through Tel Hai, the Second Aliyah, the kibbutz and the Histadrut, the ghetto uprisings and the Holocaust, smuggling of refugees, the rebellion against the British, the Palmah, the establishment of the State of Israel, the War of Independence, and the Sinai campaign.

The Inter-Kibbutz Haggadah has thinned down this historical content considerably, and added the Six-Day War. Following kibbutz precedent none of the wars of Israel is glorified, magnified, or exalted. Readers of *Siah Lohamim* (translated into English as *The Seventh Day*) will understand the background for this reluctance to turn war into a cult.

A thirty-two-page booklet, the Haggadah follows the Passover pattern of ceremonials before and after the festive meal. The section before the feast is composed of a few summary historical selections leading from the prophets to Herzl, David Ben-Gurion, and the Declaration of the Independence of Israel. Nothing is included that reflects the traditional longing of Diaspora Jewry for return to the Holy Land. After the meal, poems and songs of the 1948 war are followed by the more recent literary and musical output generated by the Six-Day War, including, of course, the now classic song "Jerusalem the Golden." The Haggadah concludes with a call for peace, in phrases taken from the traditional prayer book, from Isaiah, and contemporary phraseology.

Although this Haggadah is intended to relate the story of Israel's independence, it does not have the narrative quality of the Pass-

## Holidays and Rites of Passage 189

over Haggadah. Because the historical experiences related are so contemporary, no need is felt to follow a developmental line of explanation. Each song and poem arouses a wealth of instant associations. The Independence Haggadah is at the very beginning of its ceremonial development, when ritual and life are inextricably intertwined. The decline of a number of kibbutz festivals indicates the effect that social change and new circumstances can have upon a holiday in a relatively short time. Once peace arrives and some of the aura of the Israeli army fades, Independence Day ritual will undoubtedly be revised.

More activity is packed into Independence Day than into the seven days of Passover. At Ramat Yohanan, as throughout the entire country, the Independence Day ceremonies begin a day before, with a memorial for those who fell in battle. Since Jewish holidays begin after sunset, the memorial service is held at nighttime. It is announced nationwide by the blast of an air-raid siren at eight o'clock. By that time kibbutz members have assembled at a memorial stone standing in a field outside the settlement. In 1947, when the kibbutz was under siege, a brief but costly battle fought in the area of the monument relieved Ramat Yohanan. An honor guard from a local air-force school stood at attention at this spot. The area was illuminated by flames from helmets filled with flammable material, creating a dramatic setting. Unfortunately, the effect was flawed by garbled readings of some of the participants, particularly the youth. The flatness of this potentially moving ceremony painfully illustrated the price paid for maximum participation.

At the end of Memorial Day another siren blast signals the beginning of Independence Day. The dining room of the kibbutz was decorated with the flags of the State of Israel and of the different corps of the Israeli army. As a rule a festive meal is served with an accompanying ceremony. On this particular year, a special meal was served at the regular hour, as on *Shabbat*, with a program scheduled for 9:30 P.M. after the small children were in bed. This opened with a few serious readings, then shifted to light humorous sketches lampooning the dress and behavior of the 1948 generation and its predecessors. Community singing followed. The folk dancing began only after the conclusion of the formal program and continued until after midnight. The morning was set aside for the small children with a miniature luna park having been built on the lawns. Games, booths, races, and a children's train drawn by a tractor assured a pleasant morning for the youngsters and their parents alike. The kibbutz again assembled at about 4:00 P.M. for the traditional Independence Day picnic in the adjoining forest. Family groups built bonfires for grilling meat eaten in pitah, the flat Arab-style bread so popular in Israel. Preceding the cookout, competitive games were held between members of different branches of the kibbutz economy. People began to drift home toward sundown. The younger couples put the small children to sleep and later joined other members in the dining room to watch TV. On Independence night the yearly Israel Song Festival is broadcast from Jerusalem. New songs especially composed for the occasion are performed by the top performers of Israel's entertainment world. A panel of judges selects the "best song of the year." This program attracts national interest, and members of Ramat Yohanan remained in the dining room until the early hours of the morning, glued to the TV set.

Comparison with Independence Day in urban Israel quickly reveals the special relationship the kibbutz has to this holiday. In the city many families simply wander through the streets looking for something to do. For example, in Haifa the Neve Shaanan district built a platform for entertainers, while the main street was cordoned off so that the youth could dance. With the creation of a community center, the focus of the day has moved there. A fair was built with rides for children and puppet shows. At no point is any effort made to introduce a serious theme or ceremony. Especially noticeable is the passivity of the crowds, whose aimless wandering through the streets is in striking contrast to the tightly communal character of the day in the kibbutz. But it is more than the cohesive nature of kibbutz society that permits it to turn Independence Day into a full and satisfying holiday. The kibbutz and the State of Israel have always had a special relationship to each other, which explains the unique importance of the day for kibbutz society.

The production of a kibbutz Haggadah for Independence Day is no mere coincidence. Israel and the kibbutz are almost synonymous. Not that the four percent of Kibbutz society is representative of all of Israel, but rather that the kibbutz is inconceivable without Israel and Israel inconceivable without the kibbutz. Both exist in symbiotic relationship. Whatever the functions of the kibbutz in present-day Israeli society—and they are considered problematic by many—everyone agrees that the state could not have arisen without the contributions of the kibbutz to defense and settlement. In a sense, the Jewish community gained its rights to the land not through historical antecedents, but by living and working on it. Had the Jewish community remained only urban, its fate might have paralleled that of the Crusaders, who abandoned the countryside to the Arabs.

The pioneering sacrificial image remains a high value of Israeli society at large, including the military, whose drive and spirit can be directly attributed to the high number of kibbutzniks in positions of command. The democratic spirit of the Israeli army, which is a genuine people's army, can also be ascribed to the penetration of the kibbutz spirit. The major youth movements functioning in the city are kibbutz-affiliated, with counselors from among the kibbutz youth, who not only fulfill their terms of military service, but also contribute an additional year of service. This year may be given as a worker on loan to a young, struggling kibbutz, or as a counselor in the federation urban youth group, or in a development town or city. The kibbutz has contributed greatly to the formation of a Hebrew culture and, in doing so, to the molding of the character of the Israeli. The heritage of kibbutz creativity in song and dance is a permanent contribution. Furthermore the kibbutz as a communal society materialized only in Israel and its fate is linked to the Jewish state. Only here has it arisen and developed and only here does it have a future. With such profound historical, emotional, and intellectual attachments to Israel it is no wonder that Israeli Independence Day penetrates to the deepest levels of a kibbutznik's commitment to his world.

## *Shavuot*

Shavuot was the first of the Jewish holidays to be reinstituted in the kibbutz, but contrary to expectations, it has failed to achieve a stable tradition and, in fact, is undergoing a decline. In many kibbutzim the festival of Shavuot has become a remnant of the kibbutz past, observed primarily out of a sense of duty. The decline is especially ironic in the light of its rare success as one of the few kibbutz holidays that actually penetrated urban life. In the early 1930s the city of Haifa invited kibbutzim from the surrounding area to parade through the city displaying their agricultural products. Bikkurim—the first fruits—were presented to the Jewish National Fund. After a few years this practice was discontinued, and the kibbutz Shavuot left the city and returned to the rural areas from which it had originated.

The suitability of Shavuot as a holiday appropriate to kibbutz life was evident from the very beginning, when, shortly after World War I, agricultural schools instituted the ceremony of Bikkurim. Shavuot had been the least of the three pilgrimage festivals, both in biblical times and during the Exile from the Holy Land. Known as Hag Hakatzir, the Harvest Festival, Shavuot lost its agricultural base after the Jewish people stopped farming. The major theme of the festival, not mentioned in the Bible, became Mattan Torah—the giving of the Torah. Obviously the synagogue, in its ceremony and ritual, emphasized the latter, nonbiblical motif of Mattan Torah, paying lip service to the earlier agricultural motif by decking itself in greenery and flowers, a pale shadow of the agrarian origins of the holiday. When Shavuot was first revalued in the kibbutz movement, the historical motif of Mattan Torah receded, and the holiday reverted to its agricultural origins, but on a grander scale than in biblical times. During the biblical period Shavuot was considered an epilogue to Passover. The barley harvest, begun on Passover and signified by the Omer, was concluded on Shavuot, when the wheat harvest commences. Two loaves of bread baked from the new crop were offered as sacrifices in the Temple, as the first fruits of the harvest. When the kibbutz presented its Bikkurim they were more than the fruits of the grain harvest. Each productive sector of the kibbutz economy bestowed the fruits of its labor. The extension and expansion of the agrarian motif of Shavuot discloses the role of biblical precedent as primarily suggestive. The Bible was not to be blindly imitated, but to serve as an aid, stimulating the imagination in the conception and creation of new ceremonies. The kibbutz Shavuot was hardly an epilogue to Passover, but a unique ceremony in its own right. Its founders and practitioners sincerely believed that, given time, their ceremony would become firmly entrenched in the emerging folklore of resurrected Jewish farming and become a fixed entity in the Hebrew cultural renaissance. Unhappily time did not suffice. Within the lifetime of the founding generation the Bikkurim have taken a deep plunge. The performance of the ceremony becomes more and more difficult with the passing years, and in a number of kibbutzim Bikkurim has been cancelled. Shavuot is still observed as a holiday through choreographic presentations of the Book of Ruth, visits to the different agricultural divisions, or in other ways, but the bringing of the first fruits is often deleted from the program.

The problem of the agricultural festivals has been discussed elsewhere, as well as the competition from Sukkot, which is benefiting from the renewed regard for the holidays of Tishri. But it is not only the decline of agriculture as a central value that is to blame for the diminishment of Bikkurim. The advances of agriculture in research, technology, and mechanization have liberated the farmer from his almost absolute dependence upon nature's cycles. Crops of grain, fruit, and vegetables can now be harvested during months when it would formerly have been impossible. Apple trees can be "put to sleep" and "reawakened," vegetables grown out of season, etc. In other words, Bikkurim no longer "overlaps the agricultural reality of our times." In addition, fatigue may have set in, depriving Shavuot of the full attention it deserves. Preparation for Bikkurim in a kibbutz is a complex undertaking, requiring coordination between schoolchildren who dance and sing in the program, adults who are responsible for arranging the procession with the first fruits, and for the construction of platforms and arrangement of sites for the ceremony itself.

This writer witnessed Bikkurim in 1971, in a field of Kfar Hamaccabi. An area had been cleared for the purpose, a stand built for the readers and a small orchestra, and a symmetrical pile of bales of straw set in the middle of the field. The ceremony began with the customary selection of biblical readings and Shovuot songs. Only the kindergarten children danced, each carrying a small basket of fruits and vegetables. At the conclusion of their dance the children centered on the mound of straw, placing their baskets on its tiered sides. Then came the procession of first fruits, with gaily decorated tractors drawing wagons that displayed banana stalks, citrus fruits, chickens, sheep, etc. The crowd, seated along the edges of the field, was roused out of its passivity by a tractor-drawn rotor, used for spraying trees, which now sprayed everybody with perfumed water. When the procession ended, the afternoon's ceremony was over.

The *Vatikim* agreed that this Bikkurim ceremony was only a dim afterglow of ones they recalled, when adults participated in song and dance, symbolically re-creating the biblical past, acting the part of pilgrims bringing first fruits to the priesthood. Today, they said, the holiday has become a children's festival, and with that view this writer must concur. As is often the case, the blame is laid upon the younger generation, now responsible for the cultural life of the kibbutz. Dissatisfied with Bikkurim, they performed it with little conviction of its worth, yet have arrived at no clear alternative. Some *Vatikim*, as indulgent parents, say that each generation must find its own mode of expression, however unsatisfactory it may be to their elders. Shavuot evening was set aside for Israeli folk dancing, which is reserved for holidays and festive occasions.

What have some kibbutzim done to rectify the imbalance resulting from the slow decline of Bikkurim? A few kibbutzim have timidly moved toward reinstating the Mattan Torah motif. At Degania Bet, the figure of Moses was re-created for a Shavuot ceremony, while at Revivim, biblical stories and episodes are dramatized. This may be done in parallel with the customary Bikkurim ceremony. Attempts have been made to replace Bikkurim with Hag ha-Sadeh, a field festival consisting of visits to the different branches where a picnic, with competitive games and entertainment is held. The Book of Ruth holds an honored place in Shavuot ceremonials, whether as a reading or for dramatic, choreographed presentation. Ruth fits into the agricultural setting of Shavuot because the story takes place against the background of the harvest festival.

One kibbutz, however, has moved boldly into the Mattan Torah motif. At Yifat, in the western Yizrael Valley, the traditional custom of studying all Shavuot night has been revived and reinterpreted. The person behind this innovation was Meir Ayali, the former principal of the regional kibbutz high school. In his youth he studied at an Orthodox yeshivah in Frankfurt and has continued to stress the importance of Talmud Torah—study of the Torah—as a value for all Jews, Orthodox or not. In 1966 he instituted Tikkun L'eyl Shavuot, which traditionally was marked by the study of texts from the range of Jewish learning during the whole night of Shavuot. At Yifat new content has been poured into this form. The session begins at 11:30 P.M. with a lesson in Talmud led by Ayali. Copies of the section for study are distributed in advance. The lesson is followed by a talk by a guest lecturer, usually a faculty member from the Hebrew University. The subjects vary. This writer participated in three *Tikkunim*—one devoted to Franz Rosenzweig, the other to Hasidism, and the third to the relationship of modern Jewish thought to the Bible.

Contrary to the customary approach towards kibbutz holidays, the *Tikkun* is not aimed at a mass audience. It appeals only to a select few who have the interests and background for a confrontation with the topics discussed and the material studied. The *Tikkun* was held in the social club of Yifat, which can accommodate about 150 people. While most members of Yifat did not participate, the *Tikkun* drew a large proportion of younger people. The creation of Tikkun L'eyl Shavuot and the interest it aroused indicate that intellectuals within the kibbutz movement cannot always find satisfaction in holiday celebration based upon a search for a common denominator for all members. This writer believes that if other kibbutzim were to follow the example of Yifat by devoting part of Shavuot to study, the response would be positive, even though limited to only a small proportion of the population.

The very gradual return of the historical motif of Mattan Torah should not be overestimated. Study will interest only a small minority. If the celebration of Mattan Torah is ever to be introduced into a kibbutz Shavuot, it would have to be presented by means of all the dramatic, musical, and artistic tools at the disposal of the kibbutz.

Often the remark is overheard: "Yes, we want Mattan Torah, but how are we to go about it?" With the centrality of agriculture undermined and the wobbly belief in Mattan Torah only beginning to gain strength, the future of Shavuot in the kibbutz should be an interesting study in the power of the rejected historical past to intrude its beliefs and customs upon the most consciously innovative of societies.

## The Extinct Holidays*

Until recently the High Holy Days fitted into the category included in the title of this section. The four minor fasts—Asarsh B'Tevet, Shivah Asar B'Tammuz, Tisha B'Av, and Tzom Gedaliah—will probably go unnoticed in the future as they were in the past. The holiday of Simhat Torah (the Joy of the Law) will probably also be fated to the same oblivion as the four fasts, unless the growing interest in the Mattan Torah (Giving of the Torah) theme of Shavuot could possibly lead to a renewed appreciation of Simhat Torah.

But the kibbutz need not look only to tradition for holidays or customs that have risen and declined. It can turn to its own limited experience for examples of festivals that sprang up, blossomed briefly, faded, withered, and perished. Some of these holidays were artificially created and transplanted onto the body of kibbutz life, but failed to "take," and so were sloughed off. Others, like the

*The material for this section is drawn, unless otherwise noted, from articles by Mattityahu Shelem: "The Vineyard Festival" in *Niv ha-Kevutza* of September 1968 and "The Shepherd and his Festival," *Niv ha-Kevutza* of June 1961.

first of May, still exist in a truncated form, devoid of content and meaning, but nevertheless formally maintained on the calendar.

A few kibbutzim attempted to initiate a number of holidays connected to special agricultural branches of their economy. One was called the Vineyard Festival, another the Shearing Festival. Although two kibbutzim in particular, Ein ha-Shofet and Kiryat Anavim, engaged in ambitious projects designed to make the Vineyard Festival a living celebration, they were unable to ensure a consistent observance of the holiday. Despite persistent efforts the Vineyard Festival barely succeeded in taking a breath of life before it disappeared from the kibbutz scene.

Before the kibbutz movement was even dreamt of, a vineyard festival had originated in Rishon LeZion, one of the first Jewish agricultural settlements in Eretz Yisrael. In the last decade of the nineteenth century their first celebration was held in the light of the central position of grape cultivation in the economic life of that community. This initial attempt to create a popular holiday was unsuccessful, for no determined effort was made to renew it every year. A sister settlement of Rishon LeZion, Zichron Yaakov, another community that was almost totally dependent on grapes and the wine industry, had also sought to inaugurate a wine festival. It, too, had little success, primarily because it lacked the social and cultural base necessary to produce a genuine holiday.

Another attempt to create a permanent wine festival was made by the generation of kibbutz settlers of the 1920s who took upon themselves "the mission to set down the foundation for renewed cultural and folkloristic values." They had hoped that, among other festivals, it would become a permanent cultural asset. The wine festival, however, was one of the abortive efforts in their attempts to reconstruct traditional holidays that have had a continuous history of practice and to renew ancient ones that had fallen into disuse. It is the latter category of holidays that failed to take hold.

The idea of a wine festival was based upon a reference in the Mishna (Taanit 4:8) that on the fifteenth day of the Hebrew month of Av "the daughters of Israel would go dancing in the vineyards." They were followed by young men, who would use this opportunity to pick a wife from among the girls. There is some speculation that this "youth holiday" was characterized by a chase, with the men in pursuit of the women. This type of folk holiday was probably frowned upon by the rabbis, who wrote that from the day the Temple was destroyed the joy described in Taanit was nullified. Joy was henceforth to be derived from the study of the Torah.

Whatever the veracity of this explanation, the kibbutz generation of the 1920s and 1930s hoped to restore the joy of the fifteenth of Av by celebrating the grape harvest of the summer months. A few kibbutzim with extensive vineyards prepared ceremonies and in some instances succeeded in performing them. In Kiryat Anavim (City of Grapes), whose arable land is heavily planted with vineyards, its thirtieth anniversary served as an opportunity to renew the fifteenth of Av as a vineyard festival. Ten years later, in 1960, the ceremony was repeated, although on a markedly reduced scale in comparison with the 1950 celebration. Since then no attempt has been made to revive the day. The only reminder of the fifteenth of Av appears on the *Shabbat* prior to that date, when sections of the ceremony are inserted into the *Kabbalat Shabbat* program.

Two kibbutzim, Degania Alef and Yotvatah, the former the oldest of kibbutzim and the latter a relatively young one, have made intermittent efforts to revive the fifteenth of Av not as a vineyard festival, but as a festival of love. Here as well the festivities have been random, appearing suddenly and disappearing. The celebration described below took place in Yotvatah in 1957.

The festivities were conducted in the following order: After dinner the members moved out to the date plantation. It was a dark night, and only on the arrival of the young women were torches lit and the chase of girls and boys begun. When the couples were formed they broke into a circle dance and upon its completion declared: "The festival of love has arrived—let us greet it with love." The artistic part of the program followed, composed primarily of songs and dances based on the Song of Songs. Rockets were set off to declare the beginning of a beauty contest, phrased, however, in biblical terms. The winner was not entitled a beauty queen, but rather "the most beautiful among women." All the young girls, led by the boys who "kidnapped" them, received biblical names, such as the Rose of Jericho, the Rose of Sharon, the Morning Star, and so on. By one in the morning the festivities were over in the date plantation, but continued in the dining room.

The spectacle of a "Jewish Festival of Love," even though based on biblical precedent and making lavish use of the Song of Songs (in its original context), nevertheless raises misgivings among Jews accustomed to those disciplines of Jewish life which frowned upon open expression of impulses that convention has kept under control and surveillance. Some, on the other hand, might conceivably rejoice in the liberation of the Jew from the chains of past custom that made him unnecessarily wary of his own feelings and introduced excessive guilt feelings. The Festival of Love at Yotvatah was not, after all, a pagan orgy with magical and mythical overtones. But Jews seem incapable of sustaining even the mild festival form described above, for little has been heard of it since. The heritage of self-discipline and restraint so evident in Jewish tradition, which the kibbutz has inherited, sets up emotional barriers to the creation and representation of a vineyard or love festival.

The Shearing Festival had its origin in the romantic notions current in the Second and Third Aliyah, which idealized and glorified the new Hebrew shepherd returned to the land where his forefathers had tilled the soil and led vast herds of sheep across the hills and valleys. Unlike most romantics, however, those pioneers combined a practical streak with their emotional intensities, harnessing a naive belief in the purity of a shepherd's life to the very immediate historical mission of settling Jews in Eretz Yisrael.

Jews were not shepherds in the Diaspora and generally considered shepherds to be the epitome of boorish primitivism and cultural simplicity. Determined to be shepherds without these traits (two of the most learned and intelligent men in Ramat Yohanan are shepherds), they learned the "trade" from local Bedouins and from self-study. Their romanticism was encouraged by the wealth of biblical references to sheep and shepherds. The idea of a Shearing festival arose in response to biblical verses describing the celebrations and feasts accompanying the shearing of sheep (1 Samuel 25). Apparently the biblical festival was limited only to the villagers who took the sheep out to grazing pasture. In other words, it was a popular local holiday unconnected with the official priestly institutions of ancient Israel's religious life. This festival seemed ideally suited for the emerging shepherds of modern Israel and indeed, when the shepherds' associaton was formed in 1930, ceremonies for the festival were composed. The time set for its practice was just before Shavuot, appropriate primarily from the viewpoint of the sheep. But was there really a necessity for such a festival? The question was answered (in 1961) by Mattityahu Shelem thus:

> In our days also there is a need to express the joy of labor, and mutual relations between man and living things, between the shepherd and his sheep.

Despite the meager references in biblical sources to a shearing festival, the decision to initiate this holiday was tantamount to the creation of an entirely new festival. Like the Wine Festival, it was not to be limited solely to the workers in that branch, but was to be celebrated by the entire kibbutz. At Ramat Yohanan a kibbutz-wide celebration was held, with mutton served for dinner and a ceremony performed in honor of the occasion. As with the Wine Festival, there was no continuity and within a short time the Shearing Festival had withdrawn to the sheep pen again, where it was celebrated only by the people who worked there and a few invited guests. This kibbutz shortly eliminated the sheep herd from its economic divisions simply because no one could be found to replace the aging shepherds.

In the earlier, more hopeful and heady years it was believed that a new holiday could be constructed even though its foundation in the historical past might be flimsy. Carried away by the enthusiasms of the creative decades of the 1930s and 1940s, the innovators of kibbutz holidays boldly initiated festivals that they believed could be integrated into the way of life they were developing. They could not anticipate, however, that their way of life would move in a direction contrary to their expectations, and at a pace that barely gave their new holidays an opportunity to bud before the change in the social climate cut them down. In his article on the Shearing Festival, Mattityahu Shelem outlines the most preferable approach to initiation of new holidays:

> We must not behave arbitrarily in the determination of new holidays. Sources are important, and weight should be given to continuity and sections of tradition. There is a special importance to popular historical motifs, to vestiges of ceremonies, to hints of form and custom. It is best that the new shape be based upon ancient foundations. In this way comes the continuity which fertilizes the imagination and elevates the content.

Experience has been a harsh tutor in the kibbutz. The theory for constructing new holidays has failed the test. Antiquity is not enough. Were this the case, Yom Kippur could also be celebrated by dancing in the vineyards. These failures are a valuable lesson, not only for students of Jewish culture, but for those actively involved in its perpetuation.

## Shabbat

> Today, it must be confessed, observance of the Jewish festivals faces a major challenge. Since the dissolution of the Jewish state in 70 C.E. the festivals have existed in a

> kind of cultural vacuum, expressing far more the spirit of a tradition than the temper of a living and distinctive society. They have become, to a large extent, a mechanism for conserving artificially what was once a natural and organic cohesion. For the modern Jew, this lends a certain air of remoteness and tends to make of their observance an act of sentimental piety rather than of positive and inevitable self-expression; more often than not, the modern Jew speaks of "keeping up" the festivals rather than simply keeping them.
> How far this state of affairs will be altered by the reestablishment of a Jewish state in Israel and by the consequent reintegration of the festivals into a distinctive Jewish life, is at present premature to discuss; but the bare fact that such alteration will take place can scarcely be doubted. Moreover it will issue from a natural cultural development, and not from the fiat of any central authority—a sanhedrin or a college of rabbis. For Judaism is not a creed, to be determined or imposed in such a fashion, it is the spirit of an entire people attuned to hear a voice beyond the thunders and ready, even while it stands in a wilderness, to answer together: "We will do and we will hear" (Exodus 24:7).
> —Theodore H. Gaster,
> *Festivals of the Jewish Year*

*Shabbat* is unquestionably a special day in kibbutz life, but it is not approached with the awe, reverence, and trepidation characteristic of Orthodox or other religious Jews. *Shabbat* in the kibbutz may be compared in mood to *Shabbat* as it is conceived and observed among liberal religious movements in Judaism. In movements not committed to *halakhah*, the final verdict on the permitted and forbidden of *Shabbat* and holiday practices lies in the hands of the community as a whole and of the individuals who make it up. In kibbutz parlance, "*Shabbat*" has come to mean release from work, or time off. If someone can arrange a day off in the middle of the week, then he has gained a *Shabbat*. A half-day off is half a *Shabbat*. This lighthearted usage does not detract from the uniqueness of the day, for while *Shabbat* in the kibbutz has little of the intensity felt in Orthodox practice, it is different from the remaining days of the week for more reasons than mere physical rest.

The modern Hebrew essayist, Ahad Ha-Am, once remarked that the Sabbath has kept Israel more than Israel has kept the Sabbath. According to this approach, the *halakhah* was designed to ensure the survival of the Jewish people, to assure them a "portable fatherland" no matter among what nations they live or what cultures surrounded them. This classically Zionist attitude could lead to only one conclusion, that the halakhic way has served its purpose, since the Jewish people now have a land of their own. In a Jewish state the halakhic *Shabbat* is unnecessary. But what is to come in its place? In modern urban Israel *Shabbat* is no different from what it is in the United States. Commercial establishments are indeed closed and there is no public transportation, but *Shabbat* itself is little more than a day with no work; it is not yet a day of spiritual rest. Many Israelis spend the day driving through the country, going on picnics, or swimming. The Israeli living in a kibbutz, should he leave his kibbutz and settle in a city, would probably glide effortlessly into the *Shabbat* patterns current among his urban neighbors. In other words, the kibbutznik has no commitment to *Shabbat* different in range or depth from that of his urban counterparts. He travels on *Shabbat*, does not attend public worship, does not say kiddush in his home, and does not practice any of the rituals that permeate the day. Yet there is a feeling that *Shabbat* cannot be permitted to become a day for pleasure trips alone (not that this element is lacking in the kibbutz *Shabbat*).

Social changes within the kibbutz and the growth of a more diverse, heterogeneous community have given a new significance to *Shabbat*. At one time members had more constant contact with each other, not only at work, but socially, and at the weekly general assembly meetings. Today the increasing division of the kibbutz into small family cells has directed social energies toward the intimate family and away from the extended family. Attendance at the general assembly meetings has declined precipitously in many kibbutizim, and in some cases this forum now meets bimonthly instead of weekly. In other words, opportunities have been decreasing for the type of kibbutz-wide events that bring all members together as one body. In kibbutz parlance, the sense of *yahad*, oneness and togetherness, is in danger of gradual attenuation unless something is done to reverse this troubling trend.

Holidays, festivals, weddings, Bar Mitzvah celebrations are all examples of community-wide ceremonies that contribute significantly to the cultivation of *yahad*. The kibbutz is not content with sporadic events. Once a week almost the entire membership appears for a film showing. But this is an unsatisfactory form of encounter, since nothing is required other than passive gazing at the screen. Thus, the Sabbath is being reconsidered as a means of reinforcing kibbutz *yahad*. It is on *Shabbat* evening, in most kibbutzim, that the entire community sits down together to a meal. During the work week each meal is served within a two-hour duration because of the wide variation in individual work schedules. On *Shabbat* evening the entire membership squeezes into the dining room (except in kibbutzim where the meal must be eaten in shifts because the dining room is too small). Wherever the entire community can be seated together at tables arranged for *Shabbat,* the setting is appropriate for the *Kabbalat Shabbat.* This has become the core of *Shabbat* ceremony in the kibbutz. As a rule the brief ceremony centers around some aspect of Jewish cultural heritage.

When did the *Kabbalat Shabbat* ceremony begin in the kibbutz? Certain kibbutzim, particularly Degania Alef and Geva, served as pacemakers, Geva being the first to institute a *Kabbalat Shabbat.* Other kibbutzim did not follow suit until the 1950s when the custom spread widely, particularly in the Ihud federation. In a sense the ground for *Kabbalat Shabbat* had been prepared through its introduction in kindergarten and the children's houses, where it was celebrated simply. This groundwork was undoubtedly instrumental in the shift to an adult ceremony. (The children add immeasurably to the *Shabbat* atmosphere in a kibbutz, as they leave their dwellings after their *Kabbalat Shabbat,* dressed in white shirts or blouses.)

The Sabbath in the kibbutz is not celebrated only by a *Kabbalat Shabbat.* The cultural life of the community is concentrated on this day, as most kibbutzim devote Friday evening to *m'seebat leyl Shabbat,* the Sabbath eve gathering. The evening is devoted to lectures, plays, concerts, light entertainment—a mixture of activities that are the responsibility of the cultural committee. In Ramat Yohanan this tradition is so firmly planted that many members grumble if there is "no program for Friday evening." Many kibbutzim follow a set pattern: *Kabbalat Shabbat* before the meal, which usually has somewhat better food including wine, and is served on white tablecloths. Later in the evening there is the *m'seebat leyl Shabbat.* The Sabbath day itself is free for individual members to do as they please. A few go to synagogue, most stay at home, receive guests, visit family, go on trips, take the children for a walk or a ride in a wagon pulled by a tractor. There is no kibbutz equivalent of the traditional *havdalah* ceremony separating the holy Sabbath from the secular week, but for the kibbutz the Sabbath is over, and the week begins when the general assembly meets at about 9:30 on Saturday night, to hear and debate the problems of its society. That is *havdalah.*

In the weekly bulletin of the Ihud, *Iggeret,* there appeared from the very inception of the federation in 1951 letters and short articles in favor of some way of separating the Sabbath from the rest of the week. The first official meeting in the movement on the subject of the Sabbath was in 1951, held for cultural committee chairmen. Representatives of fifty kibbutzim attended, to search for ways of enlivening and enriching the Sabbath. Proposals were adopted for the introduction of a *Kabbalat Shabbat,* in approximately the same pattern as it exists today. The recurring theme throughout that early period, and to this day, is the quest for some way of absorbing that *neshama yetayrah,* the additional soul, with which the Sabbath imbues those who are capable of understanding its spirit.

Conversations with kibbutzniks on this subject evoke a wide range of response. Some are satisfied with the Sabbath as lived in the kibbutz today, others suffer a vague gnawing, a blurred and amorphous feeling that there is more to the Sabbath than they are experiencing. Visits to Orthodox kibbutzim often strengthen this longing, which, however, is rarely given any concrete expression. There are others who, having had contact with tradition in their youth before immigration to Israel or through studies, are convinced that Sabbath holiness is the attribute the kibbutz must seek. This special quality can arise out of a configuration of practices and customs that no kibbutz is able to include in its way of life. Some individual members do observe a traditional Sabbath, but only in isolation.[105]

The kibbutz hopes that by practicing *Shabbat* the way it sees fit it will eventually achieve a Sabbath holiness comparable in mood and texture to the tradition. However, since no kibbutz or section of its population has as yet succeeded in realizing this elusive quality of holiness, the inescapable conclusion, at least of Orthodox Jewry, is that the Sabbath can be kept only traditionally, or not at all. This Orthodox view is usually supported by the *Vatikim,* who refuse to attribute holiness to any sort of experiences other than the traditional ones.

> I do not like to use the word holiness out of respect for terms which represent values deriving from a certain experiential belief world. Only a person spiritually identified with that world may be permitted to use its terminology without engaging in deception.

The composer of this quote, Mattityahu Shelem, would eliminate "holiness" from the vocabulary of the kibbutz, but would be willing to substitute Yirat Kavod, which is closer to reverence or awe of the Sabbath. Here is his image of what the Sabbath should be:

> I would like to see the Sabbath in the State of Israel defined as a day of spiritual and physical rest and a day of social and cultural preoccupation. This includes: sports, trips and games, meeting with family and friends, *Kabbalat Shabbat*, study, lectures, discussions and symposiums (primarily on Jewish subjects), esthetic experience, exhibitions, dances, music, including in this sphere whatever can extend the intellect and gratify the soul. . . . As a member of a kibbutz I enjoy and attend all cultural events arranged on Friday evenings. Saturday afternoons are given over to family gatherings.

Mention of the synagogue is conspicuously absent, but Shelem remarked that young men from the kibbutz returning home after a stay in the United States were often impressed by Conservative and Reform synagogue services. He predicts a future period when something like a synagogue will be built on a regional basis for a group of kibbutzim. At present there is no move in that direction by any of the second generation, including those who have spent time in America. As yet the brief *Kabbalat Shabbat* ceremony is the closest parallel in the kibbutz to both the synagogue and the family Friday night around the table. In spirit it is closer to the latter, though a few minor elements of the synagogue service do enter, such as readings from the Torah section of the week.

Many kibbutzim have no *Kabbalat Shabbat* ceremony at all; others perform it perfunctorily, while some have an established usage dating years back. Of the latter, Degania Bet has woven a ceremony whose structure and purposes are explained by their poet, Levi Ben-Amitai, in the paraphrase below. *Kabbalat Shabbat* in the version of Degania Bet has fixed and changing sections. The fixed pieces include opening songs chosen for their appropriateness to kibbutz life, values, and visions such as "How good it is for brothers to sit together"; "How goodly are your tents"; "Purify our hearts"; "Spread over us your canopy of peace." After the opening melodies the kibbutz sings three verses of *"L'Kha Dodi,"* "Come Sabbath Bride," which was picked as the permanent *Kabbalat Shabbat* hymn. This is followed by short readings on the holiness of *Shabbat*, extracted from the prayer book. Levi Ben-Amitai explains the reasons for his choice of verses:

This is our thanksgiving for the holiness of the Sabbath, which You have blessed of all days and sanctified above all times. "Accept our rest"—our Sabbath rest as we are able to practice it at this time. "We have been sanctified by Your commandments" for we indeed observe great mitzvot. "Give us our portion in Your Torah" for we esteem the Torah and bestow it as an inheritance to our children.

And afterwards a verse of prayer so very kibbutzlike:

Satisfy us in Your goodness and make us rejoice in Your salvation, and purify our hearts to serve You in truth for we are still struggling with ourselves and the great truth of our lives.[106]

The next section of the ceremony fluctuates in content, although its form remains the same. It is composed of a reading from the section of the week with a short addition from the *aggadah*. The conclusion is entitled "Sabbath Poem" and varies from week to week. From poems written in honor of the Sabbath throughout all ages and periods of Jewish history one is chosen for reading each Sabbath. Candles are lit, but no blessing is said over them, although in some kibbutzim short blessings have been composed.

The very gradual change in attitude to the Sabbath, as evidenced by the introduction of *Kabbalat Shabbat*, received additional confirmation through the acceptance of Friday-night cultural programs. At one time Friday was the night for screening movies, but a growing distaste for this practice built up within a small, determined minority, who convinced many members that this was incompatible with the spirit of the day. The quality and substance of the special programs vary widely in the light of the diverse backgrounds, interests, and age levels of kibbutzim. The general approach is to balance them with light and serious subjects. Of essence is the feeling that the Sabbath should not be spent on activities that would fail to differentiate it from the workday week. Kibbutzniks who have written on this subject invariably stress the socially beneficial results of Friday evening programs and in their campaign of persuasion they point to the fact that social tensions and problems have decreased following the creation of successful and permanent series of Friday evening events. There are no means of evaluating the accuracy of this statement unless a kibbutz were to be suddenly deprived of these programs. My own experience has tended to justify the contention that a rich Sabbath cultural program reinforces the ties between a member and his kibbutz. Sabbath culture is a need and right of its people that the kibbutz must satisfy if it is to ensure a gratified membership.

In the sparse literature of the kibbutz movement on the Sabbath only two restrictions are mentioned as essential for the defense of the Sabbath against encroachments of the workday week—limitation of work and the weekly projection of films on Friday night. Showing a film on an occasional Friday night is not deemed harmful to the quality of life, but when a kibbutz consistently shows movies on *Shabbat* the indications are clear as to that community's cultural tone. Both these abstentions arose out of the realization that there would be no distinction between the Sabbath and the rest of the week in the kibbutz unless these prohibitions were enforced. The kibbutz, which had originally constructed its Sabbath according to positive commandments, has now reluctantly accepted the above prohibitions as part of its search for a richer Sabbath. However, a certain minimum of labor is required on this day in a number of branches—in the cowshed, the chicken coops, the kitchen, and in factories with expensive equipment that cannot be turned on and off. The atmosphere of Sabbath rest is disturbed when too many members are observed moving around in their work clothes. Nevertheless, should a special piece of work have to be done for which the week is not sufficient, a kibbutz can declare a call-up of members to donate a number of hours of work on the Sabbath to finish or speed along that particular job. In other words, a kibbutz will feel free occasionally to violate its general principle of Sabbath rest, should conditions warrant it.

The physical calm and gentle rural setting of a kibbutz help to fashion a quiet and restful Sabbath—attending *Kabbalat Shabbat* together, participating in the evening cultural program, waking up late in the morning, taking walks with the children, napping in the afternoon. All these small activities, when experienced together, have the cumulative effect of setting a Sabbath atmosphere that is singular to the kibbutz. While the mood and tone of an entire community at rest—better dressed, enjoying their families, receiving guests, gaining cultural profit, and released from personal worries and communal anxiety—is not the Sabbath of traditional Jewry, it is nevertheless felt as a day apart. Here a "practicing community," a group with similar life-style, make the Sabbath an easier day to experience.

## Bar Mitzvah

In all ceremonies relating to rites of passage other than birth, the kibbutz takes a major part. When a child is born the kibbutz holds no special naming ceremony. For a male the family invites a *mohel* from a neighboring community, who circumcises the baby, initiating it into the covenant of Abraham. The family may post a notice on the bulletin board at the entrance to the dining room inviting all members to rejoice with them at the ceremony. At no point, however, does the kibbutz take official notice other than including some lines in the local bulletin congratulating the parents. This rite remains, therefore, a private family function no different from the ceremony held in Jewish communities throughout the world. Nor does there seem to be any interest in communalizing the ceremony and moving it into the public realm.

The next rite of passage, Bar Mitzvah, that in modern times has assumed an importance it never had in antiquity or later times, has undergone a complete transformation in the kibbutz and would not be recognizable in its present form to anyone accustomed to the traditional synagogue ceremony. Only a few kibbutzim have retained the traditional custom of sending a boy "up to the Torah" upon his thirteenth birthday for the reading of the prophetic portion of the week. Kfar Maccabi, for example, observes this practice and follows the procedure common in cities: brief lessons in chanting the Torah portion of the week and introduction of the laying of *tefillin*. Not that there is any expectation of the youngster's continuing the practice. The aim is only to acquaint him with the Bar Mitzvah ceremony and to gratify parents. The majority of the kibbutz movement does not provide a traditional Bar Mitzvah to families that request it. If a kibbutz has a synagogue, a family can use it for their son's Bar Mitzvah, but it remains a private affair, unconnected with the broader community. When there is no synagogue, or the local kibbutz synagogue is unappealing, some families take their sons to synagogues in the city, including Reform synagogues, for the Bar Mitzvah ceremony. These are isolated occurrences. The majority of kibbutz children pass through a dual Bar Mitzvah. Firstly, they have a joint ceremony for all seventh-grade youngsters, held in the dining room in the presence of the entire kibbutz. There is no fixed date, the Bar Mitzvah taking place when the entire class has completed its preparations for the occasion. The second ceremony takes place in the school, usually during Shavuot, and offers a résumé of the Bar Mitzvah study program that the class has completed. Parents and teachers are present. Privately, some parents may mark their child's thirteenth birthday by inviting family and friends to a modest reception in their room, but this is done at their own initiative.

Bar Mitzvah has become firmly established in the ceremonials of kibbutz life, and this is attested by the size of the informative booklet issued on this ceremony, entitled *Yalkut Bar Mitzvah* ("a Bar Mitzvah collection"). This abundance of material can be attributed to the child-centered nature of the holiday, which inevitably involves large numbers of parents and children in its preparation and performance and, most significantly, kibbutz educators, who are responsible for equipping the children with the skills they need for the completion of their Bar Mitzvah year. The *Yalkut Bar Mitzvah* is in fact addressed to educators and counselors, and not chairmen of cultural or holiday committees.

In his introduction the writer of this collection states the aim of Bar Mitzvah in the kibbutz: "We seek to adapt the Bar Mitzvah period to our approach, as a part of our educational system and our secular way of life."[107] As it has done with the entire calendar year and personal life cycle, the kibbutz has removed Bar Mitzvah from the synagogue and moved it into its school system. This transfer is highly significant, for it reveals the position held by the school within kibbutz society. The regional school of the Zevulun Valley, which serves three kibbutzim, is not known by the commonly accepted Hebrew term for school, *Bet Hasefer* (literally, "house of the book"), but is called *Bet ha-Hinuch*, ("house of education"). The obvious implication, and one accepted by kibbutz educators, is that their school is a purveyor of values as well as a transmitter of knowledge.

In the kibbutz world, where a sense of *mitzvah* is an absolute necessity, a Bar Mitzvah would seem to be almost an essential, if not indispensable, ceremony. The awareness of a kibbutz *mitzvah*, however, has barely penetrated its public consciousness and as a result the Bar Mitzvah year and its ceremonial conclusion rarely touch upon this aspect. Although objections are no longer raised against a Bar Mitzvah ceremony, kibbutz educators still remain uncertain about its appropriate form and content. Ritual patterns have taken shape, as has a program of study, but their execution varies widely throughout the movement. The doubts raised from time to time by kibbutz educators are not a retreat from Bar Mitzvah as an integral part of kibbutz life, but rather a "sacred uncertainty" that leads them into constant reevaluation and reappraisal. The kibbutz has cause to be proud that despite its own unceasing self-trial and examination, some elements of its Bar Mitzvah program have been proposed for introduction into Israel's urban schools, significantly enough, by the Center for the Fostering of Jewish Consciousness of the Ministry of Education and Culture.[108]

The traditional Bar Mitzvah accords new rights (or obligations) to the thirteen-year-old when he achieves his religious majority, allowing him to lay *tefillin* and be called to a reading of the Torah. Though he was far from assuming his place as a responsible member of the Jewish community, he could at least be counted among ten for a quorum. In effect, Bar Mitzvah was a minor occasion among traditional Jews because it was not a rite of passage that constituted a radical change, as from puberty to adolescence, or from bachelorhood to marriage. The child was not initiated into the religious obligations of adult society, because he had already taken part in many of them, so Bar Mitzvah ceremonially sealed the youngster's long-standing involvement in religious practices. For the average non-Orthodox youngster in Western society, Bar Mitzvah is a momentary interference in his personal life. The content and form of the ceremony are often totally unrelated to his lifestyle.

When Bar Mitzvah began to be observed in the kibbutz, the question was raised whether Bar Mitzvah really fitted a collective society as it did an Orthodox society. Clearly it did not. This led not to abandonment, but to the creation of new forms. "This is the only organized experiment in a secular Israeli community to deal with the content of the Bar Mitzvah holiday from all aspects: study, societal action, national consciousness, involvement in the movement."[109] But before this development could occur, objections had to be overcome. The most commonly voiced were *(a)* thirteen-year-olds are not genuinely responsible; *(b)* there is no need to stress or emphasize intellectual or sexual maturation by holding a special ceremony; *(c)* nothing actually changes for a kibbutz child; *(d)* a holiday irrelevant to the reality of kibbutz life would be empty of content; *(e)* mere attachment to parental memories is a danger.

Whatever the validity of some of these objections, the view eventually prevailed that Bar Mitzvah deserves an honored place in the kibbutz year and in the life cycle of the kibbutz child. The ultimate justification for introducing Bar Mitzvah, as summarized in the report of a kibbutz educator's conference, was "fulfillment of commandments." Bar Mitzvah was perceived not as just a social holiday, but as preparation and training for the implementation of "personal and societal tasks, plus many and different *mitzvot*." In the Bar Mitzvah collection, buried under mounds of material, there is a variation of a traditional blessing whose concluding formula was the centrality of *mitzvah*. "Blessed is He who has kept us in life, has preserved us, and enabled us to see our sons bearing the yoke of kibbutz *mitzvot*."[110]

Not all educators have agreed with the use of the term *Bar Mitzvah* for the program of ceremony, study, and implementation of specified social tasks. It has been proposed that the term *Bar M'seemah* ("Son of the task," or "mission") replace *Bar Mitzvah* ("son of the commandment") because *mitzvot* require a continuity, while the *m'seemah,* or task, is generally coupled to a specific goal. Once the goal is achieved, the task is completed. The term *Bar M'seemah* implies the termination of a mission, while *Bar Mitzvah* suggests the daily practice of kibbutz commandments.

At Ramat Yohanan the Bar Mitzvah took place on a Friday evening and the entire kibbutz appeared for the festivities, jamming the dining hall. A colorful, tastefully decorated stage was erected. The master of ceremonies opened the festivity by introducing a program that emphasized the unity of the generations, with each set of parents and children appearing on the stage in some joint activity. A family with musical talent performed, while other families with no special artistic skills read a literary section together. The master of ceremonies made clever use of sources from Jewish literature by connecting the name of each child with biblical or Midrashic verses where his name appears. After this, each boy returned to his classmates for the presentation of short, entertaining sketches, and then the general secretary of the kibbutz presented each child with a watch. The prevailing atmosphere was festive, light, and convivial.

The serious side of Bar Mitzvah was reserved for school, when the class reported on the projects it had completed and the subjects it had studied. At Ramat Yohanan, Bar Mitzvah had once been the exclusive province of the school, but the members requested that it should become a kibbutz holiday as well. Parallel observances, in school and in the kibbutz, are a recent development and have in essence added another holiday to the kibbutz calendar. In kibbutz literature Bar Mitzvah is called *hag* ("holiday"), whereas in traditional Judaism a Bar Mitzvah and a wedding are not considered holidays because they are limited solely to family circles. Through a communal celebration, the kibbutz has transformed Bar Mitzvah and marriage into holidays for the entire community. The feeling for the "kibbutz family" receives additional social support.

The example of Ramat Yohanan is not necessarily applicable to other kibbutzim, which may succeed in imparting an entirely different character to their ceremonies. At a conference of educators of Ihud ha-Kibbutzim held in 1964 on the subject of Bar Mitzvah, some of the participants described ceremonies in their kibbutzim that emphasized "Jewish consciousness."

Kibutz Hatzerim, where traditonal Rosh Ha-Shanah and Yom Kippur services have been held in the past few years, is continuing that trend by presenting a Bar Mitzvah ceremony composed by Judah Sharett, a resident of Kibbutz Yagur since 1926, who has composed numerous selections for kibbutz holidays. His Bar Mitzvah ceremony makes generous use of traditional materials, among them chants of biblical readings according to the traditional melodies. A connection with the synagogue rite is maintained by including sections of the blessings said before reading the prophetic portion. This kibbutz has no ideological or philosophical objections to hearing their youth chant, "Blessed are You, Lord our God, King of the Universe," or sing melodies with words such as "There is no God as magnificent as our God." As David Maletz, veteran member of Ein Harod, remarked, "We are able to include God in our ceremonies because we are not afraid of Him."

This review of the various practices in different kibbutzim did not include Bar Mitzvah material from Ha-Kibbutz ha-Artzi. There were not more than nine reproductions of Bar Mitzvah ceremonies in the *Bar Mitzvah Collection*. The editor undoubtedly wished to avoid duplication. In Ha-Kibbutz ha-Artzi there is a ceremony for thirteen-year-olds, but its emphasis is on *aliyah la'tnuah*, ("entrance into the movement"). Its literature on kibbutz Bar Mitzvah is meager, and constitutes mostly a defense of its refusal to follow in the direction taken by the other kibbutz movements. The Kibbutz Artzi tends to accept those objections to Bar Mitzvah which the other movements rejected as inconsequential.

Planning of Bar Mitzvah is spread out over the entire school year of the seventh graders, for experience had taught educators that it was not feasible to pack the preparation into a brief period of six to eight weeks. The focus of the Bar Mitzvah is the implementation of *m'seemot* or *mitzvot*. There is no unified approach in usage of this terminology. Some kibbutz schools use one term to the exclusion of the other. Some use both. The number thirteen occasionally appears as a framework for the *mitzvot*, while other schools classify them according to subject, without straining to fit them within precisely thirteen *mitzvot*.

In Kibbutz Afikim the *mitzvot* were divided into thirteen (this example is from 1962). The first on the list was "knowledge of the Jewish tradition." This *mitzvah* was not composed of a full study course, for the children already studied Bible and Jewish history, but was aimed at acquaintance with synagogue practices, such as the order of weekly readings, special Sabbaths, how to read from the Torah and Haftorah, some Rashi, legends of the Bible, *tefillin*, and finally *mitzvot* between man and his neighbor. Not all kibbutzim include this *mitzvah* in their list, although today there is a growing consciousness of the need to use the Bar Mitzvah year as a means for inculcating larger doses of Jewish consciousness into the school.

The second *mitzvah* is "knowledge of the history of the Jewish people," the third, "knowledge of Israel and of the local region"— this means acquaintance with both geography and economic, political, and security problems. The fourth is "the movement," which includes a study of problems faced by the member kibbutzim of the Ihud as well as an introduction to the urban youth movement of the Ihud, the Working and Studying Youth. The fifth *mitzvah* is entitled "in the family," the sixth, *bahevrah* ("in the group"), which for kibbutz youth refers to their own separate children's society. This *mitzvah* is twofold, including private lessons to children in need of them, and organizing a party.

*Mitzvah* number seven is devoted to the economic and work problems of their kibbutz, and is followed by the eighth, "security," which obligates the thirteen-year-olds to be on guard duty one full night and to make rudimentary acquaintance with a rifle. The ninth *mitzvah* is known as "personal trial." In its first part the youngster is left alone in a field a few kilometers from the kibbutz for one day, with the necessary equipment, and is required to prepare his own meals. In other words, he is challenged to shift for himself until picked up in the evening. The second part of the ninth *mitzvah* is called "acquaintance with another style of life" and entails a study of, plus a visit to, a *moshav*, or a settlement composed primarily of new immigrants. In the reality of present-day Israel, this usually means an introduction to communities populated by Oriental Jews. Number ten, "acquaintance with our neighbor," involves a visit to a nearby Druze or Arab village and a meeting with their youth. The eleventh, "operation savings," requires the children to collect old newspapers, kitchen utensils, bottles, etc. for a practical purpose. For number twelve they are asked to operate the kibbutz meteorological station and to be responsible for cleanliness in specific areas in the kibbutz. This *mitzvah* is known as "projects." The final one requires a written piece on a research topic. Comparisons with other kibbutzim reveal no basic difference in essence, but only in terminology or in the specific expression a particular *mitzvah* may manifest, depending on local resources and opportunities. The only activity absent from the thirteen *mitzvot* of Afikim that appeared with regularity in other listings is best entitled "good citizenship," which demands an acquaintance with the institutions of local government, i.e., the regional council, police, law courts—and also to profer aid to persons who are blind or deaf.

The Bar Mitzvah year has an extension in the year of service expected of a boy or girl before or after military service. Instead of returning to his kibbutz and entering into an economic branch, or continuing with advanced studies, a kibbutz youth is asked to donate a year to the movement, either by working at a young and struggling kibbutz or by serving as a counselor among new immigrants in development areas or major cities.

Without entering into the details of each *mitzvah*, their aim appears to be a nurturing of social responsibility. There was no personal *mitzvah* in the list other than writing a research paper. Even the trial of spending a day isolated in the field remains ultimately a social *mitzvah*, for if one knows how to protect one's own life, one is better equipped to protect the lives of others. *Mitzvot* must be social to be genuine. The *mitzvot* reviewed above tally with the realities of kibbutz life, in some cases parallel to kibbutz life processes, in others either ahead or behind the kibbutz lifestyle.

The *mitzvah* requiring study of Jewish tradition has little followup in later years, though Jewish history and knowledge of Israel remain a constant preoccupation throughout school. Whether there is any continuity after graduation from high school is difficult to determine, though a reasonable conjecture is that knowledge of Israel and its geography is more avidly pursued in adulthood than is Jewish history. The varying tasks to be performed within the kibbutz itself, like work, acquaintance with different branches of the economy, etc., are lessons in the mutual responsibility on which the kibbutz is nurtured. Here, too, there is continuity, with these *mitzvot* becoming a regular part of kibbutz life, as the Bar

Mitzvah youngsters mature. The *mitzvot* aimed at encouraging an alertness to the problems of others—not only the Arab and Druze, but the Oriental Jew as well—lag behind. Here is a case where the ideal encased in the *mitzvah* has failed to diffuse its meaning. In the opinion of a member of the psychology department of BarIlan University who conducted studies on kibbutz youth in the army, they show little concern for the problems of Oriental Jews, often remaining aloof from them. Therefore the aim of this *mitzvah* is to change an existing attitude and create understanding. The *mitzvah* "operation savings" is a remnant of mild asceticism, which is threatened by the abundance in today's kibbutzim. Saving papers and bottles in the well-to-do settlements seems anachronistic at first, but it too has a social purpose, for this waste material is then sold and the money put to a social use. Collection of old objects may also be intended to inculcate a respect for used things that may still retain their value.

With the rise of a new generation clamoring for more individuality, it was inevitable that a more individual, familial Bar Mitzvah be developed. Such an experiment took place recently at Kibbutz Ayelet ha-Shahar. A teacher proposed that each child celebrate his Bar Mitzvah alone. The kibbutz accepted her proposal, although with grave reservations arising out of fear that individual ceremonies would injure the communal character of the festivity. She claimed, however, that the communal Bar Mitzvah festival itself was a failure.

> All the experiments and efforts expended in creating new content for the old vessel have not been successful. In place of a warm and intimate ceremony we put on an impressive performance in a large crowd, a ceremony whose grating pathos only disguises the lack of genuine content. The community and parents of the children know that nothing has happened which justifies such frenzied preparation. In addition, the child has no opportunity to express himself, and what is demanded of him in that festive form is beyond his capabilities.[111]

It was suggested that Bar Mitzvah be practiced in the spirit of the Jewish tradition, but not as Orthodox Jews. By approaching the Bar Mitzvah is this fashion it could be observed in a traditional spirit without becoming a religious event. This argument probably appeared to allay fears that religious ceremonialism was infiltrating the kibbutz. The clinching argument made use of the sacred cow of psychology. In a traditionalistic ceremony, with maximum participation by the parents, "the feeling would be 'I matured,' in contrast to 'we matured'; the knowledge that the *mitzvot* 'fall on me personally' has supreme importance to a kibbutz boy." This is not only a personal trial, but also "a nursing of the feeling of personal uniqueness so lacking among pupils in communal education."[112] This rejection of the communal Bar Mitzvah is no indication of a trend, though it raises the question of whether the family could be restored as an independent and active unit in kibbutz festivities.

Bar Mitzvah often confronts a kibbutz family with tests of principle. Most families have relatives in the cities and these relatives, invited to the kibbutz Bar Mitzvah, follow the accepted urban pattern of bringing gifts to the youngster. But a kibbutz youngster may not make use of every gift he receives, otherwise he may infringe or breach the principle of equality. One kibbutz appointed a special Bar Mitzvah committee to decide what gifts are acceptable and what gifts must be turned over either to the kibbutz or the Hevrat Yeladim, the children's society, for common use. In some cases the kibbutz recommends preferred gifts to relatives and friends to avoid creating conflicts for the boy. Preferred gifts are usually books or camping equipment, which the youngster would receive from the kibbutz in any case. A "one-time" pleasure is also acceptable, such as a trip to Eilat, or a ticket to the theater, ballet, or opera. Cash gifts above thirty Israel lirot must be handed over to the kibbutz. In short, Bar Mitzvah is an opportunity to undergo the personal trial of observing a kibbutz *mitzvah*, the equal distribution of goods. Adherence to this *mitzvah*, with flexibility, will be fateful for the future of kibbutz identity.

## Marriage

In his two volumes on *The Jewish Holidays* and *The Lifetime of the Jew*, Haim Schauss included marriage in the latter work as one of the rites of passage between birth and death. This classification is correct for Jewish society in general, but does not hold completely for kibbutz society. While marriage is unquestionably an individual ceremony, a landmark in the personal history of a Jew, it is also a holiday for the entire kibbutz and is indeed known in kibbutz literature as Hag ha-Klulot ("the marriage holiday"). The communal character of the festivity is what underlies this transformation of marriage, which in effect is an event in both the life of the individual and of the kibbutz community.

In nonkibbutz society a couple's marriage ceremony is a combination of the legal and the social, with the rabbi, as representative of the State and of Jewish tradition, formally consecrating the marriage and conferring legal force upon it. Family rejoicing follows in the wake of the rabbinical ceremony. For the great majority of kibbutzim, however, a young man or woman about to be married is not only the child of his parents, but also that of the entire community. With the exception of only a few kibbutzim, marriage, like Bar Mitzvah, has become a community celebration. Unlike Bar Mitzvah, the marriage festival in the kibbutz occurs more than once a year. Although no clearly definable pattern has yet emerged, the general practice is to have kibbutz weddings a few times a year, depending upon the number of couples involved. Couples who intend to be married are asked to set their wedding for one of the dates during the year determined by the kibbutz as suitable for weddings. Why does the kibbutz consider it necessary to have group weddings? The services of Orthodox rabbis are available during the entire year. The decision to hold a group ceremony is dictated by the conditions of kibbutz life, and not by the availability of rabbis. To have a separate ceremony for each couple is a heavy burden on the cultural committee and their subcommittees. A kibbutz wedding is a ceremony in its own right, including more than food, drink, and dancing. It demands planning and preparation, involving dancers, a choir, sketches, and the composing of light banter appropriate to the couple.

Ha-Kibbutz ha-Artzi kibbutzim sometimes insist upon the exclusion of the traditional ceremony required by Israel law. They differentiate between the requirement of Israel law—consisting of rabbinic sanction, a ceremony that they reject in principle—and their own kibbutz ceremony, where the community fills a social obligation, but not a legal one. Couples will travel to a rabbi in a neighboring community to be officially married, and then return home. For Ha-Kibbutz ha-Artzi, therefore, their own ceremony is infinitely more significant than the traditional one, but not every kibbutz follows in this pattern. There are a number who raise no objection to performing the traditional ceremony in the kibbutz, which is to be followed immediately by the kibbutz marriage. Indeed, in a few isolated instances kibbutzim have sought to integrate the traditional ceremony into their own.

The willingness of some kibbutzim to search for a synthesis between the traditional way and the kibbutz way is a significant reminder of the cultural hold still retained by Jewish tradition. In this context a wedding in Ramat Yohanan is an instructive example of the unexpected effects of life upon principle. At first, the Orthodox ceremony was mocked and scoffed at and only accepted as a necessary evil prior to the major ceremony held shortly afterwards. In the course of time, however, the traditional *huppah* and *kiddushin* began to attract members as well as the immediate family. The scoffing came slowly to an end, and the traditional ceremony is now firmly emplaced as introductory to the kibbutz ceremony.

There is a kibbutz that has waived marriage as a kibbutz festival, returning it completely to the family. This is Yagur, one of the largest kibbutzim in Israel, with a population of close to 2,000 people. Having decided they were unable to organize and host community weddings properly, the kibbutz agreed to budget a certain sum to each family and leave the responsibility for the wedding in the hands of the parents. This practice is followed in many kibbutzim when a young man or woman has left the kibbutz, while his parents remain. The kibbutz declines to provide a community wedding, but it will budget a sum that the parents may use for a "private" reception in the kibbutz itself. These two poles, the personal and the communal, illustrate the problem facing the kibbutz, of striking a proper balance between marriage as an individual and as a social communal concern.

In 1966 the Inter-Kibbutz Committee on Holidays and Festivals published a booklet containing material for the use of cultural committees planning a wedding. It contained examples of ceremonies and two illustrations of the type of kibbutz *K'tubah* presented to a newly married couple by their community.

The focus is the *Ma'amad haHithay'vut*, a ceremony of mutual obligation. It takes place in the center of the platform erected in the dining room, or if the wedding is held out of doors, at some centrally located position. The couple is called up in a number of ways, depending upon local kibbutz custom. Some couples are accompanied by parents and relatives, others by best men. Often they arrive on foot, but in some instances are brought in a decorated wagon pulled by a tractor. If the ceremony is held near fish ponds, the couple may arrive in a small boat. The area surrounding the ceremonial platform may be decorated by arches hung with appropriate wedding verses. In place of the traditional bridal canopy, one kibbutz built a canopy enveloped in greenery. Another kibbutz constructed a canopy from the branches of date trees, basing itself upon a verse from the talmudic tractate *Kiddushin:* "Be sanctified to me by this date tree."

The *Ma'amad haHithay'vut* is included in every rite but takes different forms: a scroll, registration in a book of marriage, passing on a marriage cup, and the like. The scroll and book are generally embellished with ornaments. The names of married couples have been engraved on the cup and passed on from one couple to another. When a couple receives a marriage scroll, it is a kibbutz parallel to the traditional *K'tubah*. The language is not legal, as in the tradition, but it is a formula of moral obligation, with the couple promising to build their home and family in the kibbutz. This was revised when it was observed that married couples were leaving their kibbutzim. The genuineness of their obligation was in question; the content of the marriage scroll was therefore changed in the light of the new circumstances, which invalidated and annulled the obligatory character of the document. In more recently composed marriage scrolls couples do not obligate themselves to build their home in the kibbutz, but rather the kibbutz requests or appeals that they continue their life there. A kibbutz *K'tubah* now invites a couple to build a home in Israel as well as a home in the kibbutz—an admission of reality's toll upon the kibbutz.

The ceremony is a mixture of short prose and poetry readings, songs and dance, the main subjects being love, youth, and springtime. Biblical readings are generally from the Song of Songs, as are songs and dances. Any literary selections pertaining to the subject from Jewish literature are put to profitable use. At the conclusion of the ceremony the couple receives a gift from the kibbutz, often an artistically illustrated album of the Song of Songs. Some weddings include short plays that touch on marriage, taken from the works of modern Hebrew writers.

When the ceremony is over, food is served and this is followed by an entertainment of short satirical sketches, parodies, comic games, and folk dancing. This brief résumé cannot capture the aim of the marriage ceremony, "to enrich the content of matrimonial joy through a cultured and value-bearing expression. The subjects of the celebration are the joy of youth, the joy of fathers and sons, the joy of society. We do not yet have a set pattern or a crystallized framework."[113] The artistic part of the ceremony and the entertainment are dependent upon the amount of talent available in a particular kibbutz, and a willingness to participate and perform. The general atmosphere, as at a wedding anywhere in the world, is joyous.

Examination of the different verbal formulas used in the kibbutz marriage scrolls and *K'tubot* reveals a combination of traditional style and kibbutz content. A *K'tubah* has no real meaning in a kibbutz, for should a marriage fail, the wife does not need a legal contract from her estranged husband guaranteeing minimum support. Her kibbutz ensures physical sustenance on a level no lower than she had before separation. The *K'tubah* is retained in the marriage ceremony, but is given an entirely different content. The fiction of a legal document is retained by use of the term *brit*, or "covenant." One *K'tubah* begins "today we have entered into a covenant of marriage." When a couple signs the *K'tubah* their covenant is not limited to them alone, but encompasses their kibbutz as well, for the terms of their *brit* include building a home and family in the kibbutz, living their lives according to its principles, and devoting their energies and talents to its success. Some *K'tubot* follow the traditional pattern of requiring the signature of two witnesses, while others ignore this procedure and call to witness the heavens above and the earth below. The geographical location of a kibbutz is sometimes included:

> May this scroll be evidence of the covenant between you into which you have entered, to build a house in Israel in Kibbutz Afikim, which dwells by the banks of the Jordan and Yarmouk in the Valley opposite Golan and Gilad.[114]

Marriage is vital to the kibbutz for a number of reasons. It refills the human reserve that is depleted by losses to the city and by the drying up of external sources. To be single in a kibbutz is not a desirable status, so the kibbutz movements operate a matchmaking service through tours, conferences, seminars, etc., where young single people may meet. Should local sources of marriageable youth decrease, a bachelor may be sent to work outside the kibbutz. In her article "Mate Selection in Collective Settlements," the late Yonina Talmon lucidly analyzes the marriage pattern of second-generation youth. She concludes that the prevalent pattern of marriage combines in a delicate balance out-marriage (exogamy) with in-marriage (endogamy).

> By combining "exogamy" and "endogamy," the second generation reconciles dissociation with identification and maintains a flexible balance between rebellion and loyalty. . . . A combination of exogamy and endogamy militates against insulation, yet safeguards distinctiveness.[115]

The terms "exogamy" and "endogamy" are carefully defined in her work, for in kibbutz life they assume special meanings. For our purposes, however, they may be more generally understood as encompassing marriage between kibbutz and nonkibbutz youth. Kibbutz parents impelled by the understandable desire to see their social creation continue prefer marriage between their youth and those from other kibbutzim. Marrying a nonkibbutznik poses the danger of losing a youngster to the nonkibbutz world. In one sense the kibbutz is in a position somewhat similar to Orthodox Jewry: for both groups in-marriage is a significant force in preserving group unity and cohesion. For the kibbutz movement out-marriage balances the danger of insularity and provincialism by bringing into the kibbutz individuals who can constitute an important connection between the kibbutz and the surrounding society it wants to influence. Marriage patterns of the second generation have been a successful compromise between social self-preservation and an individual's vacillation between permanency in his kibbutz and the allure of the outside.

Fifteen to twenty years ago the kibbutz began to expend its creative energy on fashioning a wedding ceremony. This arose with the emergence of the second generation and the increased permanency of kibbutz life. Many of the *Vatikim* had never gone through the formal procedures of a religious ceremony. They simply moved into a "family room." With the gradual return of the family nucleus to kibbutz society, and the ascendancy of kinship ties, the children of the *Vatikim* began to request a wedding ceremony. These inclinations were reinforced by their parents, who felt that their own marital pattern—common-law marriage—no longer fitted the kibbutz scene. Thus began the search for a compatible ceremony to legitimize the marital attachments of the second generation and intensify the generational tie. Further, the *Vatikim*, as parents, sought a socioceremonial outlet for the joy they felt when their children announced an intention to marry.

Because the kibbutz feels that it has created a unique life-style, it is unable to lean upon the ceremonials developed by others under different conditions. Impelled by this ideological stance, the flow of circumstance, a need to ritualize its values, and the human urge to mark decisive moments in life history, the kibbutz has sought to create a marriage ceremony that has roots in its way of life. Kibbutz marriage is a successful example of the organic manufacture of a ritual.

## Mourning

In death, as in life, the kibbutz insists upon a measure of separation between its members and the surrounding community. Unlike the average Israeli, who can expect to be laid to rest in a municipal cemetery and whose remains are entrusted to the final care of the local *Hevra Kadisha* ("burial society"), a kibbutznik will be buried "at home." Kibbutzim have their own cemeteries, often situated on the outskirts in a small grove planted for that purpose. The care of a kibbutz cemetery is in the hands of members, so an unkempt cemetery, with tilting tombstones and overgrown weeds, is not part of the kibbutz scene.

The kibbutz has taken first steps toward initiating a culture of remembrance. As in their approach to holidays, kibbutz spokesmen, in writing or speaking of mourning procedures, claim that because the practices of traditional Judaism are unsatisfactory and inappropriate, the kibbutz is forced to probe into its own mores to discover methods or mechanisms for the guidance of the mourner and the community. The Jewish tradition cannot be so summarily dismissed from a subject as elemental as death and mourning, where past memories, future fears, and burdens of guilt all combine to overcome even the most devout and consistent rationalist. Recognizing the confusion that prevails in many kibbutzim in matters pertaining to mourning, and hoping to contribute to the evolution of another kibbutz tradition, the Inter-Kibbutz Committee on Holidays and Festivals produced a booklet on this subject, entitled *Mourning*. It notes the need to impart to the coming generations a form of communal mourning that will teach them mutual responsibility. This fundamental principle of the kibbutz applies to death as to life, including not only close relatives and members of the family, but all members of the kibbutz. Failure to educate the young in their obligation to participate, in some fashion, in mourning for each kibbutz member who dies, would constitute a serious setback to the tie between the individual and society. In urban society death and mourning are considered the province of family and friends, but in the kibbutz, events, customs, and practices are evaluated for their intrinsic merit and also for their effect on kibbutz solidarity. Were mourning to be relegated only to those who are directly affected, the extended family would lose another of its functions to the biological family, moving the kibbutz closer toward making the family cell the exclusive unit of kibbutz life.

A defined set of customs in this sphere, as in holidays and festivals, would release members from uncertainty. A mourning tradition would present the necessary guidelines for honoring members. The need for a stable, perhaps even static tradition is stronger in this sphere than in any other area of kibbutz ceremonial practice. A return to the past, particularly to its superstitious folk practices, is out of the question. The religious concept of death, as understood by the editor of *Mourning*, is not suitable for the kibbutz, thereby invalidating the Kaddish prayer with *Tzidduk ha-Din*—acceptance of the judgment of death as God's will. This does not imply that mourning is to be mute, for if appropriate forms are not found and the present vacuum not filled with kibbutz customs, "foreign or undesirable content could enter."

As customary in the kibbutz when cultural questions of Jewish import are elevated to become important issues, the heart and the head pull fiercely in opposite directions. In death, however, human emotions are not so liable to compromise or surrender to the dictates of a rationalism, which overlooks the mysteries of human existence. Following a burial at a large and veteran kibbutz in the Jezreel Valley, a quarrel broke out that was reported in the pages of the Ihud movement's weekly bulletin. At this funeral skullcaps were worn, but one of the members refused to put one on and took his argument to the internal kibbutz press. In a column entitled "Profanation of the Sacred, or Self-deception," he asked why he should be forced to wear a skullcap and hear the prayer *El Male Rahamim* at the graveside when he knew that the person lying in the grave would have objected. This may only be a supposition, for even confirmed rationalists have been known to request religious ceremonials at their burial. Not everyone is willing to pay the price of consistency. A compromise was achieved by asking a religious functionary from a nearby community to perform the traditional ritual at the graveside. Using the services of a stranger could well have been the outcome of the custom once practiced among some kibbutzim of standing silently by the open grave. The gloomy and melancholy mood that this must have engendered probably led to the conclusion that without some ritual, funerals could become unbearable.

The difficulties occasioned by public mourning for every death in the kibbutz constitute another problem. Its concept of communal mourning requires a temporary halt in the pace of kibbutz life on the funeral day itself or for a period of three or seven days, depending upon the practice of the individual kibbutz. Work is to cease during the funeral, while cultural and social activities are curtailed for the three- or seven-day mourning period. In most countries public mourning of this sort is decreed only for heads of state or unusually distinguished figures, but in the kibbutz all members are thus honored. As some kibbutzim have grown into big and settled communities with many elderly people, the question is raised whether kibbutz life should be allowed to become periodically paralyzed as the number of yearly deaths increases. In addition, the effect of a death on holiday observance has to be solved. Here the problem is not what the family should do, as in Orthodox Judaism, but how the entire community should behave. In Ramat Yohanan when a death occurred two weeks before Purim, all decorations were at once removed, to be later restored in time for the festivities. Grumbling and complaints about the inconvenience caused by temporary cessation of activity is no indication that the kibbutz will reverse itself, even though the social reality of a large, heterogeneous kibbutz population makes death a matter primarily for those directly affected. Yet the ideal of communal mourning remains institutionally in force so that the present system of work and cultural stoppage might very well continue.

It should not be expected that every funeral or memorial ceremony in a kibbutz is a solemn, dignified occasion. Letters and extracts from kibbutz bulletins that appear in *Mourning* reveal indifference, lack of interest, conversation about everday affairs while at the cemetery, etc. Everyone has observed indifferent or even frivolous behavior in cemeteries, which serves as a form of self-protection against dejection and depression. Jewish tradition provides standard phrases to be uttered when meeting mourners, thereby solving the problem of how to behave in the presence of mourners. Because mourning customs are usually couched in religious language, many young people brought up in a secular society do not know how to act when comforting a mourner.

> I heard the best of our young men, dumbfounded, asking how is one to behave in a case of mourning? How is sympathy expressed? From whom can they learn when there are no accepted customs? It is said that the accepted customs are the fruit of superstition, or of religious beliefs which we reject. But have we not adopted the greeting "Mazal Tov," which is an ancient magic relic without any tie to Jewish belief? There is a general participation in the joy of a member when a son is born to him; or when there is a marriage. Participation in joy—yes, so why not participation in mourning? An ancient and wise proverb says: In sorrow

a friend is known. Certainly all members of a kibbutz are friends to each other. . . . In the eyes of outsiders we look like a big family, but organized economic cooperation is not enough. This cooperation is the basis for the growth of customs which fit it. We would do well to foster such customs, for thus the genuine culture of a society grows, when it gives expression to the real needs of its members during every hour of their life, including those moments of mourning we can all expect.[116]

If the kibbutz has, by its own testimony, succeeded in developing a culture of remembrance, then what accounts for the plaintive tone of the above quotation? A kibbutz culture of remembrance does indeed exist, but it remains communal, outlining and proposing how the kibbutz, as a body, should act. There always remains a fear of dictating to the individual, which might possibly result in an intrusion on his conscience. Forms of mourning by individuals or families remain their private affair, outside of kibbutz moral jurisdiction. Among the different elements in the kibbutz culture of remembrance—memorial ceremonies, archives of the deceased, memorial booklets, gravestones, statues—an interesting and unusual change is occurring in the composition of the memorial booklets. A booklet in memory of the deceased is customarily distributed to all the members after one year has elapsed. These booklets were often written in the spirit of the eulogies that appeared in the back sections of the federation quarterly—caricature of real people whose frailties are instantaneously erased by death, or so it would seem to a reader of this eulogistic literature. Obviously, it is the family friends who are responsible for these lifeless portraits—and they are not to be blamed for continuing in a traditional and time-honored fashion. Lately, however, particularly under the influence of the young intellectuals associated with *Shedemot,* one discerns a new direction in this type of literature. Eulogies are giving way to a different means of perpetuating the deceased in communal memory.

A year after the conclusion of the Six-Day War the Ihud published a book of remembrance in honor of all members of Ihud kibbutzim who fell in the war. Edited with taste and reverence, this book is a departure from accustomed practice. In place of the glowing terms so characteristic of this literary genre ("Sing to the dead before they die," writes the Hebrew poet Yitzhak Shiloh), an attempt is made to sketch a living portrait of each of the sixty-seven men eulogized. Entitled *B'Darkam* ("In Their Way"), it is an uncommon piece of literature. The editors correctly assumed that a living image of the dead would be more faithful to their memory than turning them into a community of saints. Consequently no classical eulogies appear in *B'Darkam*. The editors talked with friends and family, tape-recorded conversations about the deceased as he was remembered, and requested the right to publish letters or other documents. Some families objected to this method and were reluctant to disclose personal letters, preferring the traditional and conventional mode of remembrance. Despite some opposition, the book, as finally published, succeeds in achieving the editors' aims. *B'Darkam* is more than a collection of memorial material; it is also "a book of witness, for it creates a collective bibliography of a young kibbutz generation."[117]

Every kibbutz home in the Ihud has a copy of *B'Darkam* not only because it was widely distributed, but because it has assumed a significance beyond the emotional reach of the mourning families. It has become, in a sense, a part of the kibbutz sacrificial heritage, a part of its living memory. "We shall return to this book more and more, again and again." *B'Darkam* is a valuable and human contribution to one aspect of a kibbutz culture of remembrance. The other aspects—memorial ceremonies, archives, gravestones—receive generous attention in *Mourning*. Considerable space is devoted to literary material that could be used for Yizkor, the yearly memorial ceremony in honor of the deceased. As a rule it is held in many kibbutzim on Yom Kippur evening. The suggested poetry and reading are almost exclusively from modern Hebrew literature, with only biblical quotations representing the tradition. In place of the customary Yizkor prayer a kibbutz Yizkor has been composed by a few kibbutzim. It is not a prayer in the customary sense, but rather a ceremonial of remembrance and identification with the departed.

Sections are also devoted to proper methods of inscribing tombstones, and examples are given. From kibbutz archives illustrations are provided of the proper documentation of death and the correct cataloging of all literary and artistic remains. Conspicuously absent are examples of graveside ceremonies and suggested means for comforting mourners. Nevertheless, *Mourning* does contain sufficient material for a kibbutz seeking a guide for public and communal demonstrations of mourning. There are slight differences in practice among the various kibbutzim, but the overall approach is similar. To illustrate, a partial summary is offered below of the proposals of the committee on mourning customs of Ramat Yohanan.

The proposals are to be brought to the attention of the general assembly that may add to or modify them. Upon approval, they become the law of the kibbutz. These are some of the proposals: When a death occurs, a mourning notice will appear on the bulletin board. The coffin is to be accompanied from the hospital and will be placed on the lawn in the summer and in the library in the winter. There is to be silent communion. An automobile will convey the coffin to the cemetery, accompanied by members. During the funeral all work will cease so that everyone may pay final respects. By the graveside there is to be only one eulogy and a reading from the Bible. If the deceased worked outside the kibbutz, or if the family requests it, another eulogy may be added. Recitation of the Kaddish will be according to the wishes of the family. Regarding all ceremony at the graveside, prior consultations should be made with the family. It is suggested that plots should not be reserved, although maximum consideration will be given to such a wish. On the seventh day, family and friends alone visit the grave. By the thirtieth day a tombstone should be in place. There are two possible ways of remembrance: at the unveiling of the tombstone or by a memorial ceremony in the dining room. In the latter case a corner will be prepared in honor of the deceased. Members will enter silently at a set hour. In conclusion there will be a musical selection, and members will disperse after the family leaves. After a year, the deceased will be recalled yearly in the kibbutz bulletin in a special column in remembrance of the dead. Relatives and close friends of the family visit the grave and announce it on the bulletin board. The community will determine a suitable time for a general and communal memorial service, which may be on Yom Kippur eve, on the day celebrating settlement on the land, or the national Day of Remembrance on the eve of Independence Day. On the yearly memorial day the names of all those who died that year will be mentioned, and that day will also serve as a personal day of remembrance.

The publication of a bulletin in honor of the deceased is to be done at home (in the kibbutz). Should the family request an alternative method for perpetuation of the memory of the deceased, it will be done in conjunction with kibbutz institutions.

## General Remarks

1. Tombstones are to be uniform in size, shape, and inscription for all the deceased other than those killed in battle.
2. The cemetery is to be carefully tended.
3. A person is to be appointed (part-time) for general care of the cemetery.
4. Notice of death and date of funeral will be announced in one daily newspaper *(Davar)* and one afternoon newspaper; a notice in another paper will be published at the request of the family. Notices are to be written in one style and are to be of equal size.

At the graveside on burial day, practices vary widely, from silence to a eulogy accompanied by Kaddish and El Male Rahamim. Readings from Psalms may also be included. One kibbutz has special graveside readings for children and another for the elderly, in both instances taken from modern Hebrew literature.

This summary of kibbutz custom is based on the handful of kibbutzim whose practices are noted in *Mourning*. The remainder are not mentioned, either because they failed to respond to the editor's request for a written outline or because they could add little to the picture already drawn. It may reasonably be inferred that the variations in custom cover the range of kibbutz practice at this juncture. The actual atmosphere during the funeral rites and the consistency in observance of these guidelines is difficult to determine. In conversations some members noted the cold and severe atmosphere prevailing at funerals in certain kibbutzim, while other communities reap praise for the humane and merciful character of their rites.

An observer with no prior knowledge or experience of the kibbutz could gain an excellent insight into the social concepts of kibbutz life through a perusal of the mourning customs. The communal character of the kibbutz breaks through time and again. At no point is the individual member guided, for what a man does in his own room is considered his own affair, to be determined by his own conscience. In one community, for example, a mourner invited a rabbi to his home to lead a lesson in Mishnah. The only overlap between the individual and the public realm occurs during the exhibition of the kibbutz Book of Remembrance, usually laid out on a table on Yom Kippur, or whatever day a kibbutz has decided upon. This amounts to a community and individual *Yahrzeit*.

In the light of the severe psychological shock suffered by a mourner, the mechanisms of traditional Judaism seem singularly successful in reintroducing him gradually to a new reality while deprived of a major human support he may have taken for granted. The fears and unspoken guilts erupting at that critical moment need an outlet lest they lead to self-destruction. Therefore the mourner is surrounded by family and friends, and goes through a ritualistic absolution by remaining unshaven, unwashed, sitting on a low stool, and so forth. The kibbutz has ignored this entire realm of the individual expression of mourning out of solicitude for individual conscience. Is mourning therefore a more difficult, wrenching experience for a kibbutznik deprived, in most cases, of the consolations offered by the traditional rituals of the home? Does the communal stance of the kibbutz supply the solace so necessary to the mourner suddenly faced with the burden of loneliness? What comfort does he gain from the cancellation or postponement of public functions during the mourning period? Does a public declaration of communal mourning functionally serve as an indicator that he is not alone, and that the community is willing to change its order of life for a few days out of respect for his departed? Does the kibbutz way of mourning more effectively soften the blow inflicted by death? The answers to these and other questions could help evaluate the kibbutz way of mourning and determine its implications for the human encounter with death.

# 9
# *Conclusion*

> The individual who is joined by the roots to the collective is destined, either visibly or invisibly, to shape the life of the community. The level of collective religion—certainly for Judaism and the present time—is no longer alive and not to be revived, because there are no individuals who by their genuine numenous experience, can stir the collective.
> —Erich Neuman, "Stages of Religious Experience and the Path of Depth Psychology," *Israel Annals of Psychiatry and Related Disciplines* 18, no. 3 (December 1970)

## *The Meaning of the Kibbutz in Jewish Life*

Despite its small size, Israel is accustomed to being a center of global attention, a front-page item for much of the world's press. Although many Israelis devoutly wish their country would be relegated to the back pages, or appear primarily in tourist advertisements, many of them secretly harbor a slightly perverse pleasure at the constant attention that their country gains. Whatever the immediate sources of the world interest in the existence and fate of this numerically small people—political, military, strategic, social, or religious—it has a long history. The common view, to a great extent justified, bases this historical interest of the Western world in Jewry upon the common cultural heritage arising out of the biblical past. The existence of a religious language common to Jews and Christians had undoubtedly played an important part in binding Jewry culturally to different peoples and nations. Max Weber, however, probes more deeply into the relationship between the Jewish people and the nations of the world:

Ritually correct conduct, i.e., conduct conforming to caste standards, carried for the Indian castes the premium of ascent by way of rebirth in a caste-structured world thought to be eternal and unchangeable. . . . For the Jew . . . the world was conceived as neither eternal nor unchangeable, but rather as having been created. Its present structures were a product of man's activities, above all those of the Jews, and of God's reaction to them. Hence the world was an historical product designed to give way again to the truly God-ordained order. The whole attitude toward life of ancient Jewry was determined by this conception of a future God-guided political and social revolution. . . . There existed in addition a highly rational religious ethic of social conduct; it was free of magic and all forms of irrational quest for salvation; it was inwardly worlds apart from the paths of salvation offered by Asiatic religions. To a large extent this ethic still underlies contemporary Middle Eastern and European ethic. World-historical interest in Jewry rests upon this fact.[118]

Now that a small but influential segment of world Jewry has reestablished a Jewish state and named it after a biblical predecessor, "world-historical interest in Jewry," has undergone a resurgence. For reasons that are not difficult to understand, Israel stands as the contemporary representative of a biblical ethic of social conduct that has only recently begun to take serious root in religious circles of the Western world, although in a "secular" form. Somehow there exist expectations that Israel society would be more just and more equitable than other societies. Whatever the truth or falsity of these expectations, Israelis accept them as legitimate, despite their longing to be "as all other nations."

In this context the kibbutz becomes a showpiece for the social quality of Israel society, and visitors to Israel are often taken to kibbutzim not to see farms and factories, but to observe and absorb the operations of this egalitarian society. Oddly enough, the pride in the kibbutz evinced by Israelis finds its expression in contacts with non-Jewish visitors to the state, or with professional people in the social sciences and humanities. Jews from outside of Israel are rarely encouraged by nonkibbutz Israelis to settle in a kibbutz. This task is performed by the official agents of the kibbutz movements. Ambivalence toward the kibbutz is a well-known phenomenon in Israeli life.

On the basis of this study, the kibbutz should open itself to a new and different type of visitors and researchers—to Jews who, through a study of Jewish life, are seeking a means of understanding and clarifying the significant problems and issues common to

Conclusion                                                                 231

concerned and thinking Jews everywhere. Previously, the kibbutz was considered the realm only of Jewish socialists or Zionists, but not of Jews with any religious identity. It is hoped that this study of certain aspects of kibbutz society will assist in creating among Jews a fuller identification with the Jewishness of the kibbutz, and in particular its confrontations with the same religious, social, and ethical questions that bear upon all thoughtful and reflective Jews. A brief sketch of these questions as they emerge out of kibbutz life will serve to adumbrate a kibbutz theology, an account of the major issues in kibbutz faith at this juncture in its development. The importance for Jewish theology of the type of life lived by Jews has been stated by by Nathan Glazer:

> In Judaism then, it is not God directly, found after an inner search, that changes man, but the example of the good and holy life, presented by the community of Jews whether in actuality or as a historical myth or as an ideal. The disciples of Hasidism in Williamsburg see this community before their eyes; the returning Yiddish writers recall it from the past. . . . All we can know from the history of Judaism is that the abstract demand to seek faith, to find God, tends to find little answer among Jews and that concrete examples of Jewish living must be given before religion has an impact on their lives. Once again, honesty requires one to say that it is likely that no satisfactory example can be given in the modern world, that those moments in Jewish history when the Jews were truly a people of priests and a holy nation required circumstances that can never be repeated.[110]

The kibbutz, an avowed social movement, has no pretensions of serving as an example of the "good and holy life" in terms similar to the Hasidim of Williamsburg, nor would it agree to its inclusion among the people of priests and a holy nation. But despite its disclaimers, the kibbutz cannot escape the imperatives of Jewish history and life that draw it into a theological realm of discourse. Often Christians who are unencumbered by the weight of contemporary Jewish history and its dichotomization into religious and nonreligious see in the kibbutz a community with an almost monastic mystique. But Christian opinion will not be the determinant in resolving the place of the kibbutz in Jewish religious history. If Nathan Glazer is right, then the quality of life as lived in the kibbutz will determine whether or not it becomes a factor in the progressive revelations of the spirit as they occur within Jewish history. These revelations did not occur in a complete and comprehensive form to any particular group, but occurred intermittently, in fragments, to small bodies of Jews. The cumulative experience of those scattered moments when small groups of Jews transcended themselves becomes part of the heritage, a part of the people's historical memory. What then of the kibbutz, a *community* in a sense that can be applied to few other groups of Jews in the world? What has the kibbutz contributed to the store of ideas and to the quality of life in the Jewish world today?

A study of the kibbutz could be an invaluable asset for Jewish theology. A society with few speculative interests, a kibbutz image of deity, if and when it arises, would probably be close in concept to a metaanthropological approach. Only out of concrete examples of living, out of man's spiritual acts, can deity emerge. In other words, God becoming God through man, evolving within the dynamics of the life impulse. The kibbutz is ideally suited to the development of such theology, for it is firmly rooted in a system that is not only based upon spiritual principles, but is actively engaged in seeking their application in daily life. There has been no thinking along these lines as yet, primarily because kibbutz thinkers have not been aware that it is possible to reflect in this fashion.

> The entire modern analysis of religion . . . has been forced to ground religion in the structure of the human situation itself.[120]

The human situation is the ground of kibbutz life, and as the kibbutz moves toward a deeper and more profound analysis of human complexity and its accumulated experience with human problems deepens its insights, it will gain the necessary tools for theological thinking. The anthropological theology hinted at as fitting the communal structure of kibbutz life is not a necessary consequence of that structure, but, as Buber's remark that "the *Yahad* is the Sinai of the future" would seem to indicate, it is close to it in spirit.

> To say, "Let us join hands and be just and merciful to one another," is a creative act bringing something new to bear on the human situation.

The endeavor of the kibbutz to create a community of fellowship, with all the difficulties it undergoes, remains another distinct contribution to modern Jewish life. Despite the present division of kibbutz society along family lines, the ideal of communal fellowship still remains powerful in kibbutz society. Without the additional communal soul, the kibbutz ceases to exist. The quality of a kibbutz can indeed be measured by the manner in which the spirit of fellowship pervades all its people and all its institutions.

> Fraternity does not mean indiscriminate familiarity. It does not exclude reserve, or scorn, or struggle, when they are appropriate and necessary, but it does exclude alienation, the thrusting aside of other men as foreign and lesser beings.[121]

Despite all its faults, the trivial pettiness, greed, and gossip that are a part of the kibbutz human scene, this society remains loyal to the basic premise of fellowship as described above. Kibbutz fellowship faces a difficult test in the years ahead, as kibbutz society becomes more heterogeneous, multigenerational, and multiprofessional,—practically a microcosmos. Can the spirit of fellowship be retained among individuals who have little in common other than a commitment to the kibbutz ideal?

Another significant contribution of the kibbutz to the modern Jewish spirit is the blow it has given to the polarization of Jewish life into the opposites of "religious" and "nonreligious." The kibbutz experience has taught the Jewish world that the most viable distinction is between belief and unbelief, with Orthodox Jews sometimes falling into the latter category. Despite its insistence upon calling itself secular, the kibbutz can be considered a member of the community of faith, even though the object of its faith is man.

The humanism of the kibbutz (which may prove insufficiently profound to some of its members) is not to be conceived as an antithesis to theism, but as an antithesis to materialism. Its essence is simple. "It is the attitude which judges the externals of life by their effect in assisting or hindering the life of the spirit."[122] Although man is considered sovereign, as testified by the moral and judicial authority of the kibbutz general assembly, this too does not mean atheism, for asserting man's creative powers is not to assert his omnipotence. Nor does this assertion imply that human powers know no regulation, either by moral imperatives or by a Supreme Being. Most Jews today, including many who are members of synagogues, would subscribe to the kibbutz humanistic theology as described in this work. The existence of a kibbutz humanism within the Jewish world is a reminder to other Jews that humanism, with its universal outlook, need not result in an abandonment of the Jewish people and its heritage.

The existence of a Jewish humanism alongside a possible theological anthropology is not a contradiction. The kibbutz has passed beyond its early period of collective conformity, whether social, ideological, political, or intellectual. Now it will make room for the divergent elements of man's cultural life and his need for faith with different forms of humanism and theism existing together, side by side.

In evaluating the religious quality of the kibbutz, the inclusive standards of judgment proposed by Winston L. King supply a useful guide.[123] He suggests three basic criteria: "The first of these would be an intellectual viewpoint or account coherent with our most assured knowledge of the environing reality." This means that statements made about history, science, the nature of man, the ultimate nature of the world must endure the criticism of the historian, the physical scientist, the social scientist, the philosopher. If a religion is to speak to men, it must persuade them it is true in the light of the other knowledge they possess. The second criterion concerns the personal values that any particular religion encourages as being in accord with our estimation of man and his values. The final consideration is the nature of living and character that this faith produces. In other words—what does a religion do for man or make of him?

Working backwards, there can be little doubt that the kibbutz passes the pragmatic test of the third and second points. All observers of the kibbutz agree that, whatever his faults, "*homo kibbutznikus*" is a worthy and humane individual. The social values of his community and their viability have encouraged him to live a life of helpfulness and mutual cooperation. In answering the first question, the kibbutz lags, not because it suffers from a shortage of intelligent and thoughtful people, but as a result of its relative youth and disinclination to engage in speculation. The creation of a metaphysics requires time and accumulation of enough concrete experience to supply sources for metaphysical speculation. Sociologists of religion differ markedly among themselves on whether and how to include naturalistic and supernaturalistic faiths under the heading of religion. Lenski[124] includes both theistic and nontheistic faiths, while Wach[125] rails against those "pseudo-religions" that substitute social efficacy for "relation to an ultimate non-finite reality, i.e. a cosmological dimension."[126] The conclusive answer to this dispute will have to wait, as is said in the tradition, until the arrival of Elijah. However, there is a clue to the answer in the Mishnah Torah of Maimonides, Laws of Repentance, chapter 3, section 2:

> A man whose sins are greater than his virtues immediately dies of his evil deeds, as is written: by your many sins. (Jeremiah 30:14)
> And also a state whose sins are great is immediately lost, as is written: the cry of Sodom and Gomorrah is great. (Genesis 18:20)
> And so the entire world; if its sins are greater than its virtues, it is immediately destroyed, as is written: And God saw how great was the evil of man on the land. (Genesis 6:5)
> This weighing is not according to the number of virtues and sins but according to their quality. There is a virtue which is over against a number of sins, as is written: Because there was found in him a good thing [I Kings 14:13] and there is a sin which is over against many virtues, as is written: And because of one transgression he will lose much good. (Ecclesiastes 9:18)

# Appendix:
# The Kibbutz and Martin Buber

Although Martin Buber's steadfast belief in Zionism has received less attention than his famed dialogical philosophy and his compilations of Hasidic stories, it was an integral part of his philosophy and the result partly of his strong identification with the kibbutz, the ideals and accomplishments of which he regarded with the utmost seriousness. His ties with the movement in fact, although uneven, remained in force until the end of his life.

Buber was not a leader in the kibbutz movement; he never joined a kibbutz and remained detached from the movement's daily problems. He was, however, one of the few prominent figures in Israel's academic world who sought a dialogue with the kibbutz. In 1945, when he organized a symposium of leaders from the kibbutz and other cooperative movements and some of the faculty of the Hebrew University, it was one of the few occasions that the kibbutz and the University faced each other as equals.

### Genuine Judaism Only in Community

Buber's willingness to speak with the kibbutz and not to it was much more than a consequence of his dialogical approach. Martin Buber believed that genuine Judaism could be found only in those movements which seek community. Distinguishing "official" Judaism from "subterranean" Judaism, he believed the latter to be truer to the spirit of Jewish teaching. Among them he placed the Essenes, the Hasidim—and the kibbutzim. All these represent the search for a communal form of life, a form that epitomizes, for Buber, the highest ideals of Judaism. Far from representing rebellion then, the kibbutz represents continuity, a socially creative Judaism.

Since this socially creative Judaism, Buber believes, can arise only within an autonomous Jewish community, Diaspora Judaism is negated. Although it served the function of preserving the Jewish heritage, it failed to create the life of righteousness and justice, the true community. That task fell to the Zionist movement, the only movement in the Jewish world that had set for itself the goal of establishing an autonomous Jewish state. The kibbutz, that part of the Zionist movement which was best equipped to achieve true community, became, for Buber, the instrument for the achievement of this life of righteousness and justice. Thus, Zionism and kibbutz are transformed into one religiosocial movement, with aims transcending the establishment of merely another nation-state, and Buber's support of the kibbutz movement is now understandable. The kibbutz, by searching for an appropriate social pattern for its humanistic faith, is for Buber evidence that God can exist without an intellectual acknowledgment of His presence.

## *The* Hevrutah

Such stress upon community does not make Buber a collectivist; he did not believe that communing with other human beings is enough for man to become fully human. Living next to people is no guarantee of being able to live with people. No admirer of either collectivism or individualism, Buber chose a middle road which he termed *Hevrutah*, which can best be translated as "community," "fellowship," or "commune." In contrast to collectivism, which raises barriers to an individual meeting with his fellowman, *Hevrutah* is the type of society in which man can meet with man on an equal basis, free from the egocentrism of individualism and free also from the personal renunciation demanded by collectivism. The type of community envisaged by Buber as the ideal setting for man meeting with man would be socialistic, founded upon equality and cooperation, providing the appropriate setting for a truly human community life. But "the establishment of a human people" is not the final end of his proposed community. God, too, is part of it—"in its midst," because the kingdom of God is no more than the kingdom of man as it shall become. What accounts for Buber's unusual faith in *Hevrutah*? And how does this faith relate to the kibbutz?

Buber sought the means of making God a living reality to his contemporaries, but realized that the traditional ways of invoking God no longer awakened an awareness of His presence. In this era, with man now occupying His place, God has retreated into the shadows. But through the medium of human action, directed to goals that are consonant with God's will, he can return from the periphery, and because our age is nonreligious, this would be accomplished through secular means. If He seeks interaction with man, God must "accommodate" Himself to the patterns that men live by, and since men live together in society, Buber believed that a mode or style of life that would draw God into it by virtue of its aims would allow God to reveal Himself, and would be conducive to a religious awakening and to some form of revelation of the living God.

What is of significance here in Buber's teaching is his belief that human striving for true communal life leads inevitably toward God, and that the search for God must lead inevitably to true community. When Buber writes of "the religion of communal living, a religion where God reveals himself in the society of man," his hopes for, and belief in, the potential of the kibbutz are underlined.

### Perfection of the Individual

But even the most successful community consists of individuals, and unless they are sound, each of and by himself, the best communal structures will eventually disintegrate. So no *Hevrutah* is really possible unless each individual in the community seeks his own inner perfection. When peace reigns within, a man can seek peace among others; thus uncontrolled flight into the heady realms of community is discouraged. Whether Buber was naive and utopian in his expectations is a question for later discussion, but published evidence indicates that the kibbutz was to serve as a testing ground for Buber's brand of religious anthropology.

A community must resist self-worship, must accept its own limitations and avoid letting its patterns of life become absolutes. When this is achieved, a real tie to "The Absolute" becomes possible. Because modern society rejects the traditional familiar language of religion, God will not appear in the theological garb familiar to us. If and when God does appear, He reveals Himself as an Absolute. The religious man has a special relationship to this absolute, whose essence, according to Buber, can be discovered only through group experience, the feeling of *Hevrutah*.

Though Buber was a man who resisted labels and pat formulations, his views could be classified as religious socialism, a unique brand, bearing the clear stamp of his personality. No kibbutz today identifies with his religious socialism. The Orthodox kibbutzim practice religion, but not as Buber conceived it. The non-Orthodox kibbutzim practice religion, also not as Buber conceived it. The non-Orthodox kibbutzim consider themselves socialist, and are not knowingly religious; and except for a few, they find Buber's philosophy quite puzzling, although by now his works have been translated into Hebrew. The attraction that he has for a few kibbutz intellectuals lies in his unification of socialism and religion, which appeals to a minority who believe that their socialism must be related somehow to the religious heritage of the Jewish people.

## Can Hevrutah Be Attained?

But Buber's teaching may be beyond human capacity. It is not surprising, therefore, that he was disappointed that the kibbutz failed to achieve *Hevrutah*. In his eyes, the kibbutz failure to reach genuine community was not only a failure for socialism, but also for Judaism, for his image of Judaism is intertwined with his socialism. If one fails, so must the other. Buber writes that a true Judaism is based on the Jewish saying, "Join in acts of creation." The task of Judaism is not "the truth in an idea or the truth in an image, but the truth in an act . . . not a philosophy or an artistic creation but a real society." Accordingly, Buber hoped that the kibbutz would realize what he considered authentic Judaism, free from the stultifying atmosphere of ritual and dogma. Known as a philosopher of the concrete and the real, Buber taught that it is presumptuous to believe in an idea without living it. But his demands upon the kibbutz seem unrealistic, for the people living in the kibbutz are only human, with the attendant human frailties.

There is one kibbutz, however, whose founding stemmed directly from Buber's philosophy. Ha-Zorea, founded in the 1930s by German Jewish youth who were his followers, was originally planned as a commune in Germany, but with the rise of Hitler it was decided that Palestine was the appropriate site. Some years after settlement on the land, the members became Marxists, joining Ha-Kibbutz ha-Artzi and, in effect, breaking their tie with Buber, who rejected Marxism and what he called "politicization of the kibbutz." To the founders of Ha-Zorea, Buber represented the highest and purest expression of the purpose of life. Lacking direction, disappointed in liberalism, dissatisfied with careerism, they turned to him for guidance. His appeal to them was personal as well as intellectual, the force of his personality playing a role as important as his literary message. The founders of Ha-Zorea were, in a sense, typical of those Buber attracted—young people from assimilated homes, remote from Judaism and searching for a means of returning to the Jewish heritage. Buber's success in drawing Jewish youth closer to their Judaism was a Diaspora phenomenon, an outcome of the problems of Jewish existence in an open, fragmented society where Judaism is only one of many options. In the early years of his settlement in Israel, Buber did not fulfill the same function, for the community was composed mostly of Eastern European Jews who had fled from what they considered to be Judaism. What possible Jewish function could Buber have in a community where being Jewish was, supposedly, not a problem?

## Buber's Dialogue with Kibbutz Youth

With the arrival on the Israel scene of a native-born and third generation, Buber's philosophy has had a modest revival. His Zionism, which led him to reject lucrative offers to settle in the affluent countries of the West, led to one of the ironies of his life: he remained a living example of the saying that no man is a prophet in his own country. Buber had few followers in Israeli society and remained virtually isolated from its mainstream. Only toward the end of his life, as young people from the kibbutz movement turned to him more frequently, did he begin to travel to kibbutzim for "dialogues," or to invite these youths to his home for conversation.

But how can Buber interest the son of a *Vatik*, an old-timer? If the father has rejected Buber, why should the son seek him out? Surprisingly, the son finds himself in the same position as Diaspora youth from central and western Europe. He is outside Judaism, and being a Jew is a problem for him. Sabra youth of today know the Bible and Jewish history, yet some of them feel alienated from their Jewish heritage. Buber is in this case a mediator between the Sabra and the world of Jewish thought and feeling.

For a few kibbutz intellectuals, Buber's appeal is partially based upon the high value he placed on the kibbutz. His religious socialism, though accepted by a few, nevertheless meant that Buber spoke the same language as the kibbutz. No kibbutz movement officially adopted any of his views, but the ideology has been enriched by Buber's thought. His writings on inter-personal relations and *Hevrutah* are relevant to this society. But it was to Buber as both Jew and Zionist that young people were attentive, for some of the native-born generation were seeking religious belief, and here Buber could help.

## Buber's Antinomianism

Buber's philosophy of Judaism, an antinomian approach, does not demand obligatory performance of ceremonials. If authentic Judaism means the creation of a truly human community, the kibbutznik who accepts Buber's theology and social ethic is faithfully fulfilling the commandments existing between both God and man and man and his neighbor. The absence of customary religious ceremony matters little, for ceremony restricts interchange between the I and the Eternal Thou. For kibbutz youth, spiritually distant and despising Orthodox Jewry, Buber's teachings provided an apologia for the kibbutz.

Copies of his dialogues, especially those held at Kibbutz Afikim in the Jordan Valley, reveal how Buber was called upon for clear and direct solutions to complex problems. A quick review of some of the questions indicates why Buber was unable to do more than hint at possible answers to these questions. He was asked, for example:

1. What can I give my son of a traditional atmosphere?
2. My parents expect more of me than my emotional relation to them permits. What am I to do?
3. What is the mission of the Jewish people?
4. How can we create a sense of Sabbath holiness in the kibbutz?
5. How can I expose my youngster to Jewish values of which I am not sure myself?

Buber's answers were sometimes evasive, sometimes direct, sometimes disappointing, especially those to the first and fourth questions. He had not lost his spiritual insight, but during his years of isolation in Jerusalem, he had lost contact with the kibbutz reality and no longer really understood it. That is the tragedy of Buber's "return" to the kibbutz: when the kibbutz needed him and was ready for him, he was no longer able to help.

What other elements in Buber's philosophy drew the young to him? Especially attractive was his rejection of institutional forms as a means of improving the quality of human relations. The young people observed that the forms of kibbutz life have not succeeded in drastically revising interpersonal relations. In the last analysis, every man must stand by himself and depend upon himself. In a collective society, this insight needs constant reemphasis. The general trend in the kibbutz movement today is a search for more outlets for individual expression.

On the thirtieth day following Buber's death, Kibbutz Ha-Zorea held a memorial service. One of the speakers, a Marxist, praised Buber as the only man who had provided an acceptable non-Orthodox answer to the question of "What is a Jew?" Buber's idea of Judaism was acceptable to the Marxist Ha-Zorea of today because its members envisage Judaism in social, not metaphysical terms, but for Buber being a Jew meant realizing the Kingdom of Heaven on earth. This interpretation, of course, ignores Buber's religious philosophy and his call for a relation to the Absolute.

## *Mutual Disappointment*

Buber's influence on Ha-Zorea is exceptional. The kibbutz movement as a whole has had little dialogue with him. Unlike A. D. Gordon or Berl Katznelson, he never took an active part in the struggles of the labor movement. His German origin may have been the cause of his isolation, for the leadership of the Jewish community in pre-State Israel came from Eastern Europe; the differences in origin and educational background made it understandably difficult for him, and many *Vatikim* complained that his style was, perhaps, too abstract.

Such divergent backgrounds explain the defection of Ha-Zorea. Menahem Gerson describes the Buberian phase of the kibbutz as a form of "neoreligiosity." But Gerson points to what he terms the "Promethean experience" as the cause for the decline of Ha-Zorea's neoreligiosity. During the economic struggle for existence that so completely monopolized the members, the philosophical questions that had engaged them in the more leisurely atmosphere of comfortable middle-class German-Jewish life seemed totally irrelevant. When one is struggling to live, the aims of life need no commentary. Interest in Buber could reawaken only when the kibbutz became a settled community, with the time to ask questions.

## Ideal and Reality

Another factor in their alienation from Buber was disappointment in the naiveté of his teachings on communal life. Instead of an ideal life, with an overabundance of humanity, friendship, and mutual help, communal living sometimes produced aggressiveness, indifference, and ambition. This disappointment found expression in the turn against Buber. His spiritual world was unreal, it was said to be a fool's paradise. Buber seems to have realized this, too. Speaking with Buber before the older man's death, Gerson reports that Buber agreed that his earlier works had lacked the realism he strove to include in his later writing.

Not surprisingly the disappointment was mutual—not only toward Ha-Zorea for becoming Marxist, but toward the entire kibbutz movement. At one time Buber saw in kibbutz life a favorable omen for the entire community that he believed would eventually be reflected also in urban life. The kibbutz would blossom into a redemptive society founded on neighborliness and human relations. With the passage of time his hopes and dreams vanished, for, he said, "a freshness of life has been cut off from the kibbutz movement."

Buber's vision of the kibbutz is not unlike the famous comment on Job in Jewish tradition—that he had never existed. Criticism of the kibbutz for falling into decline is pointless, since it had never reached the stage of communal brotherhood that he writes of. A study of early kibbutz history shows that those small, intimate, homogeneous groups were not free of friction or interpersonal quarreling. In fact they remained small only because personal rivalry and conflict blocked their further growth. In the first thirteen years of Degania, 415 people passed through it, the stable number remaining 20 to 35. Consequently, interpersonal relations were temporary, with few opportunities for the type of I-Thou relations proposed by Buber.

## Buber's Romantic Idyll

For the *Vatikim* to gaze upon the past through idealizing lenses is certainly understandable, but Buber fell into that trap as well, and built a romantic idyll of early kibbutz life that lacked any substantive basis. Criticism of the present-day kibbutz for over-institutionalization and the strangulation of possible I-Thou relationships becomes easier when it can be shown that such a relationship had once existed. But Buber's criticisms are inapplicable because, despite occasional moments of spiritual elevation, the past of the kibbutz in effect was no different from the present.

Buber's portrait of I-Thou relationships in the communal brotherhood is actually a visionary goal and cannot serve as a definition of an existing social reality. Buber admitted that such expectations are unrealistic. Once Western man has passed through individualism, it is highly unlikely that he can ever fully return to true community. Therefore Buber's true community remains a higher value, a vision, which can only direct us within the changing social reality.

Buber's is a dual approach, condemning the kibbutz yet admitting that an unattainable vision is the basis for his condemnation. This type of criticism fits into a classic pattern of chastisement and rebuke, not only for failure to achieve the humanly possible, but also the superhumanly possible. Performance of the commandments of Jewish tradition is no easy task, nor is everyone capable of it; yet maximum fulfillment remains the ideal. So the kibbutz sets standards of interpersonal relations, as Buber sees them, that are almost utopian. Failure to achieve them does not demand their ultimate rejection, for if realism were the sole standard, then the kibbutz itself would disappear. Buber's contribution is to regard the kibbutz from the point of view of eternity.

## Sources

Martin Buber. *Israel and the World*. New York: Schocken Books, 1963.

———. *Pointing the Way*. New York and Evanston: Harper Torchbooks, 1963.

———. "The Communal Brotherhood." *Niv ha-Kevutza*. March 1967.

———. "Decision and Realization." *Shedemot* 5–6 (February 1962).

Menahem Gerson. *Education and Family within Kibbutz Reality*. Tel Aviv: Sifriyat ha-Poalim. Menahem Gerson (interview).

Amram Ha-Yisraeli (interview).

Yaakov Horowitz. "A Meeting with Martin Buber." *Hedim*. August 1963.

Ehud Luz (interview).

"Memorial Service in Honor of Martin Buber at Kibbutz Ha-Zorea. *Hedim*. January 1966.

Ofra. "Dialogue and Socialism in the Writing of Buber." *Niv ha-Kevutza*. December 1968.

Uri Osri. "Progress and Cooperation." *Niv ha-Kevutza*. September–December 1968.

"Yaakov Raz Speaks about Martin Buber." *Iggeret* 695 (July 22, 1965).

Avraham Shapira. "Gog and Magog and Our Life Experience in the Kevutza." *Iggeret* 714 (December 16, 1965).

"The Social Image of the Hebrew Village." Symposium at the Hebrew University, 1945.

Harry Viteles. *A History of the Cooperative Movement in Israel*. Book 2. *The Evolution of the Kibbutz Movement*. London: Vallentine Mitchell, 1967–68.

# Notes

1. Shmuel Joseph Agnon, *Samuch V'Nireh* (Jerusalem: Schocken Books, 1960), p. 5.
2. Abraham Joshua Heschel, *The Earth Is the Lord's* (Cleveland, New York, Philadelphia: Meridian Books and the Jewish Publication Society of America, 1963), p. 100.
3. Mark Zobrowski and Elizabeth Herzog, *Life Is with People* (New York: International Universities Press, Inc., 1952), p. 229.
4. S. N. Eisenstadt, *Israeli Society* (London: Weidenfeld and Nicolson, 1967), pp. 9–10.
5. Joseph Baratz, *A Village by the Jordan* (London: The Harvill Press, 1954), p. 100.
6. Henrik F. Infield, *Cooperative Living in Palestine* (London: Kegan Paul, Trench, Trubner and Co., Ltd., 1946), p. 19.
7. *Sefer Ha-Shomer ha-Tzair* (Merhavia: Sifriyat HaPoalim, 1956), p. 106.
8. Erich Fromm, *Man for Himself* (New York: Fawcett World Library, 1968), p. 208.
9. Gordon Allport, *The Individual and His Religion* (New York: Macmillan Co., 1960), pp. 130–31.
10. Gideon Elad (interview).
11. David Maletz, "The Spiritual Sources of Our Educational System," *Shedemot* 25 (Spring 1967): p. 41.
12. Martin Buber, *The Social Image of the Hebrew Village* (Hebrew University, Symposium, 1945), p. 237.
13. Lewis Mumford, *The City in History* (London: Penguin Books, 1966), p. 313.
14. Eliezer Schweid, *Until Crisis* (Jerusalem: S. Zaks and Co., 1969), pp. 27–28.
15. Mattityahu Shelem (interview).
16. Razya Ben Gurion, "On Yuzik of the Hugim Group," *Shedemot* 32 (Winter 1969): 85.
17. David Maletz as quoted in Martin Buber, *The Social Image of the Hebrew Village* (Hebrew University Symposium, 1945): 235.
18. Rivka Gurfein, "The Distinction between the Temporary and the Permanent," *Hedim* (82) (January 1966): 29. There remains a regret that, while most European peoples have gradually become secular without losing the spiritual treasures of their religious heritage, the Jewish people were unable to make this slow transition, and thus their sudden rebellion resulted in alienation from their heritage.
19. Shmuel Tzur, "The Generation of Immigrants and Israeli Youth," *Shedemot* 5–6 (February 1962): 46.

20. Yohanan Greefilian, "The Imaginary Redemption," *Shedemot* 29 (Spring 1969): 37–39.

21. Gordon Allport, *The Individual and His Religion* (New York: Macmillan Co., 1960), pp. 116–17. In kibbutz literature this same point was made in 1961 by Meir Mendel of Kiryat Anavim. In *Niv HaKvutza* of March 1969, p. 32, he pointed out discernible signs of an interest in religion long before the Six-Day War.

22. Ephraim Reisner, "In the Struggle for Values," *Shedemot* 9–10 (June 1963): 29.

23. Stanley Meron (interview).

24. Israel Bitman (interview).

25. Moshe Kerem (interview).

26. Eliezer Goldman (interview).

27. Nathan Rotenstreich, "The Genuine Problem of Values," *Niv ha-Kevutza* (August 1959), p. 394.

28. Yehuda Erez, "A Meeting with Someone like That," *Shedemot* 30 (Summer 1968): 53–59.

29. Quoted in: Zvi Singer, "The Good Society," *Focus* 4, no. 2 (1963): 19.

30. Yehoshua Manoah, "Between Us," *Iggeret* 556 (November 18, 1962): 10.

31. David Maletz (interview).

32. Yitzhak Maor (interview).

33. Boaz Cohen, *Law and Tradition in Judaism* (New York: The Jewish Theological Seminary of America, 1959), pp. 208–26.

34. Morris Lazarus, *The Ethics of Judaism* (Philadelphia: The Jewish Publication Society, 1900), 1:122.

35. Ibid., 2:1.

36. Ibid., 1:3.

37. Boaz Cohen, *Law and Tradition*, p. 225.

38. Ehud Luz, "Utopian Aims in the Zionist Movement," *Shedemot*, 21 (Spring 1969): 70–71.

39. Alex Barzel (interview).

40. Martin Buber, *On Zion* (New York: Schocken Press, 1975).

41. Martin Buber, *Paths in Utopia* (London: Routledge and Kegan Paul, 1949), p. 9.

42. R. H. Tawney, *Religion and the Rise of Capitalism* (London: Penguin Books, 1966), p. 73.

43. Jacob H. Agus, *The Vision and the Way* (New York: Frederic Ungar Publishing Co., 1966), p. 337.

44. *Kabbalat Shabbat Adar Aleph and Adar Beth* (Ramat Yohanan: Institute of Festivals and Holidays).

45. Yehoshua Manoah, *The Kvutza and Its Image* (Tel Aviv: Am Oved, 1966) p. 59.

46. Yitzhak Maor, "The Kevutza under Trial," *Niv Ha-Kevutza* (September 1961), p. 34.

47. Avraham Aderet (interview). In a slim volume entitled *Objections to Humanism* (London: Penguin Books, 1965), p. 50, Professor Ronald Hepburn writes: "There are certain types of religious experience, senses as of the 'holy,' some forms also of mystical experience that, for some people at least, can continue to occur even in agnosticism. They seem in this sense to be 'autonomous,' not belief- dependent, experiences. Even if they are not seen as yielding new knowl-

edge of the world, insights into 'ultimate truth,' they can still make a profound mark on a person's moral outlook, by nourishing a sense of wondering openness to new ways, new possibilities of life. They implant a disturbing restlessness, a nisus towards the transformation of ideals, an intensified dissatisfaction with the mean, drab or trivial." He proceeds further in stating that theistic belief is not a prerequisite for the type of mystical experience that is an "experience of reconciliation, the breaking down of barriers of individuality." It can be brought into intimate relation with movements of thought and feeling, such as sympathetic identification with others, escape from egocentricity to the stance of charity.

48. Asher Maniv, "A Living and Not a Dead Tradition," *Bulletin of Maayan-Zvi* (January 23, 1965, December 31, 1965). Also "Seekers without a Compass," *Iggeret* 854 (November 13, 1968): 10.

49. George Friedman, *The End of the Jewish People* (London: Hutchinson, 1967), p. 56.

50. Stanley Meron, "Separation and Charity," *Niv Ha-Kevutza* (May 1968), p. 39.

51. William K. Frankena, "The Concept of Social Justice," in *Social Justice* (Englewood Cliffs, N.J.: Prentice-Hall, 1962), p. 27.

52. R. H. Tawney, *Equality* (New York: Capricorn Books Edition, 1961; first published in 1931), p. 47.

53. Louis Finkelstein, "Human Equality in the Jewish Tradition According to Biblical and Rabbinic Tradition," in *Aspects of Human Equality* (New York: Harper, 1956), p. 179.

54. Eliezer Schweid, "Secularism from a Religious Viewpoint," *Petahim* 7 (January 1969): 29. The remainder of the discussion on Rav Kook is based upon this article by Dr. Schweid.

55. Zalman Dudai (interview).

56. Israel Bitman, ed., "Sources for the Origin of the Kibbutz" (Yifat: Regional High School of the Western Valley, no date; mimeographed), 1: 5.

57. Amram Ha-Yisraeli, "Remarks Made at a Meeting of Tzavta of the Hefer Valley, *Shedemot* 33 (Spring 1969): 24.

58. Menahem Rosner, "Principles, Types and Problems of Direct Democracy in the Kibbutz," Social Research Center on the Kibbutz, Givat Haviva (March 1965), p. 2 (mimeographed).

59. David Maletz, "Culture in the Kibbutz," *Sefer Busel* (Tel Aviv: Tarbut V'Hinuch, 1960), p. 16.

60. Mattityahu Shelem (interview).

61. Zvi Ra'anan, "Holiday Patterns and Tradition," *Yedi'on* (January 1967), p. 3.

62. Jack J. Cohen, *The Case for Religious Naturalism* (New York: The Reconstructionist Press, 1958), p. 150.

63. Gershon Scholem, *On the Kabbalah and Its Symbolism* (New York: Schocken Books, 1965), p. 120.

64. Israel Bitman (interview).

65. David Maletz, "Our Spiritual Image," *Shedemot* 9–10 (June 1963): 7.

66. Maletz, "Culture in the Kibbutz," p. 20.

67. Ibid., p. 24. To illustrate the kibbutz way of sanctifying the mundane Maletz uses the dining room. As in Hasidism the petty and unrewarding become holy, so work ordinarily considered unattractive—such as waiting on tables—is transformed into a service to the kibbutz community that is building its joint life.

In this fashion the material and the profane attain merit and are ennobled and sanctified.

68. Ze'ev Gazit (interview).

69. Erich Fromm, *Psychoanalysis and Religion* (New Haven and London: Yale University Press, 1960), p. 111.

70. Aryeh Ben Gurion, "Partial Meditations on Holidays in the Kibbutz," *Yedi'on* (March 1970), p. 3.

71. Haim Schauss, *The Jewish Festivals* (New York: Union of American Hebrew Congregations, 1938), p. 112.

72. *Rosh Ha-Shanah* (Tel Aviv Inter-Kibbutz Committee on Holidays, 1966), p. 22.

73. *Masekhet Rosh Ha-Shanah*, edited by the Inter-Kibbutz Committee on Holidays (Tel Aviv: 1970).

74. Philip Birnbaum, *High Holiday Prayer Book* (New York: Hebrew Publishing Company, 1951), p. 343.

75. *Masekhet Rosh Ha-Shanah*.

76. Ibid.

77. Ibid.

78. Philip Birnbaum, *High Holiday Prayer Book* (New York: Hebrew Publishing Company, 1951), p. 286.

79. *Masekhet Rosh Ha-Shanah*.

80. Zvi Ra'anan, "Why is there no Yom Kippur in the kibbutzim of Ha-Kibbutz ha-Artzi?" *Yedi'on* (August 1964), pp. 7–8.

81. Ibid.

82. Yitzhak Maor, "The Holidays of Tishri," *Yedi'on* (October 1964), p. 14.

83. Yaacov Raz, "Yom Kippur Evening," *Iggeret* 703–4 (September 26, 1965). The first two lines of the paraphrase were not changed in the Hebrew and are ordinarily translated: "With the consent of the Omnipresent One and with the consent of this congregation." In their kibbutz context, however, the word *Makom* could only be translated as "place" and *Kahal* as "community."

84. Theodor H. Gaster, *Festivals of the Jewish Year* (New York: William Sloane Associates, 1952), p. 150.

85. *L'Yom Ha-Kippurim, Alef*, presented by Y. Ron-Polani (Ramat Yohanan, The Holiday Division of Ihud ha-Kevutzot ve-ha-Kibbutzim, 1966), p. 3.

86. Y. Ron-Polani, "On the Kol Nidre Night Assembly," *Iggeret* 896–97 (September 12, 1967): 10.

87. *L'Yom Ha-Kippurim, Bet*, p. 9.

88. Ibid., *Alef*, p. 4.

89. "The Kibbutz and Tradition," *Petachim* (August 1969), p. 9.

90. Haim Schauss, *The Jewish Festivals* (New York: Union of American Hebrew Congregations, 1938), p. 171.

91. *Sukkot* (Tel Aviv: Inter-Kibbutz Committee on Holidays, 1966), p. 31.

92. Schauss, *The Jewish Festivals*, p. 208.

93. Ibid., p. 230.

94. Mattityahu Shelem, "The Holiday of Light," *Niv ha-Kevutza* (November 1962), p. 729.

95. *Passover Haggadah* (Tel Aviv: Ihud ha-Kevutzot ve-ha-Kibbutzim Passover Haggadah, Ha-Kibbutz ha-Me'uhad, 1971).

96. *Iggeret* 21 (March 20, 1952): 4.

97. *Haggadah of Passover*, translated by Maurice Samuel, with an introduction

by Louis Finkelstein (New York: Hebrew Publishing Co., 1942), p. 13.

98. *Haggadah Shel Pesach* (Ha-Kibbutz ha-Artzi, 1964).

99. Mattityahu Shelem, "The Four Questions and Their Solution in Kibbutz Haggadot," *Niv ha-Kevutza* (March 1969), p. 124.

100. Mattityahu Shelem, "The Revival of the Omer Festival," *Niv ha-Kevutza* (March 1961), p. 67.

101. *The Seventh Day: Soldiers Talk about the Six-Day War* (London: André Deutsch, 1970), p. 164.

102. Zvi Ra'anan, "Deepening Israel Independence Day," *Hag Ha-Atzma'ut* (Tel Aviv: Inter-Kibbutz Committee on Holidays, 1967), p. 3, of the section entitled "Essence and Content."

103. Shlomo Lavi, "An Official Holiday or a Popular Holiday," ibid., p. 2 of the section entitled "How We Should Celebrate."

104. Yehoshua Gevani, "Independence Day in Alonim," ibid., p. 5 of the section entitled "Holiday Readings."

105. "Symposium on Shabbat," *Petahim* (November 1970), pp. 29–30.

106. *Leyl Shabbat: Kabbalat Shabbat* (Tel Aviv: Inter-Kibbutz Committee on Holidays and Festivals, 1967), p. 3.

107. *A Bar Mitzvah Collection:* "Bar Mitzvah and Entrance into the Movement," ed. by Aryeh Ben Gurion (Education Department of the Ihud and Education Committee of Ha-Kibbutz ha-Me'uhad, 1967), p. 2.

108. Ibid., p. 68.

109. Ibid., p. 2.

110. Ibid., p. 42.

111. Aviva Opaz, "Bar Mitzvah as a Family Festival," *Shedemot* 33 (Spring 1969): 87.

112. Ibid., p. 88.

113. Mattityahu Shelem, ed., *Klulot* (Tel Aviv: The Inter-Kibbutz Committee on Holidays and Festivals, 1965), p. 4.

114. Ibid., p. 63, of "Tokhniyot." The marriage scroll of Afikim suggests that a covenant is entered into by the couple not only between themselves, but also between the couple and *ha'eyda ha-kibbutzit*, the kibbutz brotherhood.

115. Yonina Talmon, "Mate Selection in Collective Settlements, *American Sociological Review* 29 no. 4 (August 1964): 491–508.

116. *Mourning*, ed. Aryeh Ben Gurion (Inter-Kibbutz Committee on Holidays and Festivals, 1963), p. 11.

117. Avraham Shapira, "The Culture of Remembrance in the Kibbutz," *Iggeret* 834 (June 19, 1968): 5

118. Max Weber, *Ancient Judaism* (Glencoe, Ill.: The Free Press, 1952), pp. 3–5.

119. Nathan Glazer, *American Judaism* (Chicago: University of Chicago Press, 1957), pp. 147–49.

120. Robert Bellah, "Religious Evolution," *American Sociological Review* 29 (1964): 358–74.

121. Albert Hofstadter, "The Career Open to Personality: The Meaning of Equality of Opportunity for an Ethics of Our Time," *Aspects of Human Equality* (New York: Harper and Brothers, 1956), p. 114.

122. R. H. Tawney, *Equality*, p. 84.

123. Winston, L. King, *Introduction to Religion* (New York: Harper and Row, 1954), pp. 479–82.

124. Gerhard Lenski, *The Religious Factor* (New York: Doubleday and Co., 1963), pp. 330–31. He defines theistic and nontheistic faiths as religious because of the striking similarities between them: "To begin with, all are social phenomenon, involving groups of men. Second, all are systems of faith . . . accepted on the grounds of faith, not empirical or logical demonstration. Third, all are systems of faith by means of which men seek to cope with the most basic problems of human existence."

125. Joachim Wach, *The Sociology of Religion* (Chicago: University of Chicago Press, 1944), p. xxxiii. Gershon Scholem, in his Hebrew article, "The Possibilities of Jewish Mysticism in Our Day," *Amot* (October–November 1963), pp. 12–18, claims that this generation is ready for a real and authentic religious experience because it is a crisis generation and mysticism finds inspiration when history provides a crisis. For the Jew mysticism does not entail unity with the Godhead—that would be too insolent. For the Jew mysticism is experiental recognition of divine matters. Generations must pass after a crisis; it took two or three generations for the Kabbalists of Safad to arise. However, today most Jews are secular. Is mysticism a possibility? Can it be revealed in nontraditional forms? Rav Kook saw Jewish secularism as a great mystic experience. Today the powers of the Jewish people are absorbed in building their new life. In former years this energy and force would have found an outlet through traditional means, perhaps as mysticism. Professor Scholem's remarks are not a conclusive reply to Joachim Wach, but they temper the extremism of his conception.

126. Gordon Allport, *The Individual and His Religion* (New York: Macmillan Company, 1950), p. 69. He remarks: "Yet, even from a psychological point of view, we see that the ground covered by any secular interest, however vital, falls short of the range that characterizes a mature religious sentiment which seems never satisfied unless it is dealing with matters central to all existence. A cause may be absorbing, but it seldom includes the whole of a mature individual's horizon. Residues are left over which only religion can absorb."

# Glossary of Hebrew Terms Used in the Text

**Aggadah:** The body of Jewish legend and the nonlegalistic sections of the classical literature.
**Apikorsim:** Skeptics, freethinkers, and heretics.
**Bar Mitzvah:** A religious ceremony for a male Jew thirteen years of age by which he becomes a formal member of the community.
**Bet Hamidrash:** A house of study. A place for religious services and study.
**Bikkurim:** First fruits.
**Haggadah:** A collection of prayers, readings, and songs used for the ceremony surrounding the evening meal on the first night of Passover.
**Hakafot:** Circularly carrying Scrolls of the Law within the synagogue on Simhat Torah.
**Halakhah:** Jewish law as developed down through the ages by the rabbis.
**Halutz:** Pioneer.
**Hanukkah:** Holiday commemorating the victory of the Maccabees.
**Hasidim:** Followers of the religious revivalist movement founded in eighteenth century in Eastern Europe.
**Haver:** Member or friend and comrade.
**Heder:** Religious elementary school among orthodox Jewry in Eastern Europe.
**Hilonim:** The secular Jews of modern Israel.
**Histadrut:** Israel's labor federation.
**Hovot:** Obligations.
**Huppa:** Wedding canopy under which the marriage ceremony is performed.
**Kabaalat Shabbat:** In the kibbutz a brief ceremony performed prior to the festive Friday night meal.
**Kaddish:** A prayer recited by a mourner following the death of a close relative.
**Kavanah:** Concentration of the mind upon an act about to be performed. In religious terminology refers to intention in prayer.
**Kehiliyateynu:** A book published in 1922 containing letters, notations, and confessions of members of Kibbutz Alef. See the section on *Kehiliyateynu* in chapter 1.

**Kibbutz** (pl. **kibbutzim**): Israeli communal settlement.
**Kibbutznik:** Member of a kibbutz.
**Kiddushin:** Marriage.
**K'tuba:** Marriage certificate.
**Mattan Torah:** Revelation of the Torah at Sinai. Traditionally celebrated during Shavuot.
**Me'ah She'arim:** A residential quarter of Jerusalem that serves as a center for an ultra-orthodox sect that rejects the existence of the State of Israel.
**Minhag:** Religious custom as distinct from religious commandment.
**Mitzvah:** Religious commandment, meritorious deed.
**M'sorati'im:** Segment of Israeli society with inclinations toward traditional religious practice but who do not identify with the organized orthodox community.
**Purim:** Holiday based upon the Book of Esther commemorating the deliverance of the Jewish people from its enemies.
**Rav:** Rabbi.
**Rosh Ha-Shana:** Fall holiday celebrating the beginning of the Jewish calendar year.
**Seder** (pl. **Sedarim**): The festive meal on the first evening of Passover. In the Diaspora on the first two evenings of Passover.
**Shabbat:** Sabbath.
**Shabbes Goy:** A non-Jew who does work on the Sabbath that is prohibited to Jews.
**Shavuot:** Feast of Weeks. Both a Harvest Festival and a commemoration of Mattan Torah.
**Shechina:** Divine Presence.
**Shtetl:** Small town.
**Shulhan Arukh:** The most authoritative codification of rabbinical law, compiled by Joseph Caro in the seventeenth century.
**Sukkot:** Feast of Booths. A fall harvest holiday.
**Takkanon:** Code of kibbutz principle and practice.
**Tefillin:** Phylacteries—leather cases containing quotations from the Pentateuch, worn on the forehead and on the left arm during morning prayers.
**Torah:** The entire body of Jewish teaching and wisdom.
**Vatik** (pl. **Vatikim**): Veteran. A term applied to the founders of kibbutzim.
**Yahad:** Oneness.
**Yeshivah:** Rabbinical academy.
**Yom Kippur:** Day of Atonement.

# *Bibliography*

The Kibbutz journals *Niv ha-Kevutza, Shedemot, Iggeret, Yedion*, and the publications of the Committee on Holidays and Festivals (Inter-Kibbutz) supplied the majority of the Hebrew sources consulted. In addition, relevant material appeared in *Hedim, Ba-Derekh, Ba-Shaar*, and *Amudim*. The nonkibbutz journal *Petahim* also contributed valuable information. Interviews were conducted with thirty-two kibbutz intellectuals and three Israeli thinkers who maintain close ties with the kibbutz movement.

Admanit, Tsuriel. "Religious Community." *Shdemot* 7 (1977): 30–33.

Allport, Gordon. *The Individual and His Religion*. New York: Macmillan Co., 1960.

Amir, Yehuda. "The Effectiveness of the Kibbutz-Born Soldiers in the Israel Defence Forces." *Human Relations* 22, no. 4 (1969): 333–44.

*Among Young People*. Tel Aviv: Am Oved, 1969.

Ayali, Meir. "The Image of our Holidays." *Shedemot* 31 (Autumn 1969).

Baer, Yitzhak. *Yisrael Ba'Amim* [Israel among the Nations]. Jerusalem: Mosad Bialik, 1955.

Bahad. "From Rodges to Yavne." *TVA Ideological Series*. London: Brit Halutzim Datiyim, 1944.

Baratz, Joseph. *A Village by the Jordan*. London: The Harvill Press, 1954.

Bendix, Reinhard. *Max Weber: An Intellectual Portrait*. London: University Paperbacks, Methuen and Co., 1966.

Ben Gurion, Aryeh. "Shabbat: Origin and Interpretation." Inter-Kibbutz Committee on Festivals, 1967.

Ben Josef, Avraham. *The Purest Democracy in the World*. New York, London: Herzl Press and Thomas Yoseloff, 1964.

Berger, Peter; Berger, Brigitte; Kellner, Hansfried. *The Homeless Mind*. New York: Random House, Vintage Books, 1974.

Bergman, Samuel H. *Faith and Reason: An Introduction to Modern Jewish Thought*. Washington, D.C.: B'nai B'rith Hillel Foundations, 1961.

Bettelheim, Bruno. *The Children of the Dream*. London: Macmillan Co., 1969.

## Bibliography

Blasi, Joseph. *The Communal Future: The Kibbutz and the Utopian Dilemma*. Norwood, Pa.: Norwood Editions, 1978.

Blockham, J. H. J. *Objections to Humanism*. London: Penguin Books, 1965.

Bondheimer, Aryeh. "On Seeing Aim in Life." *Shedemot* 30 (Summer 1968).

Brandt, Richard B., ed. *Social Justice*. Englewood Cliffs, N.J.: Prentice-Hall, 1962.

Bryson, Lyman; Faust, Clarence, H.; Finkelstein, Louis; and Maciver, R. M. *Aspects of Human Equality*. New York: Harper and Brothers, 1956.

Buber, Martin. *The Social Image of the Hebrew Village*. Hebrew University, Symposium, 1945.

———. *Paths in Utopia*. London: Routledge and Kegan Paul, 1949.

———. *Between Man and Man*. London: The Fontana Library, 1961.

———. *Israel and the World*. New York: Schocken Books, 1963.

———. *Pointing the Way*. New York and Evanston: Harper Torchbooks, 1963.

Clement, Leslie S. "The Kibbutz." *The Rift in Israel, Religious Authority, and Secular Democracy*. London: Routledge and Kegan Paul, 1971.

Cohen, Boaz. *Law and Tradition in Judaism*. New York: The Jewish Theological Seminary of America, 1959.

Cohen, Jack J. *The Case for Religious Naturalism*. New York: The Reconstructionist Press, 1958.

Cohen, Reuven. "Between God and Satan." *Shedemot* 29 (Winter 1968).

Cohn, Norman. *The Pursuit of the Millennium*. New York and Evanston: Harper Torchbooks, 1961.

Diamond, Stanley. "Kibbutz and Shtetl. The History of an Idea." *Social Problems* 5 (2) (1957): 71–99.

Douglas, Mary. "The Effects of Modernization on Religious Change." *Daedalus* 3, no. 1 (1982): 1–20.

Dupre, Louis. "Spiritual Life in a Secular Age." *Daedalus* 3, no. 1 (1982): 21–32.

Durkheim, Emile. *The Elementary Forms of the Religious Life*. New York: The Free Press, 1965.

"Education towards an Attachment to the Jewish People." *Hedim* 81 (July 1965).

Eisenstadt, S. N. *Israeli Society*. London: Weidenfeld and Nicolson, 1967.

Erez, Yehuda. "The Bible and Traditions in the Jewish Labor Movement." *Niv ha-Kevutza* (September 1954).

———. "Meeting with Three like That." *Shedemot* 30 (Summer 1968).

Etzioni, Amitai. "The Organizational Structure of the Kibbutz." Ph.D. diss., University of California, 1958.

Fishman, A., ed. *The Religious Kibbutz Movement: The Revival of the Jewish Religious Community*. Jerusalem: Religious Section of the Youth and Hehalutz Department of Zionist Organization, 1957.

Fishman, Arieh. *The Religious Kibbutz Movement*. Jerusalem: The Religious Section of the Youth and HeHalutz Department of the Zionist Organization, 1957.

Fishman, Aryeh. "The Religious Kibbutz: A Study of the Inter-Relationships of Religion and Ideology in the Context of Modernization." Ph.D. diss., Hebrew University, 1976.

———. "Comparative Economic Performance of the Religious and Secular Kibbutz." Paper read at Bar Ilan University Sociology Seminar, January 1980.

Fleik, J. "Israeli Kibbutz-Model for Religious Orders." *America* 11 (1971): 143–46.

Frankena, William M. "The Concept of Social Justice." *Social Justice*. Englewood Cliffs, N.J.: Prentice-Hall, 1962.

Friedman, Maurice S. *Martin Buber: The Life of Dialogue*. Chicago: The University of Chicago Press, 1955.

Fromm, Erich. *Man for Himself*. Greenwich, Conn.: Fawcett Publications Inc., 1968.

———. *Psychoanalysis and Religion*. New Haven and London: Yale University Press, 1950.

———. *The Sane Society*. New York: Fawcett World Library, 1968.

Fuchs, Yitzhak, ed. *The Religious Kvutza*. New York: Bnei Akiva, 1960.

Gabovitch, B. "Les Origines Communautaries Dans L'Israel D'Aujourd'hui." *Archives Internationales de Sociologie de la Cooperation* 9 (1961): 18–33.

Gadon, Shmuel. *N'tivay Ha-Kevutza V'ha-Kibbutz* [The Path of the Kevutza and the Kibbutz]. Tel Aviv: Am Oved, 1958.

Gaster, Theodor H. *Festivals of the Jewish Year*. New York: William Sloane Associates, 1952.

Gazit, Zeev. "On the Concept of Secular Faith." *B'Shaar* (September 1964).

Gelb, Sa'adia. "Kibbutz and Religion." In *Kibbutz: A New Society?* pp. 212–14. Ichud Habonim, 1971.

Gerson, Menahem. *Hinukh v'mishpaha B'mitziut ha-Kibbutz* [Education and Family within Kibbutz Reality]. Tel Aviv: Sifriat HaPoalim, 1968.

Glazer, Nathan. *American Judaism*. Chicago: University of Chicago Press, 1957.

Golomb, Naphtali, and Katz, Daniel. *The Kibbutzim as Open Social Systems*. Ruppin Institute, Israel, no date.

Graubard, Stephen, ed. "Religion." Special Issue of *Daedalus* 3, no. 1 (1982): v–xi.

Gurfein, Rivka. "The Reply to a Challenge." *Shedemot* 20 (Winter 1966).

Ha-Cohen, Eliezer. "The Imprint of the Kibbutz on the Israeli Image." Council of Ha-Kibbutz ha-Artzi, 1964.

*Hanukkah*. Inter-Kibbutz Committee on Holidays, November 1966.

*Ha-Sho'ah V'ha-Mered*. Edited by Mattityahu Shelem. Inter-Kibbutz Committee on Holidays, March 1963.

Heineman, J. *Prayer in the Period of the Tanaim and Amoraim*. Jerusalem: Magnes Press, 1966.

Herzberg, Arthur. *The Zionist Idea*. New York: Doubleday and Co., 1959.

Heschel, Abraham. *The Earth Is the Lord's*. Cleveland: Meridian Books, 1963.

Ihud Ha-Kevutzot V'ha-Kibbutzim, Education Department. "Bar Mitzvah Report of a Conference of Educators." December 1964 (mimeographed).

Infield, Henrik F. *Cooperative Living in Palestine*. London: Kegan Paul, Trench, Trubner and Co. Ltd., 1946

Jacobson, Chanoch. "The Social Determinants of Secularity. An Empirical Study of Deviance from Religious Norms." Ph.D. diss., University of Wisconsin, 1969.

Johnson, F. Ernest. "The Concept of Human Equality." *Aspects of Human Equality*. New York: Harper Brothers, 1956.

Kadushin, Max. *Worship and Ethics*. Northwestern University Press, 1964.

Katz, Jacob. *Tradition and Crisis*. Glencoe, Ill.: The Free Press, 1961.

*Kehiliyateynu* [Our Community]. Kibbutz Alef, 1922.

Kerem, Moshe. "The Kibbutz: The State of the Dream." *Judaism* 22 (1973): 182–93.

Kerem, Moshe; Maton, Stanley; Tzur, Muki. "Judaism in the Non-Religious Kibbutz, A Dialogue." pp. 1–8. Ammi, World Union for Progressive Judaism, 1978.

King, Winston L. *Introduction to Religion*. New York, Evanston, and London: Harper and Row, 1954.

Krieger, Joseph. "More on Tradition and Faith." *Iggeret* 703 (September 26, 1965).

Langer, Michael. "Religious Pioneering." *Shdemot* 7 (1977): 34–37.

Lazarus, Morris. *The Ethics of Judaism*. Philadelphia: The Jewish Publication Society, 1900.

Lehrman, Z. "Changing Rural Culture." *Shedemot* 7–8 (November 1962).

*L'Hag ha-Shavuot*. Inter-Kibbutz Committee on Holidays, May 1962.

Lenski, Gerhard. *The Religious Factor*. Garden City, N.Y.: Anchor Books, Doubleday and Co., Inc., 1967.

Lichtheim, George. *The Origins of Socialism*. London: Weidenfeld and Nicolson, 1962.

Luz, Ehud. "Beloved Is Man for He Was Created in the Image." *Shedemot* 22 (Summer 1966).

———. "Between Necessity and Will." *Shedemot* 40 (Winter 1971).

Luz, Kadish. *Avney Derekh* (Pathstones). Tel Aviv: Tarbut V'Hinukh, 1962.

Maletz, David, ed. *Ha-Adam B'Hityashvut* [Man in the Settlement]. Mifleget Poalei Eretz Yisrael, 1948.

———. "The Bequeathing of Values." *Niv ha-Kevutza*, November 1965.

———. "The Spiritual Sources of our Educational System." *Shedemot* 25 (Spring 1967).

Maniv, Asher. "Friday Evening in the Kibbutz." *Iggeret* 666 (November 24, 1964).

———. "On Tradition in Our Life." *Niv ha-Kevutza* March 1966.

Manoah, Yehoshua. *Ha-Kevutza V'Dmuta* (The Kvutza and Its Image). Tel Aviv: Am Oved, 1966.

Maor, Yitzhak. "The Society of Man." *Niv ha-Kevutza*, December 1954.

———. "Equality and Effort." *Iggeret*, January 4, 1962.

———. "The Kevutza as a Way of Life." *Niv ha-Kevutza*, September 1963.

Margalit, Ephraim. "The Beginning of ha-Shomer ha-Tzair in Israel and Its Contact with the Environment." *BaDerech* 3 (December 1968).

Maron, Stanley. "Kibbutz and Utopia." *Shdemot*, 8 (1978): 77–82.

Marx, Karl. *Early Writings*. Toronto, London: McGraw-Hill Paperback, 1964.

———. *Selected Writings in Sociology and Social Philosophy*. Toronto, London: McGraw-Hill Paperback, 1964.

*Megilat Hag L'Yom ha-Atzma'ut*. Inter-Kibbutz Committee on Holidays, 1971.

Melman, Seymour. "Industrial Efficiency under Managerial vs. Cooperative Decision Making." Ha-Kibbutz ha-Artzi ha-Shomer ha-Tzair Industrial Department (mimeographed).

"Memorial Ceremony in Honor of Martin Buber." *Hedim* 82 (January 1966).

Meron, Stanley. "The Jewish Roots of the Kibbutz." *Niv ha-Kevutza*.

———. "Content and Frame." *Iggeret* 855 (November 1968).

Miller, Daniel. *The Religious Kibbutz*. Oxford: University of Oxford Press, 1962.

Moore, George Foot. *Judaism*. Cambridge: Harvard University Press, 1954.

Mumford, Lewis. *The City in History*. London: Penguin Books, 1966.

Neubauer, Peter B. *Children in Collectives, Child Rearing Aims and Practices in the Kibbutz*. Springfield, Ill.: Charles C. Thomas, 1965.

O'Dea, Thomas F. "Five Dilemmas in the Institutionalization of Religion." *Religion, Culture and Society*, edited by Louis Schneider. New York, London, and Sydney: John Wiley and Sons, 1964.

Palmani, Oved. "Equality According to Effort." *Iggeret*, October 26, 1961.

Passamanick, B. "Some Observations on the Moral Ideology of First and Second Generation Collective and Non-Collective Settlers in Israel." *Social Problems* 11 (2) (1963): 165–78.

Ra'anan, Zvi. "Culture and Entertainment." *Hedim* 83 (April 1966).

Rabin, A. I. *Growing Up in Israel*. New York: Springer Publishing Co., 1965.

Ron, David. "Bible without God." *Niv ha-Kevutza*, March 1952.

Rosner, Menahem. "Principle Types and Problems of Direct Democracy in the Kibbutz." Givat Haviva Social Research Center on the Kibbutz, March 1965 (mimeographed).

Rosner, Menachem; Ben-David, J.; Avnat, A.; Cohen, N.; and Leviatan, U. *The Second Generation: Continuity and Change in the Kibbutz*. Tel-Aviv: Sifriat Ha Poalim (in Hebrew), 1978.

———. *The Second Generation: Continuity and Change in the Kibbutz*. Cambridge, Ma.: Harvard University's Project for Kibbutz Studies Monograph, 1978.

Rotenstreich, Nathan. *Humanism in the Contemporary Era*. The Hague: Mouton and Co.

Schweid, Eliezer. *Ha-Yahid. Olamo Shel Aleph Daled Gordon* (The Individual. The World of A. D. Gordon). Tel Aviv: Am Oved, 1970.

———. *Ad Mashbair, Ha-Yahadut V'Tzionut B'Medinah* (To the Point of Crisis, Judaism and Zionism in the Jewish State). Jerusalem: S. Zaks, 1969.

Scholem, Gershon. *On the Kabbala and Its Symbolism*. New York: Schocken Books, 1965.

*Sefer Busel* (Essays in Honor of Yosef Bussel). Tel Aviv: Mifalei Tarbut V'Hinukh, 1960.

*Sefer ha-Shomer ha-Tzair* [The Book of the Young Guardians]. Merhavia: Sifriyat ha-Poalim, 1956.

Shapiro, Avraham. "Spiritual Life and the Secular Atmosphere of the Kibbutz." *Shedemot* 31 (Autumn 1969).

Shelem, Mattityahu. "The Shepherd and His Festival." *Niv ha-Kevutza*, June 1961.

———. "Passover in the Kevutza." *Niv ha-Kevutza*, March 1962.

———. "The Holiday of Light." *Niv ha-Kevutza*, November 1962.

———. "The Vineyard Festival." *Niv ha-Kevutza*, September 1968.

———. "The Four Questions and Their Solution in Kibbutz Haggadot." *Niv ha-Kevutza*, March 1969.

———. "Pattern and Search." *Iggeret* 896–97 (September 12, 1969).

———. "Passover Haggadah in Kibbutzim." *Niv ha-Kevutza*, March 1970.

Shua, Zvi. "The Question of the Evaluation of the Non-Jew according to the Jewish Outlook." *Shedemot* 28 (Winter 1968).

Shur, Shimon; Beit-Hallahmi, B.; Blasi, J.; and Rabin, A. *The Kibbutz Bibliography*. Norwood, Pa.: Norwood Editions, 1980.

Siah Ein Shemer (mimeographed).

Snarey, John. *The Social and Moral Development of Kibbutz Founders and Sabras: A Cross-Sectional and Longitudinal Cross-Cultural Study*. Cambridge, Ma.: Harvard University's project for Kibbutz Studies, 1982.

Soan, Gadi. "The Festival of Love at Yotvatah." *Iggeret* 292–92 (August 23, 1959).

Spiro, Melford. *Children of the Kibbutz*. New York: Schocken Books, 1958, 1965.

Spiro, Melford. *Kibbutz: Venture in Utopia*. Cambridge, Ma.: Harvard University Press, 1956.

———. *Kibbutz—Venture in Utopia*. New York: Schocken Books, 1963.

Talmon-Garber, Yonina. "Differentiation in Collective Settlements." *Scripta Hierosolymitana* 3: 153–78. Jerusalem: Hebrew University 1956.

———. "Histapkut B'Muat: D'Fusey T'Murah Idealogit" [Ascetiscism: Patterns of Ideological Change]. *Ha-Mivneh ha-Khevrati Shel Yisrael* [The Social Structure of Israel]. (Jerusalem: Akdemon, 1966).

———. "Mate Selection in Collective Settlements." *American Sociological Review* 29, no. 4. (August 1964): 491–508.

———. "The Family in a Revolutionary Movement." *Ha-Mivneh ha-Khevrati Shel Yisrael* [The Social Structure of Israel]. Jerusalem: Akdemon, 1966, pp. 396–435.

Tawney, R. H. *Equality*. London: George Allen and Unwin, 1962.

———. *Religion and the Rise of Capitalism*. Penguin Books, 1938.

"The Haggadah, Past and Present." *Studies in Bibliography and Booklore*. Vol. 8. Cincinnati: Hebrew Union College–Jewish Institute of Religion, 1965.

"The Kibbutz and Tradition. A Conversation at Givat Haviva." *Petachim* 5 (10) (1969).

*The Seventh Day: Soldiers Talk about the Six-Day War*. London: André Deutsch and Steimatsky's Agency, 1970.

Tillich, Paul. *Dynamics of Faith*. New York and Evanston: Harper Torchbooks, 1958.

Troeltsch, Ernst. *The Social Teachings of the Christian Churches*. New York and Evanston: Harper Torchbooks, 1966.

Twersky, David. "Movements to Merger." (Excerpts from an article in the *Jerusalem Post*, 4.4. 1979) In *Kibbutz Studies*, 1 Sept. 1979, pp. 3–6.

Tzur, Shmuel. "Ascetism in the Second Aliyah." *Shedemot* 34 (Summer 1969).

Una, Moshe. *Shootfut Shel Emet* (True Cooperation). Tel Aviv: Moreshet, 1965.

Unna, Moshe. "The Elements of the Religious Kibbutz." In *Kibbutz: A New Society?* pp. 45–51. Ichud Habonim, 1971.

Vlastos, Gregory. "Justice and Equality." In *Social Justice*. Englewood Cliffs, N.J.: Prentice-Hall.

Wach, Joachim. *The Sociology of Religion*. Chicago: University of Chicago Press, 1944.

Weber, Max. *The Sociology of Religion*. Boston: The Beacon Press, 1964.

Weingarten, Murray. *Life in a Kibbutz*. Jerusalem: Zionist Organization, Youth and he-Halutz Department, 1959.

Wilson, Bryan. *Religion in Secular Society*. Penguin Books, 1969.

Yadlin, Aaron. "The Kevutza in the State." *Niv ha-Kevutza*, August, 1969.

Yassour, Avraham, ed. *Kibbutz Members Analyze the Kibbutz*. Cambridge, Ma.: The Institute for Cooperative Community, 1977.

Yinger, Milton. *Sociology Looks at Religion*. New York: Macmillan Co., 1966.

Zborowski, Mark, and Herzog, Elisabeth. *Life is with People*. New York: International Universities Press, 1952.

# *Index*

Aderet, Avraham, 100
Aggadah, 80–82, 92, 128, 141, 162, 205
Agnon, Shai, 32, 33, 155, 157
Agus, Jacob B., 87
Akiva, Rabbi, 157
Aleichem, Shalom, 32
Allport, Gordon, 35, 47
Apikorsut, 61
Asarsa B'Tevet, 195
Ayali, Meir, 194

Bachelor of Kibbutz, 55
Baratz, Joseph, 36, 37
Bar Mitzvah, 207–15, 216
Ben-Amitai, Levi, 204
Ben-Gurion, Aryeh, 127, 141, 188
Bet Alfa, 38, 40, 41, 112
Bet Ha-Midrash, 58
Bet Ha-Shittah, 127, 145, 148, 161
Bergman, Ingmar, 167
Bergman, Professor S. H., 156–57
Bettelheim, Bruno, 134
Bialik, Haim Nahman, 81, 82, 121, 128, 173
Bitman, Israel, 96, 97, 98
Brandeis, Justice, 154
Breuer Yeshivah, 79
Brinton, Crane, 109
Buber, Martin, 35, 36, 41, 51, 52, 60, 93, 155, 157

Chagall, Bella, 131

Degania, 31, 36, 82, 115, 197, 202
Diaspora, 33, 43, 57, 59, 61, 71, 74, 78, 98, 135, 185, 186, 188, 198

Ein Harod, 51, 61, 178, 180, 211
Ein Ha-Shofet, 154, 155, 196
Ein Shemer, 161
Essenes, 89

Finkelstein, Louis, 111
Friedman, George, 105
Fromm, Erich, 46

Gaster, Theodor H., 154, 184, 200
Givat Haim (Ihud), 158
Gazit, Ze'ev, 46, 47, 139
Givat Brenner, 188
Glazer, Nathan, 231
Goldberg, Leah, 148
Goldman, Eliezer, 70
Gordon, A. D., 52, 58, 59
Guri, Haim, 157

Ha-Am, Ahad, 155, 200
Ha-Aretz, 43, 44
Haganah, 166
Haggadah, 169–82, 187, 188, 190
Halakhah, 80–83, 92, 102, 113, 120
Ha-Levi, Yehuda, 175
Halutz, 35, 37, 81
Hanukkah, 163–67
Ha-Zorea, 127, 152
Heftzi-bah, 180
Herzl, Theodor, 58
Heschel, Abraham Joshua, 33
Histadrut, 48, 166
Holocaust, 166, 176, 182–84, 188

Iggeret, 115, 203
Ihud, Ashdod Yaakov, 153
Independence Day, 184–91
Inter-Kibbutz Committee, 125, 127, 141, 142, 182–83, 187, 217, 221
Inter-Kibbutz Education Committee, 105
Inter-Kibbutz Festival Committee, 162

Kabbalat Shabbat, 131, 199–206
Katznelson, Berl, 48, 90
Kavanah, 130

Kehiliyateynu, 38, 39, 40, 41, 42
Kerem, Moshe, 69
Kibbutz Afikim, 212
Kibbutz Bet Ha-Shittah, 60
Kibbutz Ha-Artzi, 38–41, 46, 51, 61, 62, 65, 70, 71, 78, 102, 113, 139, 152, 154, 166, 175, 176, 211, 216
Kibbutz Hatzerim, 50
Kibbutz Me'uhad, 173–75, 176, 177
Kibbutz Tel Yosef, 177
Kibbutz Yagur, 211, 217
Kibbutz Yifat, 60
Kibbutz Ramat Yohanan, 60, 127, 138, 151, 152, 155, 160, 162, 165, 166, 176, 180, 181, 183, 189, 199, 211, 217
King, Winston L., 234
Kiryat Anavim, 197
Kook, Rav, 58, 59, 112, 113
K'tubah, 217, 218, 219
Kvutza, 37, 38

Lazarus, Morris, 88
Lenin, Nikolai, 155
Luz, Kadish, 89, 90

Maayan Tzvi, 127
Maletz, David, 51, 52, 61, 68, 69, 85, 123, 136, 138, 139, 178, 211
Marriage, 215–30
Marx, Karl, 155
Massada, 162, 166
Maniv, Asher, 127
Manoah, Yehoshua, 82, 98
Maor, Yitzhak, 85, 95, 153, 154
Meron, Stanley. 105, 106
Messiah, 87
Midrash, 128, 148, 171, 172
Mishmar Ha-Sharon, 146
Mitzvah, 83–86, 152, 212–15
Mourning, 221–28
Mumford, Lewis, 59

Palmah, 166, 186, 188
Passover, 169–82
Purim, 167–69

Ra'anan, Zvi, 102, 127, 128, 152, 186, 187
Rabbinic Judaism, 135
Raz, Yaacov, 154
Reisner, Ephraim, 73
Rishon Lezion, 196

Ron-Polani, Y., 155, 157
Rosh Ha-Shanah, 142–52, 156
Rosner, Menahem, 119
Rotenstreich, Nathan, 79, 80

Schauss, Haim, 142, 163, 184, 215
Scholem, Gershon, 135, 136
Schweid, Dr. Eliezer, 58
Shabbat, 199–206
Sharett, Judah, 211
Shavuot, 191–95
Shedemot, 51, 68
Shelem, Mattityahu, 127, 130, 131, 165, 198, 199, 203
Shivah Asar B'Tammuz, 195
Shlonsky, Avraham, 157, 175
Simhat Torah, 195
Simon, Ernst, 71
Six-Day War, 44, 66, 139, 155, 183, 188, 224
Soleveichik, Rav, 155
Spiro, Melford, 62, 71
Steinsaltz, Rabbi Adin, 84, 100, 117
Sukkot, 158–62

Talmon, Yonina, 219
Tawney, R. H., 93, 110
Tisha B'Av, 195
Tzom Gedaliah, 195

Una, Moshe, 98, 113
Union of Kibbutz Federations, 82
United Nations, 185

Vatikim, 31, 32, 33, 35, 36, 44, 48, 49, 54, 57, 59, 61, 63, 65, 67, 73, 75, 76, 78, 79, 84–86, 90, 91, 97, 99, 101, 104, 110, 122, 129, 133, 134, 140, 156, 157, 167–71, 174, 181, 193, 203, 230

Warsaw Ghetto, 166
Water Festival, 160, 161
*Weltanschauung*, 52, 71, 172
Werblowsky, Prof. Zvi, 139

Ya'ari, Meir, 41
Yedi'on, 144, 152
Yom Kippur, 151–58
Yotvatah, 197, 198

Zalman, Rabbi Schneur, 157
Zichron Yaacov, 196